HOW THE SUBURBS
WERE SEGREGATED

COLUMBIA STUDIES IN THE HISTORY OF U.S. CAPITALISM

COLUMBIA STUDIES IN THE HISTORY OF U.S. CAPITALISM

Series Editors: Devin Fergus, Louis Hyman,
Bethany Moreton, and Julia Ott

Capitalism has served as an engine of growth, a source of inequality, and a catalyst for conflict in American history. While remaking our material world, capitalism's myriad forms have altered—and been shaped by—our most fundamental experiences of race, gender, sexuality, nation, and citizenship. This series takes the full measure of the complexity and significance of capitalism, placing it squarely back at the center of the American experience. By drawing insight and inspiration from a range of disciplines and alloying novel methods of social and cultural analysis with the traditions of labor and business history, our authors take history "from the bottom up" all the way to the top.

PAIGE GLOTZER

HOW THE SUBURBS WERE SEGREGATED

Developers and the Business of
Exclusionary Housing, 1890–1960

Columbia University Press / *New York*

Columbia University Press
Publishers Since 1893
New York   Chichester, West Sussex
cup.columbia.edu
Copyright © 2020 Columbia University Press
All rights reserved

Library of Congress Cataloging-in-Publication Data

Names: Glotzer, Paige, author.
Title: How the suburbs were segregated : developers and the business of
exclusionary housing, 1890–1960 / Paige Glotzer.
Description: New York : Columbia University Press, [2020] | Includes
bibliographical references and index.
Identifiers: LCCN 2019043862 (print) | LCCN 2019043863 (ebook) |
ISBN 9780231179980 (cloth) | ISBN 9780231179997 (paperback) |
ISBN 9780231542494 (ebook)
Subjects: LCSH: Discrimination in housing—Maryland—Baltimore—
History—20th century. | Housing policy—Maryland—Baltimore—History—
20th century. | Suburbs—Maryland—Baltimore—History—20th century.
Classification: LCC HD7288.76.U52 B34 2020 (print) | LCC HD7288.76.U52
(ebook) | DDC 363.5/109752609041—dc23
LC record available at https://lccn.loc.gov/2019043862
LC ebook record available at https://lccn.loc.gov/2019043863

Cover design: Noah Arlow

To my grandfather, Milton Glotzer,

for inspiring my love of history

CONTENTS

ACKNOWLEDGMENTS

I began the acknowledgments to my doctoral dissertation by saying, "It takes a village." I could not imagine then just how that village would continue to grow as I transformed the dissertation into a book. One postdoctoral fellowship, one tenure-track job, and four moves later, I owe a deep debt of gratitude to the many people who helped bring this project to fruition.

There would be no book without the tireless editors at Columbia University Press. Louis Hyman and Philip Leventhal took a chance by offering me a contract when I was still a graduate student. Bridget Flannery-McCoy went so far above and beyond her job to help me revise that it is embarrassing to recall the initial drafts I thought would pass muster. Stephen Wesley shepherded the book through the production process. The book also benefited enormously from the editors of the Columbia Studies in the History of U.S. Capitalism series, Devin Fergus, Louis Hyman, Bethany Moreton, and Julia Ott. Thank you, too, to the readers who saw the manuscript's promise.

I have been fortunate to land at the University of Wisconsin–Madison as the first assistant professor and John W. and Jeanne M. Rowe Chair in the History of American Politics, Institutions, and Political Economy. Thank you to the Rowes for their generous and continued support of the history department. At UW I have the pleasure of working with some of the best historians in the world. It has been great to learn that these colleagues, formerly just names on the covers of books to me, are as kind and welcoming as they are rigorous and prolific. A special thank-you is in order for Verenize Arceo and James Meadows; our conversations have reminded me to stay focused on my scholarly commitment to center the experiences of people, no matter how much I am discussing companies and policy. Support for this research was provided by the University of Wisconsin–Madison Office of the Vice Chancellor for Research and Graduate Education with funding from the Wisconsin Alumni Research Foundation. In addition, a First Book Award from the Center for the Humanities at the University of Wisconsin–Madison allowed me to workshop the manuscript and improve it considerably. Thank you to Megan Massino and the center's former director, Gregg Mitman, for running the First Book Program, and to the workshop participants Nan Enstad, Stephen Kantrowitz, Nancy Kwak, Thomas Sugrue, and Monica M. White.

Before I came to UW, the Harvard University Joint Center for History and Economics gave me the opportunity to focus full-time on the book as a Prize Fellow in Economics, History, and Politics. (I clearly tend to gravitate to positions with long titles.) Thank you to Sunil Amrith and Emma Rothschild, and to senior fellows Abhijit Banerjee, Walter Johnson, Charles E. Rosenberg, Amartya Sen, and Richard Tuck. A weekly highlight at the center was the cross-disciplinary conversations over lunch with Shane Bobrycki, Namrata Kala, Nikhil Naik, Anne Ruderman, Evan Sadler, and Melissa Teixeira. Jennifer Nickerson is the glue that holds the center together on a daily basis.

The Joint Center for History and Economics generously supports the digital project that accompanies this book, "Building Suburban Power," as part of its Visualizing Historical Networks site. That project would have been impossible if not for Ye Seul Byeon's talent with databases, coding, and site design. Stacy Bogan at the Harvard Center for Geographic Analysis did initial work to clean up my data and make maps. Ian Kumekawa continues to be the point person for the site and Amy Price maintains it.

I have had the pleasure of being trained by amazing advisors. N. D. B. Connolly changed the way I think about the world. Mary Ryan and Angus Burgin sharpened and broadened my intellectual interests. If not for their mentorship, I do not know what type of scholar—what type of person—I would be today.

A historian cannot do anything without archivists and librarians. I learned this first and foremost at the Johns Hopkins Sheridan Libraries Special Collections, where this book began as a work opportunity to process the Roland Park Company records the summer before I began graduate school. Jordon Steele taught me how to process the Roland Park Company records and developed a vision for making the collection accessible to the public. Valerie Addonizio did most of the work to process the records, which was no easy task as company officials left everything to posterity except a guide to their filing system. It was also always a pleasure to work with Paul Espinosa, Heidi Herr, Amy Kimball, Jerome Powell, and James Stimpert. Cynthia Requardt hired me on the spot during prospective student weekend and recommended that I contact her colleague Margaret Burri to find a place to live.

In addition to the folks at Johns Hopkins, thank you to Russell Carlson, Frederik Heller, and Hathaway Hester at the National Association of Realtors® Library and Archives; Saul Gibusiwa, Edward C. Papenfuse, and Rob Schoeberlein at the Baltimore City Archives; Patricia Dockman Anderson of the Maryland Historical Society; and Sheila Scott at the Afro-American Newspapers Archives and Research Center.

Thank you to the staff at Cornell University Rare and Manuscript Collections, Enoch Pratt Maryland Department, the University of Baltimore Langsdale Library, Maryland State Archives, the National Archives of the United Kingdom, London Metropolitan Archives, Guildhall Library, Rochdale Local Studies Library, Harvard Business School Baker Library, the National Archives and Records Administration, and the underrated Legislative Reference Library in Baltimore City Hall.

Even though I already thanked Louis Hyman in his capacity as series editor, it was as facilitator of the History of Capitalism Bootcamp that he planted the seeds for a network that has continued to grow. Of my cohort, Alex Beasley and Destin Jenkins in particular have become valued collaborators and friends. Emilie Connolly, Jon Free, Emily Lundberg, A. J. Murphy, David Stein, and Jason White have all stayed in touch and helped me weather the isolation of moving four times in three years between grad school, postdoc, and job.

It really does take a village. Thank you to the many people who have read drafts, invited me to share my work, recommended readings, given me sources, cheered me on, and created community: Rudi Batzell, Dan Berger, Keisha Blain, Matthew Crenson, Alex Sayf Cummings, Joshua Clark Davis, Kate Drabinski, Jay Driskell, David Freund, Andrew Friedman, Yuri Gama, Shennette Garrett-Scott, Dylan Gottlieb, Walter Greason, Cristina Groeger, Marta Gutman, Richard Harris, Elizabeth Herbin-Triant, Thomas Shay Hill, Ben Holtzman, Andrew Kahrl, Noam Maggor, Todd Michney, Graham Mooney, Andrew Needham, Tracy Neumann, Carl Nightingale, Richard Otten, Atiba Pertilla, Eli Pousson, Garrett Power, Anthony Pratcher III, Pedro A. Regalado, Amanda Seligman, Chloe Thurston, Marc Weiss, LaDale Winling, and Xine Yao.

I also need to thank friends, mentors, and colleagues in Baltimore when I was completing the early stages of the project: Sara Berry, Toby Ditz, François Furstenberg, Louis Galambos, Rachel La Bozetta, Tobie Meyer-Fong, Judith Walkowitz, Ronald Walters, and Megan Zeller; Mary Ryan's Charm School of Baltimore Historians, Robert Gamble, Katie Hemphill, and David Schley; Ayla Amon, Katie Best, Royce Best, Katherine Bonil, Patrick Bonner, Jilene Chua, Emily Davidson, Stefanie Falconi, Patrick Giamario, Layne Karafantis, Adrianna Link, Lauren MacDonald, Guillermo García Montúfar, Roshanak Nateghi, Ayah Nuriddin, Morgan Shahan, Linda Tchernyshyov, Adam Thomas, Jessica Valdez, Luiz Vieira, Brandi Waters, Frank Wolff, and Túlio R. B. Zille.

Amira Rose Davis is my academic sister and one of the strongest and most brilliant people I know; Rebecca Stoil and I drove around Baltimore while she told me where the good bagels were and spitballed countless ideas. Mo Speller always pushed me to consider questions of equity and the built environment. Jessica Ann Levy edited the manuscript and ironed out rough spots with the prose; any that remain are due to me messing up her good work. She and Jessica Keene were the Dorothy and Rose/Blanche to my Sophia. Thank you for being a friend.

Apollo Amoko, Bernardo Cardenas-Lailhacar, Margaret Galvan, Pamela Gilbert, Susan Hegeman, Tace Hendrick, Kenneth B. Kidd, John Lowry, Barbara Mennel, Judith and Bill Page, Maria Rogal, Leah Rosenberg, Raúl Sánchez, Malini and John Schueller, Martin B. Smith, Delia Steverson, Maureen Turim, Anastasia Ulanowicz, Phillip Wegner, and Rae Yan welcomed me into their lives. Their friendships and encouragement came at a crucial time when it was unclear what the future would bring. Thanks to all of them, I am now recklessly unafraid of alligators.

Finally, my village has grown to encompass four continents. I am here because my parents' love knows no bounds. Aunt Flora and Uncle Jeff have always supported me. *Minha família brasileira* welcomed me with open arms and churrasco. My chosen family, too, fills my life with love: Norah Andrews Gharala and I have shared laughter and tears over the years. Talking with Colleen Dorsey is effortless, no matter how much time passes between seeing each other. Aleksander Shagalov deserves an entirely separate acknowledgment section for how much he has made my life better. Around him I can be myself completely. And, of course, Roger Maioli, my partner in crime and coparent to guinea pigs Johnson and Boswell, raises me up each and every day.

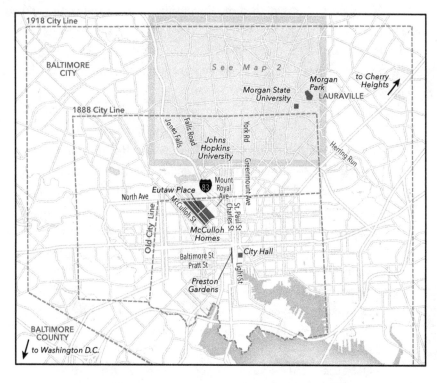

MAP 1 Map of Baltimore.

(Prepared by Tanya Buckingham, University of Wisconsin Cartography Lab)

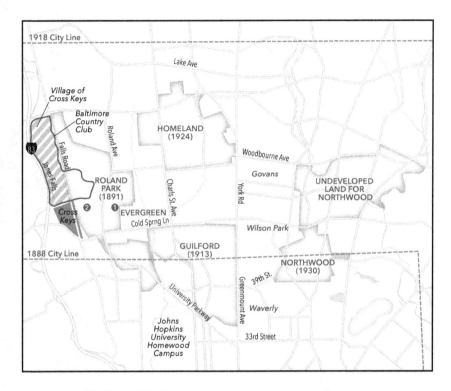

MAP 2 The Roland Park Company district and surrounding area.

(Prepared by Tanya Buckingham, University of Wisconsin Cartography Lab)

INTRODUCTION

I t will not surprise most readers that American cities are racially segregated and unequal. Throughout much of the twentieth century, majority-white urban neighborhoods tended to receive more investment and better city services in comparison to majority-nonwhite neighborhoods. Meanwhile, suburban communities grew to be even whiter and wealthier than their urban counterparts. This book examines why. What is the prehistory to the policies that helped segregate the United States? How can we account for the rise of pervasive housing segregation and why, historically, has it assumed certain forms and not others? Why, in fact, did housing segregation occur in the first place? And why and how did it persist after the elimination of legal barriers prohibiting integration?

Many of the existing explanations for the persistence of housing segregation have focused on the period after the Second World War, when a series of federal policies, white flight, and municipal fiscal crises combined to reshape the United States.[1] While not refuting this narrative, this book reveals how racial segregation was built into suburban development from the beginning. During the late nineteenth and early twentieth centuries, some of the first developers of planned suburbs experimented with racial segregation as a tactic to attract residents and augment sales at the turn of the twentieth century. In doing so, they occupied an increasingly central role in the nation's real estate industry. As more and more white Americans moved to suburbs, developers formed networks and associations where they disseminated best practices, including racial segregation. Later, when the federal government rewrote housing policy beginning in the Great Depression, developers played a central role in codifying these discriminatory practices into federal housing policy that shaped the rise of large segregated metropolitan areas after the war.

There is perhaps no better example of the rising power of developers than the Roland Park Company.[2] Founded in 1891 with British capital, the company gradually developed a 2,500-acre district in northern Baltimore, Maryland, which remained one of the top ten most populous cities in the United States for the majority of the twentieth century. Over the next several decades, the Roland Park Company garnered national recognition as a leader in suburban development, working with others like the Olmsted Brothers and Kansas City developer Jesse Clyde Nichols to give meaning to what was a relatively new form of suburban living. More than a case study of a single firm, then, the history of the Roland Park Company sheds light on how a network of investors, real estate professionals, planners, and policymakers, which emerged after 1891 and continued following the company's closure in 1959, gained a disproportionate platform on which they shaped the national housing market in ways that drew on and reinforced segregation.

In order to account for the rise and persistence of segregated suburbs and developer power, this book follows the evolution of this network, beginning with the investors who financed the Roland Park Company. It then zooms in on the company's street-level efforts with planning a suburb in Baltimore, where company officials first experimented with racial and class segregation as a marketing tactic. Even in the midst of experimenting, the company began to disseminate its practices nationally through nascent informal networks that emerged during the first decade of the twentieth century, linking real estate and planning professionals across the country. The second half of the book zooms back out to examine how the Roland

Park Company officers standardized real estate practices through national institutions such as the National Association of Real Estate Boards (NAREB) and, later, the federal government, where company executives helped codify segregation into federal housing policy. NAREB was one of several organizations that successfully influenced national debates about the role of the government and homeownership, but it proved to be one of the most successful.[3] All the while, the book tracks the impact that larger national and international changes had on the ground in Baltimore.

With this arc, *How the Suburbs Were Segregated* pushes back the chronology of suburban housing segregation, from its putative origins in the New Deal to the nineteenth century. Second, it links the global and local dimensions of housing segregation, allowing for a dynamic interplay of scale by tracing the capital, people, and ideas that gave rise to particular forms of discrimination. Finally, it bridges histories of housing with those of daily business practices to better understand how certain suburban developers gained the power to inscribe racial segregation across housing markets.

* * *

At its heart, this book is about power—how it is gained, how it is deployed, and how it shapes resource distribution. Scholars frequently emphasize the role of state power in shaping housing. Markets, like government, are "the result of power and an arena of power."[4] The practical details of suburban development also prove fertile ground for excavating the processes by which suburban developers amassed the power to make the single-family suburban house in the planned segregated suburb the most valuable type of residential property in the United States. Each chapter of the book finds developers grappling with how to make day-to-day technical and managerial decisions. On the surface, these problems—including where to run sewer pipes and how to manage labor, standardize sales forms, vet individual buyers, and negotiate with municipal governments for resources—do not seem to compare in importance to sweeping federal legislation. And yet, those processes, all of which were infused with racism and sexism, allowed developers to repeatedly create and hone narratives about which housing had the highest property value and construct exclusionary housing markets in conjunction with the state.

Recent work in the emerging field called the history of capitalism has analyzed power "from below all the way to the top."[5] *How the Suburbs Were Segregated* fits squarely within this scholarship, with its reliance on account ledgers and shareholder records and its general follow-the-money approach. But it does so with several caveats. In the quest to define what is distinctive about the history of capitalism, some of its most established proponents have, often unknowingly, delimited two things: whose work counts and what type of work counts.[6] In particular, those scholars associated with doing cultural and social history and focusing on things like women's reproductive labor, informal economies, and identity—just to name a few— have been pushed aside as part of a false dichotomy between "economy" and "culture" used to justify the field.[7]

This book, by contrast, remains committed to revealing the coconstruction of culture and economy. This commitment is particularly evident in the book's foregrounding of racial capitalism as part of its broader commitment to underscoring the necessity of racial literacy in writing histories of American capitalism.[8] Cedric Robinson developed the concept of "racial capitalism" from its original usage by scholars describing South African apartheid to explain the historical coemergence of ideas of race and capital accumulation in his monumental book *Black Marxism*.[9] As the connection to South Africa indicates, Robinson's work built on what he and others have called the Black Radical Tradition, elucidating and critiquing the ways the very structures, institutions, and cultures of the United States evolved inseparably from those of slavery and global capitalism.[10] Racial capitalism has operated differently across time and space, remaining historically rooted.[11] Despite these shifts, historians have convincingly demonstrated racial capitalism's persistence throughout American history.[12] *How the Suburbs Were Segregated* contributes to this scholarship by demonstrating how race shaped the development of a national housing market, and vice versa.

In addition to the debates about who gets associated with the field, there has been something of an attitude of existential uncertainty about whether the history of capitalism is indeed new at all. This is tied, in part, to concerns about which scholarship gets included. Such concern has produced writings that alternately announce the triumphant arrival of the new history of capitalism or declare that historians have been studying capitalism for a long time. If it is a new field, scholars question its specificity. "Is the history of capitalism the history of everything?" asks one, while another writes, "What makes the history of capitalism newsworthy?"[13]

This book cautions against any notion of triumphalism through its indebtedness to (a much older) urban history as much as the history of capitalism. Urban historians such as Arnold Hirsch focused on material relationships and political economy during the very decades of their supposed decline. The spatial turn of the 1980s and the move toward looking at structural conditions of urban inequality in the 1990s provide crucial building blocks for what N. D. B. Connolly has called a "desegregated method" of historical scholarship.[14]

How the Suburbs Were Segregated thus is the product of the history of capitalism—including the networks and initiatives that have enabled a cohort of historians interested in capitalism to get to know each other—as well as urban history and critical race studies. A primary goal of the book is to excavate and make legible some of the myriad ways racism and capital, in their historicized configurations, gave rise to segregated suburbs. There has been debate among scholars such as Lani Guinier and Ruth Wilson Gilmore about how to best understand the ways racial capitalism has been historically enacted. For the purposes of what follows, racial capitalism will be approached as a web of relationships connecting particular people, institutions, and ideas engaged in housing development.[15]

"Excavate" is a carefully chosen word for this project, as many of these relationships have been hidden over time or even from the start. Take the origins of the Roland Park Company in 1891. On paper, the company looked like it was founded by locals in Baltimore. In reality, hundreds of British investors, many of them with ties to slavery and colonialism, financed the company through a second London-based firm, the Lands Trust Company. The deeper connections between American suburbs, slavery, and colonialism become apparent when looking at these shareholders and where they got the capital they used to bankroll Jim Crow. The role that British finance played in shaping the early development of the American economy during the eighteenth and nineteenth centuries, including British investment in slave insurance and railroads, for example, is well known.[16] But British investment in suburban housing, a commodity most often associated with the twentieth century, has been overlooked. By carefully tracing the circulation of British capital that made the Roland Park Company possible, this book decenters the "American" from American housing segregation by linking the origins of both segregated suburbs and federal housing policy to a global history more expansive in time and in scope.[17] Such excavations enable American suburbs to be resituated from uniquely American places to nodes in a global circuit of capital—an outgrowth of the high degree of international financial integration at the end of the nineteenth century.[18]

A longer transnational history of capital is incomplete without a longer local history that foregrounds people and land.[19] This book begins and ends not with British investors or white developers but in historically black Cross Keys, located just down the hill from Roland Park. Over eighty years before the founding of the Roland Park Company, African Americans in Cross Keys bought and sold property, built homes, rented them, and expanded them to accommodate generations of extended family. They ran businesses, churches, pleasure grounds, and doctor's offices. The histories of Roland Park and Cross Keys became intertwined with the arrival of the company. Despite the company's best efforts to separate itself from Cross Keys, which its officials considered a necessary nuisance, the black community continued to shape life, labor, and development in Roland Park.[20]

More recently, some historians have begun to examine how housing debt could be packaged and sold on a global secondary market. In doing so, they have also shown how this repackaging reproduces racial and class inequality. Nevertheless, this literature has yet to account for how suburban development companies themselves were financed.[21] In the case of the Roland Park Company, it is clear that British investment shaped corporate decision making and priority setting in ways that proved influential for the development of suburban housing in Baltimore. While transnational capital did not replace local investment, the former allowed for the creation of development companies with far more capital than older local competitors. The larger scope of the new projects meant that these new firms faced a longer timescale for investment. As a result, company officials turned to local contexts, which included segregation, to find ways of generating profits year after year.

More work needs to be done than is possible in this book to understand how British finance affected American suburbs outside Roland Park. Absent an abundance of archival sources to document the financial origins of planned suburbs, historians have replicated the narratives developers constructed to sell suburbs in the first place.[22] Take Levittown, New York, one of the most important postwar suburbs in the United States, which was famously built on former potato farms. What happens to the story of Levittown when the starting question becomes, whatever happened to the workers on the potato farms? Did they take jobs in the malls and shopping centers that served that new development? Who were they? The web can be extended further. What happened to the people selling farm equipment? The vendors selling the potatoes? The price of vegetables? These may seem like questions that are beside the point in the history of Levittown itself, but they bring to the forefront relationships that get erased when one takes as a starting point for suburban development the empty tract of land that has been sold and cleared. These questions become even more critical when the financial history of segregated suburbs connects them to westward expansion, enslavement, and settler colonialism long before the federal policies that gave rise to Levittown.

The presupposition that developers transformed "empty land" into residential property, for example, reproduces the racial and colonial logics in the Lands Trust Company advertisements in British newspapers. *How the Suburbs Were Segregated* consequently shifts scholarly literature on suburbs away from treating them as natural arrangements.[23] Existing work deploys the "suburb" in a broad, even transhistorical manner that does not account for how historical actors themselves used it in different ways over time. As a result, these works obscure the very decision-making processes that gave rise to planned suburbs. In particular, a long-standing strand of scholarship building on research by people such as Kenneth Jackson and Dolores

Hayden created typologies of suburbs.[24] While this work has been immensely productive, this book takes a different tactic, letting actors speak for themselves and revealing debates over the definition of what constituted a suburb. As the book demonstrates, the stakes of these debates were high. Control over the discursive creation of suburbia formed one front on which developers gained power by standardizing and disseminating exclusionary practices.[25]

In addition to employing discursive strategies, companies experimented with what infrastructure was needed to develop a suburb that would net long-term returns. They turned to both racial exclusion and planning. Their initial experiments had three components. The first was deed restrictions, which also became known as restrictive covenants. These were legal contracts that set rules on how an individual piece of property could be used.[26] The second entailed finding the look and feel of the development. The third involved building physical infrastructural systems such as sewers, water, and roads. The results of all three—rules, aesthetics, and planning—had to be decided on and imposed.

Long-term planning and the company's status as a large property owner brought the Roland Park Company into contact with municipal government at the turn of the twentieth century. The company initially interacted with Baltimore officials in its capacity to secure the provision of infrastructure. They were doing so at a time when municipal government itself was being reorganized across the United States by reformers, often members of the middle and upper classes, in an effort to combat political machines. In Baltimore, as in many other cities, this was an intensely uneven and protracted process in which newly hired specialists, such as trained city planners and engineers, coexisted with elected machine legislators and appointed commissioners. These changes brought to the fore questions about democratic governance: How responsive should newly reorganized governments be to individual demands for services and goods? How much should non-elected officials be entrusted with long-term visions for the city as a whole at the expense of more local needs?

Larger-scale developers such as the Roland Park Company entered the municipal stage in a way that shaped the direction of the state and markets at what proved to be a formative moment for both.[27] The company made use of an older, haphazard city petition process to alter municipal priorities and gain preferential access to resources over other property owners. In comparison to those other property owners, the Roland Park Company had far more money, labor, and political capital at its disposal, as well as specialists on its payroll who shared training and contacts with officials in city government. Both skewed the process in its favor. Property ownership has historically been one of the foundations of political power in the United States. The shifting of the scales from individual property owners to wealthy development companies altered not only resource allocation but also citizen relationships with the very machinery of urban governance.

In 1903, British investors pulled out of the Roland Park Company. The company became locally owned while investors moved on to other locales. Though their involvement lasted only twelve years, British investors served as the catalyst for the Roland Park Company to adopt a model of development largely unseen in the United States. After 1903 the company shifted from acting on the demands of distant investors to adapting to changes in Baltimore while still retaining the business practices established to meet the long-term needs of its original backers.

These changes included increased competition and growing tensions over Baltimore's geography of race and class. By 1910, Baltimore was the sixth largest city in the United States. With a thriving industrial base and busy port, the city became a destination for blacks migrating from the rural South in search of jobs and opportunities. This created divisions between the new, largely working-class black migrants and an established black middle class that had been part of a venerable community dating to the eighteenth century.[28] Rising upward mobility for this middle class enabled them to use their wealth as lawyers, bankers, and landlords to cross the residential color line into some of Baltimore's most respected white neighborhoods closer to the center of the city. It also led to the creation of planned black suburbs as well, including one near Roland Park Company holdings.

Amid these changes the newly local Roland Park Company adopted even more stringent and exclusionary practices for their subsequent subdivisions, which they saw as potentially becoming model suburbs for a growing cadre of developers. That the company envisioned their work as having national significance was telling. During the 1890s and 1900s, the Roland Park Company began to disseminate its practices through informal correspondence networks. Developers, city planners, and government officials all began to cite the company as a direct inspiration. These networks, in turn, helped to spread the company's reputation and influence even further, along with its exclusionary planning documents and restrictive covenants. Such networks allow us to concretely trace the dissemination of ideas about housing segregation.

These networks also constituted the initial channels by which developers began to accrue the professional capital and recognition to gain a disproportionately large platform to shape tastes in housing. This is not to deny the importance of consumers or the history of consumption.[29] However, the uneven power of developers relative to other actors proved remarkable given how relatively few they were in number and how uncommon planned suburbs were at the time. The vast majority of peripheral spaces in the United States were unplanned and working-class rather than planned and affluent.[30] Even in unplanned suburbs or other areas no one considered suburban at all, two things began to happen: consumers tried to emulate the mechanics of exclusionary planned suburbs and state officials tried to reorder growth using developers' tactics.[31]

Over time, the success of Baltimore's experiment in suburban development informed the creation of a national real estate industry. In 1908, Roland Park Company officials joined those in the real estate business from around North America to form NAREB. NAREB members sought to counter the popular image of real estate agents as swindlers and scam artists by turning real estate into a profession. Citing engineers, doctors, and lawyers as groups who had successfully professionalized, NAREB leaders sought to establish barriers to entry and uniform standards. Professionalization was no easy task. The nature of members' livelihoods ranged widely. Members of the Roland Park Company, along with a cohort of similar developers, assumed early leadership roles and became some of the most vocal advocates of professionalization. The reasons for this were manifold. Reputation proved crucial for their business, especially as they targeted affluent buyers. They were also more likely to have lofty goals about setting examples for future development.[32]

As developers assumed leadership roles, they traded informal correspondence networks for institutional channels to standardize their specific business practices for all NAREB members to follow. They explicitly called for housing discrimination on the premise that segregated white neighborhoods consisting of single-family homes had high property values.[33] Their influence went far beyond occupying leadership positions. As avid players in guiding NAREB, they joined the organization's ranks in fostering an institutional culture that included a heavy dose of racism and sexism. From the songs they sang at conventions to the tours they organized as host delegations, the members of the country's largest real estate organization repeatedly affirmed their own personal and professional status through performing whiteness and masculinity.[34] Not only did best business practices come to include racial segregation, but the culture of the country's most powerful real estate institution rested on a foundation of white supremacy that superseded the beliefs of individual members and informed the growth of industry.

National efforts at standardizing practices were never totalizing. As a result, the construction of segregated housing markets owed much to the interplay between local and national scales at which business was conducted. On the ground, Realtors—members of NAREB used an uppercase *R*—made daily, often inconsistent decisions about exclusion based on local conditions. Buyers, meanwhile, sometimes attempted to subvert the barriers they surmised (or knew) existed. Local knowledge also complicated the debates at national meetings about issues such as immigration and the legality of restrictive covenants.[35] On the local level, daily business experiences influenced what information NAREB members shared about routine matters such as office organization and personnel management. These conversations filtered up through NAREB channels to the central office, which solicited member ideas. These were then vetted, packaged, and disseminated nationally. Even routine considerations such as these helped refine developers' exclusionary practices.[36] This bidirectionality resulted in the frequent remaking and redefining of the criteria of exclusion.[37]

While NAREB only partially standardized practices, it successfully cultivated an image of its members as real estate experts. When policymakers sought to address the housing crisis of the Great Depression, they turned to NAREB both as an institution and as a source for potential consultants. These Realtors differed from the social scientists and economists who have gained attention as New Deal consultants in that they appealed to an expertise rooted in practical experience rather than rigorous training.[38] Realtors then worked with federal administrators to turn their highly socially embedded, contingent, and local experiences into the common-sense principles of a supposedly objective national market. Such was the case for the Roland Park Company's second president, John Mowbray, who concurrently served as head of the NAREB Housing Committee and helmed projects in Baltimore for the two most well-known federal housing agencies of the New Deal: the Home Owners' Loan Corporation (HOLC) and the Federal Housing Administration (FHA), both of which implemented discriminatory lending practices such as redlining that gave some Americans access to mortgages on favorable terms while shutting out others.

National institutions such as NAREB never displaced the importance of local business and politics. Though the New Deal consisted of nationwide policies, they were largely implemented by locals. Like many of the measures passed during the New Deal, those pertaining to housing were implemented primarily by municipal officials and businessmen.[39] Federal legislators often devolved policy out of political expediency to appease segregationists, who saw the expansion of federal powers as a potential threat to the local racial order. Many of the HOLC and FHA agents who established the geography of federally backed discriminatory lending in Baltimore also had ties to the Roland Park Company through either their employment or their residence. The daily mechanisms of redlining showcase the central role developers played at different political scales thanks to both NAREB's success and New Deal localism.

Those roles complicate what historians have called the two-tier system of federal housing policy.[40] One tier, they contend, consisted of federal lending, primarily to white homeowners, through the HOLC and the FHA, which financed the growth of suburbs, while the other tier consisted of low-income public housing. The differences between the two tiers undoubt-edly structured many aspects of midcentury housing politics.[41] Never-theless, characterizing the system as two-tiered masks the ways public housing agencies, the FHA, and the HOLC worked together and shared similar interests. This included the business that public housing authori-ties and the HOLC conducted together. In Baltimore, beginning in 1937, Mowbray led an experimental pilot study that marshaled the joint resources of the city's public housing authority, the HOLC, and the FHA with the stated aim of keeping a neighborhood white. The project was based on model legislation NAREB and HOLC officials had been discussing for four years prior to the start of the project and the site was selected because of its prox-imity to Roland Park Company developments.

Reframing the origins of housing policy challenges the long-standing consensus about the prime role of political ideology in postwar develop-ment. I argue that neither the liberal-driven fair-housing and antidiscrimi-nation laws of the 1960s nor conservative attempts to shrink the federal housing apparatus changed a core tenet of the American housing market, a tenet that developers had helped to establish: property value was linked to race. A longer history of housing policy can, to quote from one essay on the history of finance, "hang a question mark over the when and where of value."[42] Maintaining the focus on developers into the 1950s and 1960s aids in this reframing at a time when the rise of a postwar "consumer's republic" shifts scholarly focus to individual homeowners.[43]

In Baltimore, one of the most prominent developers to gain power in the 1960s was James Rouse. Rouse was a self-described liberal whose politics and development priorities seemed, on the surface at least, to constitute a considerable break with predominant exclusionary patterns. However, Rouse's rise is precisely why a longer history of suburban power is necessary to under-stand the persistence of housing segregation. Indeed, Rouse was a part of the Roland Park Company network. Before he became famous as a devel-oper in the 1960s, Rouse began his career in the Baltimore office of the FHA and worked closely with Roland Park Company officials in business endeav-ors and government consulting. By the 1950s, Rouse and Mowbray together were in charge of spearheading federal urban renewal policy based on their work in Baltimore. This policy ultimately wreaked devastation on communities throughout the country. In Baltimore alone, urban renewal displaced over ten thousand households. As was the case around the country, the majority of those who lost their homes were African American.[44]

Often lauded both for his malls and for the racially integrated planned suburb of Columbia, Maryland, well outside Baltimore, Rouse's early and midcareer work consisted of fortifying the very socioeconomic and racial borders that the Roland Park Company had created. Nowhere was this clearer than in Cross Keys in the early 1960s, where Rouse developed a gated planned community next to Roland Park called the Village of Cross Keys after urban renewal destroyed the long-standing African American community of the same name.

Though much changed since the 1890s, the continuity of real estate networks and practices proved key to the process by which subsequent generations of developers adapted the commercial logic binding real estate's profitability to racial segregation. The following chapters, taken together, demonstrate the resilience of racial capitalism and the role that housing, in particular, continues to play as a particularly important domain for its recalibration and survival.

1

FLOWS

n 1891, a widow in Yorkshire named Emma Dixon received a check for
a 6 percent dividend on her five-pound investment.[1] Dixon was one of
four hundred British investors who owned shares in a land syndicate
called the Lands Trust Company, founded in 1888. The Lands Trust Company was one of a multitude of investment opportunities for Dixon that
year that would send her capital abroad. In many cases, these investments
helped fuel the growth of British imperialism and colonialism around
the world. In Dixon's case, her five pounds went to Baltimore, Maryland,
in the service of financing one of the first planned, segregated suburbs in
the United States, through the Baltimore-based Roland Park Company.
One of the things the company used the money for was a modern sewer
system. The sewers, which Dixon and her fellow investors funded, emptied
downhill into a popular swimming spot for black children in Cross Keys,
a long-standing black community that predated the Roland Park Company. As the children swam in contaminated water, their lives became inti-
mately intertwined with Dixon's, though neither Dixon nor the children
ever knew of each other.

Dixon's and her fellow investors' role financing the company helps to reveal the longer chronology and wider geography connecting the history of American suburbs to the global history of racial capitalism. This broader context renders legible the ways one of the first segregated suburbs in the United States resulted from a string of British investment decisions from which white investors profited by expropriating land, labor, and resources from people around the world. The sewers the Roland Park Company laid through Cross Keys degraded the land and endangered Cross Keys residents in ways that bore a striking resemblance to how the financiers of those sewers had made money for decades. More than parallels, these investments were concretely connected processes—and spaces—linked by the capital that over time, flowed from place to place before coming to the hillside near Baltimore.[2]

Before there was Roland Park there was Cross Keys, and before the Roland Park Company there was the Lands Trust Company, which financed it. Over four hundred British investors from all walks of life funneled their capital into the Lands Trust Company, which participated in land speculation. For some, this might have been the only investment they made in their lifetimes. For others, including its largest shareholders, the Lands Trust Company was simply the latest of their globe-spanning investments, funded by the ones that preceded it. Following the money that financed Roland Park brings this wider variety of actors into view and illuminates their role in the broader history of how American housing segregation came to work, from investors like Dixon to the residents of Cross Keys.

Two of the Lands Trust directors have a traceable history that reveals the prior business ventures that produced the capital that they invested and reinvested until they brought it to Baltimore. Alfred Fryer and Jacob Bright became wealthy through colonial investments in the Caribbean, Africa, Asia, and the American West. They knew each other, and there were some similarities in the nature of their business dealings. Both helmed companies centered on resource extraction of water, sugar, or land. Both imposed labor regimes on workers that closely approximated enslavement. And both purchased financial instruments, such as mortgages and bonds, backed by expropriated land and resources.

Most of the Lands Trust Company shareholders did not leave such extensive records as Bright and Fryer, but much can still be said about how they, like their more well-known counterparts, conceived of people and property together as indicators of future value. The decisions of British investors were by no means purely economic but rather were based, at least in part, on assumptions about black and brown peoples the world over.[3] Overseas investment, especially in empire, had long been popularly considered a safe and respectable source of wealth for people in Britain. With the growth in global finance toward the end of the nineteenth century, however, average British men and women began investing in unprecedented numbers.[4] With more choices than ever before, what united the hundreds of shareholders from different classes, regions, religions, and occupations in their choice to invest in the Lands Trust Company? All invested in places throughout the United States and British Empire where newspaper ads—for many British investors, the main source of information about the company—promised that the settlement of white people would increase the value of what they called empty land.[5] This notion of empty land is an artifact of settler colonialism that has persisted as a dominant narrative about suburban development in the United States.[6] It is therefore imperative to connect the intellectual work of creating the segregated suburb to a longer history of racial capitalism and settler colonialism.

Of course, Cross Keys was not empty land, nor was it even, "emptied land."[7] Instead, the area was home to black property owners and renters with businesses, kinship networks, politics, and its own civic life. The land and people on the circuits of Lands Trust capital have their own histories. Property relations at Cross Keys, as in much of Baltimore, were enmeshed in world economies: one of the earliest recorded property transactions on the hill was between a black man, tenant farmers, and wealthy enslavers. The latter, whose legal claims to the land were granted by the British proprietors of colonial Maryland, had ties to the trans-Appalachian West and to sugar refining. Then there was the proximity of Cross Keys to Baltimore City, whose growth was as much a product of global connections as it was a combination of specific environmental conditions and local financial arrangements.

The state played an integral role at each step leading to the founding of the Roland Park Company. Whether it was the imperial British government signing treaties or opting to invade countries, or Baltimore County's process for recording land titles, governments at every political scale from national to municipal were involved in creating the conditions for the emergence of the Roland Park Company. Laws from different governing bodies shaped how people transformed the material world into financial instruments and regulated how those instruments could be used. Crucially, state violence facilitated the displacement, settler colonialism, labor regimes, and resource extraction that permeate the prehistory of the company.

The late nineteenth century, however, was also a time when the role of the state was in flux. How would the municipal government of Baltimore facilitate growth? Polluted water, especially, became a recurring issue as locals debated how Baltimore should grow. What types of infrastructure should it provide, and for whom, and, crucially, who would pay for it? These and other questions informed the types of changes international capital set in motion with the founding of the Roland Park Company.

CROSS KEYS

In 1802, an African American man named Solomon Moonier bought half an acre of land at the top of a hill and became one of the first residents of Cross Keys. Named after a nearby tavern, the area that became known as Cross Keys ran from the hilltop down to a turnpike road, crossed the road, and extended to the banks of one of the Baltimore City's most vital waterways, the Jones Falls. From the top of the hill, Moonier could gaze down on the rapidly changing Jones Falls Valley. Following the namesake river south as it descended five miles to the harbor, Moonier saw Baltimore, which had become a city only twenty-one years earlier and was already the third largest in the young nation. The boundaries of Baltimore City ended far south of the hill, which was located in Baltimore County. Along the river and beyond it lay the water-powered textile mills that helped give rise to Baltimore's booming economy.

Moonier's plot of land was situated on a hill whose formation was due to the same quirk of geography that facilitated the growth of Baltimore City and enabled the Roland Park Company to use the Jones Falls as a sewer: the fall line. Along this nine-hundred-mile line the land changed from flat to hilly as the tidal ecosystem of the Atlantic met the piedmont. The result was flowing water. The piedmont's creeks and streams descended rapidly over the line on their way to the ocean. It was this flow that powered Baltimore's mills. It was also what allowed waste—be it from household sewers or industry—to be carried away on a steady descent toward the harbor. Ever since the city's founding in 1796, living upstream or away from the flow of water had always minimized exposure to the stench and disease with which those living downstream had to contend. As a result, Baltimore's geography of class and race became intertwined with its environment.

Though the fall line shaped the city's geography in a north–south trajectory along the river, property ownership in Baltimore was enmeshed in wider economies of enslavement that extended well beyond the vicinity of the Jones Falls. Moonier bought his parcel of land from a group of four white men. These men were once tenants of absentee owners, the Gough and Carroll families, two of the wealthiest families in Maryland and among its largest enslavers. The conveyancer who facilitated the transactions was a local Quaker who managed thousands of acres in the Appalachians for absentee Baltimore investors.[8]

The former tenants did not have title to the property they sold. Rather, they entered into an agreement with their landlords to buy seventy-four acres of land on installment plus interest. A single missed payment entitled the Goughs and Carrolls to repossess the acreage. Before the tenants met their obligations, they subdivided the tract into lots and sold it off. Moonier was one of the purchasers, along with a black woman named Ann Cutler who bought the neighboring half acre.[9] A decade later, in 1818, Moonier and Cutler officially received titles from the Goughs and Carrolls.[10] Cutler soon sold her land and moved away.[11] Moonier stayed and over the years built a home and established a family burial ground on the site.

It is unknown to what extent Moonier or Cutler were aware of the legal precarity of their land at the time. That Cutler moved soon after gaining title indicates that she likely did. The cases of Moonier and Cutler illuminate the centrality of property to race and class relationships in the nineteenth century. During the eras of slavery and Jim Crow, African Americans' "relationship to capitalism was not just one of exploitation but also property relations and expropriation."[12] Property ownership was widespread among African Americans of different legal statuses in the early nineteenth century, including in slave states such as Maryland. Especially in Baltimore, where one's status could sit on what Seth Rockman calls a "continuum" of freedom to unfreedom, legal recognition of property ownership could both constitute a rare buffer against dispossession and form the foundation of inheritable wealth.[13]

Race and class likewise factored into how Moonier's wealthy white neighbor to the north acquired a legally recognized property title from the outset. General Robert Goodloe Harper carved out his parcel of land from other Gough and Carroll holdings and named it Oakland. Oakland marked a new iteration of land use in Baltimore County that Baltimoreans called the country estate. Rather than productive farms, the estates were used by wealthy white families as leisure spaces centered around a large house. The families used enslaved labor to run country estates, which ranged from dozens to hundreds of acres.

Harper died in 1825, heavily in debt. His executors used Oakland's twenty-seven enslaved men and women to settle the debt and allowed his daughter and her husband, another Carroll, to keep the estate. The executors of Harper's will appraised the slaves' monetary value, and at least one of the enslaved remained at Oakland.[14] It is likely that the executors used the slaves' legal status as property to leverage their value as collateral for a loan or as the basis of a mortgage or other financial security. Such arrangements were common in the early nineteenth century as landowners relied on the enslaved not only for their labor but also as financial instruments.[15] Harper's daughter and son-in-law continued to depend on enslaved labor to run Oakland.

Enslaved labor and enslavement as finance both shaped the land surrounding Cross Keys. By the 1860s a second estate called Woodlawn was formed next to Cross Keys and Oakland. It was purchased by Hiram Wood with money he had made as a sugar refiner with business connections rooted in the same slave economies that linked Baltimore and other port cities along the eastern seaboard to the wider Atlantic world. Within two generations, property transactions had transformed the land comprised of Cross Keys, Oakland, and Woodlawn into a node that linked the Atlantic economy with the trans-Appalachian network of absentee Baltimore landowners such as the Goughs and Carrolls.

Property ownership and the environment continued to shape political activity in Cross Keys during the Civil War. The Jones Falls Valley provided a land, river, and railroad link between Baltimore and Pennsylvania. Cross Keys residents turned their homes into stops on the Underground Railroad. To do this, homeowners who had built or inherited houses modified the structures to incorporate spaces to shelter black people en route north. This was particularly dangerous given that the estates surrounding Cross Keys belonged to Confederate sympathizers.[16]

The end of the Civil War brought newly emancipated African Americans to Cross Keys, creating a more complex array of property relations and social ties. Its population swelled to include a mix of more than one hundred owners and renters.[17] Families grew and subsequent generations stayed. Long-standing residents built additions on their lots and added second or third stories to houses, further altering the landscape of Cross Keys. Moonier's children intermarried with neighbors. Some left the property where they grew up and bought or rented new homes elsewhere in the village.[18] Although Cross Keys remained predominantly African American, beginning in the 1870s its biggest landlord became a German immigrant who built a house on Falls Road next to the main path up the hill. Several of the smaller homes in Cross Keys fronted the path, which assumed his name.

In the decades after the Civil War, Cross Keys became a bustling social and political hub with ties south to Baltimore City and deeper north into Baltimore County. A string of black enclaves dotted Falls Road to the north, and it was common for Cross Keys residents to travel between them to visit extended family.[19] A local picnic grove known for its oak trees and fresh water springs played host to church revival meetings comprised of congregations from miles around. Residents did not have to leave Cross Keys to acquire the staples of daily life. Cross Keys, like many black communities in both the city and county, contained branches of clubs and fraternal lodges that became major organizers of political and civic society. A black chapter of the Workingmen's Party—one of the first Marxist-influenced political parties in the United States, which also proved popular with nearby white mill workers—organized in Cross Keys in 1877 on the heels of the Great Railroad Strike.[20]

While Cross Keys had a dynamic social structure and political life that connected residents to a wider region, work centered on the nearby country estates, marking a continuity with the antebellum economy. Most men worked as artisans, coachmen, and laborers, reflecting the community's class stratification.[21] Water proved crucial to the local economy, too; women who worked and/or cooked for nearby white families frequently took in their wash as well, using abundant water from the multiple nearby fresh springs.[22]

With its stores, amenities, and daily staples, Cross Keys was a community that defies categories often used by historians to describe peripheral spaces. It was not a bedroom community, because its residents did not commute to work despite the proximity of a railroad in the Jones Falls Valley. However, it was also not an enclave that could be explained strictly by service work, like some black neighborhoods in the vicinity of wealthy white estates throughout the country. Cross Keys and the surrounding country estates were neither rural nor urban, yet one word was absent from contemporary descriptions of them: "suburban."

That continued to be the case even as emancipation marked the start of a slow decline in country estates. In the 1870s and 1880s real estate speculators began to redevelop the area. This redevelopment was continued by the Roland Park Company, which in 1891 began transforming the area located just up the hill from Cross Keys. In doing so, the Roland Park Company broke with contemporary patterns of development, including the relatively short-lived dismantling of estates, by deploying international capital to create the first planned suburb.

CIRCUITS OF CAPITAL

Two factors characterized each stop made by the capital that ultimately financed Roland Park: investors sought to profit from racialized property and labor relations, and they did so through extraction and appropriation of resources such as land and water. This pattern can best be seen by looking at two of Roland Park's biggest investors, engineer Alfred Fryer and cotton mill owner Jacob Bright, both natives of Manchester, England. In the 1870s, Fryer was not yet looking toward Baltimore. Instead, he was working with speculators to take advantage of the emancipation of slaves in the British colony of Antigua. Fryer's entry into Antigua was facilitated by the West Indian Encumbered Estates Act (1854). Great Britain had abolished slavery in the Caribbean in 1833, providing compensation for planters but nothing for the enslaved. The 1854 act further enriched former planters by abrogating debts on the land. Once the act took effect in Antigua, planters and their intermediaries welcomed it by doing swift business to buy and resell estates. This allowed some existing estate owners to consolidate more land through chains of purchases.

It also created an opportunity for new arrivals. Fryer's Concrete Company purchased six estates and leased one from an intermediary. In total, it paid twenty-seven thousand pounds for 3,700 acres. Fryer's company purchased the land to cater to the needs of West Indian planters who were changing their modes of production amid a collapse in sugar prices. In 1846 Great Britain passed the Sugar Duties Act, which equalized import duties from British colonies. The act's gradual implementation ultimately had a devastating effect on the British Caribbean, which previously enjoyed a preferential status. As a consequence, Antigua and its neighbor Barbuda had to compete with sugar from the rest of the world, including places where it was still produced with enslaved labor.[23]

Here entered Fryer, who looked to take advantage of West Indian planters' need for cheaper ways of producing sugar, which continued to form the backbone of the Antiguan economy. Indeed, Fryer purchased the estates as sites for experiments with his recently patented sugar machine, the Concretor. He and company investors intended for the Concretor to improve the speed and efficiency of processing cane from juice and stalk into the crystallized sugar product, or "concrete," that would then be shipped to British refineries.[24] Antigua's planters already had an advantage in that Antigua's less refined muscovado sugar tended to be cheaper than that of other Caribbean islands, and the Concretor promised an even cheaper product of higher quality better suited for British refinery equipment.[25]

Curious planters became interested in Fryer's machine, which promised to process sugar cane with fewer laborers and less skill than current practices, and do so more quickly. The standard operating procedure in Antigua sugar mills was for workers to run them nonstop at harvest time. Fryer advertised that the Concretor required "only a man and a boy" to run the machine as it boiled cane juice to evaporation.[26] This was not quite the case, however. Workers still had to cut the cane, tie it in bundles, and transport it to the Concretor. Even this first step, like every other step in Antigua's sugar cultivation, proved dangerous for workers because of the planters' disregard for black lives and their desire to speed up production.

Newspaper accounts described an automated process, erasing human labor by emphasizing the work of the machine.[27] Fryer's Concretor could not have worked, however, without black labor. After workers cut and tied the cane, they carted it over to the foot of a hill where they loaded it onto the Concretor's conveyor belt made of chain and slabs of wood. The belt lifted it to machines that ground the cane and removed the solid matter via a similar conveyor belt. The extracted juice traveled through a pipe and simmered until waste material rose to the top and workers skimmed it into a cistern. More workers carried the clarified juice from a tray to the Concretor itself. The superintendent directed a worker to close or open compartments through which the juice flowed and evaporated, yielding the concrete. Yet another worker placed the concrete in containers. Still others prepared the concrete for shipment and drove it from the estate to port on a three-wheeled road-based steam engine. En route they traveled over roads that had previously been laid across the island by incarcerated black Antiguans.

Nor would Fryer have seen an opportunity for profit without Antigua's postemancipation labor, legal, and social orders, all of which were premised on the violent maintenance of racial and class hierarchy. When planters talked of speeding up work and reducing skilled labor, they were generally seeking ways to control Antigua's majority-black workforce. This was an inherently racial project. Planters, who dominated the island's legislature, lowered wages and sought to produce more in order to maintain profits as the price of sugar fell. At the same time, they also raised the prices on the most common foodstuffs eaten by black Antiguans and used the revenue to begin an immigration scheme aimed at recruiting white Portuguese laborers from Madeira. The Antigua legislature intended for the immigration scheme to quash dissent among black Antiguans and remove alternatives for mobility and employment.[28]

In addition, an engineered scarcity of property available to black Antiguans enabled planters in establishing a legal regime intended to approximate enslavement. Little land existed outside the white-owned estates, which dominated the countryside. This was coupled with a lack of access to fresh water.[29] In the past, black workers had sought refuge by leaving the sugar estates for part of the week to work in markets or in the main port settlement of St. John's. New contract laws and bad economic conditions, however, put a stop to part-time estate work. Indeed, the drive to recruit Madeiran labor was part of a broader attempt by the planter class to stem the exodus of emancipated workers from the estates. Madeirans were paid more, and unlike black Antiguans they could access credit, which enabled them to leave estate labor and build intergenerational wealth across the island, often as property-owning merchants.[30]

Planters used their political power in the legislature to reestablish the labor and legal regimes that had existed under slavery, often using the rhetoric of having to adjust sugar production in light of falling prices. Sugar workers knew they lived under laws that gave them no recourse. Whites could jail, beat, rape, and murder black Antiguans with impunity. Samuel Smith, a black Antiguan born after emancipation, observed that cattle and horses received more legal protections than black workers. Unwilling to put up with these conditions, black Antiguan women led an uprising in 1858 in which they committed acts of violence against Madeirans, police, and black Barbudans, the latter of whom were viewed as outsiders and economic competitors.[31] Much of the uprising took place in St. John's, where participants utilized the accessible roads, density of settlement, and a critical mass of people to mount public displays of dissent and dissatisfaction that were easily put down.

Fryer Concrete capital buttressed a society in which, to paraphrase Peter James Hudson, white supremacy passed as an economic rationale.[32] The business of managing a sugar estate proved inseparable from racial violence. White overseers cracked whips close to groups of cutters to speed them up, maiming people whom they hit in the eye. Planters rode horses directly into groups of workers to scatter them, trampling and killing people in the process. Smith's testimony attests to whites' indifference to the harms caused to black people.

At the time of emancipation, the land Fryer bought was worked by at least 1,137 enslaved men, women, and children.[33] Many of them came to work for Fryer's Concrete. There is little direct information about the life and labor on Fryer's sugar estates. Antigua is a relatively small island and black workers moved from one estate to another looking for the least brutal conditions, but Smith recalled that similar conditions existed from place to place. Estate workers lived in the same type of houses built for the enslaved. These wood and stone structures, forty feet wide by sixty feet long with an earthen cellar, housed several families without partitions. After emancipation, planters refused to maintain the homes because, they said, workers were now free to leave them if they were dissatisfied. Leaky roofs were a constant problem, but residents lacked access to repair supplies. Rain rotted the floorboards to the point that workers pulled them up to prevent small children from falling through into the cellar. The dirt cellar, with its mites, scorpions, and rats, became the new floor. Estate workers wrapped their feet at night to prevent bites from rats and the debilitating mite larva that ate into the skin. Each morning they awoke and gathered for roll call, after which they walked across the hundreds of acres of estate land to work.[34] Coupled with the violent strategies used by employers, estate life presented constant risks to workers' health, bodies, and lives.

Fryer invited over a hundred guests to the estate for demonstrations. These guests may have seen the substandard housing or managers cracking whips, but the focus of their attention was the Concretor. Visitors included British merchants and owners of trade magazines, sugar barons from Natal and Honduras, and refiners from Liverpool, Bristol, Glasgow, and Manchester. The head of the Manchester Chamber of Commerce, London bankers, and Antigua landowners stood shoulder to shoulder on the estate to watch the Concretor. French engineers and chemists from nearby colonies also visited, and those who could not travel requested concrete samples, which Fryer sent.[35] Planters around the Caribbean purchased the Concretor.[36] Fryer, as part of a British engineering firm, expanded business to the Dominican Republic and Puerto Rico.[37]

One of the investors in Fryer's Concrete was Alfred Fryer's friend Jacob Bright. Born in 1821 into a politically active Quaker family, he joined his father's cotton-spinning business and owned mills near Manchester, England. As the mills hummed just outside the city, he also carried on his family's political legacy as a Liberal member of Parliament from 1867 until 1895. The geographic breadth of his investments drew more places into the circuits of capital that ultimately financed Roland Park. Like Fryer, Bright chose investments centered on land and resource extraction. Fryer and Bright invested in land, government bonds, banks, and companies on four continents, sometimes together and other times separately.

In Bright's case, as a member of Parliament (and the son of a member of Parliament), his investments in the Congo and Egypt blurred the line between state action and business decision. These were just two of many stops for Bright's capital investment, especially during the 1880s. As a case in point, Bright used his platform in government to oppose the British invasion of Egypt, where he was director of the Commercial Bank of Alexandria in 1884.[38] The bank was liquidated due to political strife that ground business to a halt.

Bright also used his political position to profit in the Congo from waterborne trading, which had the effect of ushering in a genocidal regime. In 1885 Bright assumed the directorship of the British Congo Company, having helped to defeat a British treaty that would have given Portugal control over the Congo River Basin.[39] He anticipated that the company would soon gain access to the land and resources around the basin—and he was right. The 1884–1885 Berlin Conference of the United States and European powers formalized many of the mechanisms of European colonialism on the African continent. The conference gave rise to the Congo Free State ruled by King Leopold II of Belgium, who granted trading rights to the British in the river basin. The British Congo Company's boats gained access to the river and supplied material the company then exported.[40]

The boats of the British Congo Company were not the only trading ships connecting Britain to raw supplies around the world. The steamship *Jacob Bright* of the eponymous company regularly sailed out of Bright's home port of Manchester en route to the Caribbean, Central America, and the American South. Planters ranging from sugar estate owners in Antigua to owners of cotton plantations in the United States counted on ships such as the *Jacob Bright* to bolster regional economies through trade. In addition to fostering trade, steamships like the *Jacob Bright* also increasingly connected Manchester to sites of coercive labor practices based on racial hierarchies.

BRITISH INVESTORS MEET AMERICAN SPECULATORS

Thousands of miles from Egypt, the Congo, and Antigua, the same sources of British investment that would eventually find their way to Roland Park also flowed into U.S. westward expansion. White settlements in what is now Utah and Idaho were making survival increasingly difficult for local Northwestern Shoshone Indians. In 1863 federal troops retaliated for a Northwestern Shoshone raid by killing three hundred men, women, and children in the Bear River Massacre. This spurred negotiations between the Northwestern Shoshone and the federal government, opening the area to state-sponsored settlements and enabling railroad companies to run tracks through the river valley.[41] The railroads sold land near the tracks to two Kansas City financiers, Samuel Jarvis and Roland Ray Conklin, who formed the Bear

River Canal Company to supply water to towns in Utah and Idaho. The Bear River Massacre had made the valley an investment opportunity for Jarvis and Conklin. The primary customers of Bear River water were the ranchers who had settled the area and who employed Northwestern Shoshone as low-paid seasonal farm laborers and domestic servants, creating a racialized labor regime in which the dispossessed Shoshone regained access to the land as wage laborers.

Jarvis and Conklin also sold bonds to British investors for a new water system they planned for the Bear River. Fryer was one of the investors.[42] One historian who analyzed their business endeavors characterized the Jarvis-Conklin Mortgage Trust as "the preeminent institution serving as a conduit for the capital financing white settler colonialism in the U.S. West."[43] Jarvis and Conklin proceeded to accelerate both the Bear River Valley's state-backed settler colonialism and the area's integration into larger global circuits of capital. Jarvis and Conklin themselves did not displace members of the Northwestern Shoshone, just as Fryer did not enslave Antiguans and Bright did not commit atrocities in the Congo. However, they capitalized on state violence, making advantageous business decisions that reshaped the environment and maximized resource extraction and displacement.

The new water system, like the railroad before it, also brought land speculators and farmers from the Midwest.[44] With the arrival of new farmers, Jarvis and Conklin reaped further returns in Utah by conducting the main business that enriched them in Kansas City: western farm mortgages. By 1888 the trust had negotiated nearly fifteen thousand mortgages valued at $14 million.[45] During the 1880s both farm mortgage debt and the total acreage of mortgaged farmland sharply increased. These mortgages were part of what one historian called a newly impersonal moment in the history of mortgage finance marked by "attenuated" chains of financial intermediaries that handled farm mortgages.[46] Jarvis and Conklin made investments, issued mortgages, and purchased existing mortgages as a means to an end: they sold them to distant investors.

As financial intermediaries, Jarvis and Conklin pursued multiple business strategies. They sometimes sold the farm mortgages outright to an investor, likely a bank or insurance company in New England or in Britain. They also added mortgages to portfolios of the British firms for which they managed funds and profited from service fees, as when they channeled $3,252,206 in farm loans to the Yorkshire Investment and American Mortgage Company Limited, earning British investors an average return of 6 percent.[47] In a third lucrative line of business, the trust bundled farm mortgages and issued bonds against them, either selling the securities to investors or adding them to the portfolios of British clients.[48]

At least sixty other firms directed British money into American farm mortgages during the same time period.[49] The majority, including the Colonial and United States Mortgage Company, issued mortgages directly without intermediary companies like the Jarvis-Conklin Mortgage Trust. Based in Hull, England, the family that ran that company saw U.S. farm mortgages as merely one source of capital in the context of a portfolio that included investments spanning three continents. In addition to Mexican smelting factories, and a bit closer to home, the Colonial and United States Mortgage Company also invested in water and light plants in England. Like their fellow Quaker Jacob Bright, the company owners also looked toward Africa.[50] Shareholders in the Colonial and United States Mortgage Company received an average dividend of 8.3 percent throughout the 1880s.[51]

MODES OF SEEING PEOPLE AND PROPERTY

The investors who financed the Lands Trust Company when it eventually came into being in 1888 shared a vision of how racial hierarchy, land, and property combined to produce value. Specifically, they premised their investments on the idea that settler colonialism increased land value. One year prior, this tenet formed the cornerstone of an essay written by Fryer about his travels in the United States. The Jarvis-Conklin Mortgage Trust initially commissioned Fryer to journey from east to west across North America to record observations that would attract British business. Fryer published his travel account in 1887 under the title *The Great Loan Land*.

He spent much of the essay's sixty-five pages discussing how Americans had developed a character distinct from Europeans because of the relative ease with which they could purchase land to work with their own hands. Working the land, he explained, made Americans brave, hardy, and enterprising. A "wave of civilization flowed steadily and rapidly westward," he wrote. Where once only "wild animals, rattlesnakes, and red men" lived, "pioneer farmers" could sell their land for a hefty profit, presumably to financial intermediaries and land speculators such as Jarvis and Conklin.[52]

Fryer's assessment of Americans reflected contemporary thinking about white settlement and American society, promulgated by people with some of the biggest platforms of the day. Six years after *The Great Loan Land*, historian Frederick Jackson Turner delivered a speech in Chicago on his frontier thesis. According to Turner, American development—which he defined as beginning with European exploration—was shaped by successive frontier lines, at each of which white settlers eked out early stages of industrial, economic, and institutional growth, often while in violent conflict with Native Americans. Turner's conclusion was that by heading west, Americans gradually shirked European modes of custom and thought, redefining themselves into a people defined by practicality, inquisitiveness, and democratic impulses.[53] Meanwhile, Wild West shows such as Buffalo Bill Cody's trafficked in an imagined past in which the Indian Wars of the century's middle decades set the stage for American progress. Coincidentally, Turner and Cody were both present in Chicago during the 1893 Columbian Exposition, which embraced an ethnographic approach to history in which the fair's millions of attendees walked the Midway Plaisance in a procession that guided them on a journey from primitive human development, as represented by performers from around the world, to the gates of the White City, a monumental space designed to showcase America's arrival as an imperial power through its technology and culture.[54]

Needless to say, this interpretation of America's past and its attendant consequences for the present moment turned on a racial hierarchy in which its proponents erased Indians completely. The Native Americans of the Bear River Valley still lived and subsisted on the land, while providing indispensable labor to white-owned farms and homes. Closer to Jarvis and

Conklin's Kansas City base, Native Americans played central roles in forming political alliances and debating land use.[55] Nevertheless, the popular
narrative of western land as a tabula rasa subject to a march of civilization
and necessary for the making of an "American" people time and again served
the social, financial, and political goals of capital.[56]

The Great Loan Land, then, was hardly unique in adopting a perspective
that white settlement would improve the land it touched. Jarvis, Conklin,
and Fryer's adoption of it for their business, however, casts light on the intellectual work behind attracting British investment to North America
and the specific types of investment they thought would be most salient to
a distant pool of white shareholders. As an Englishman traveling in the
American West, Fryer turned narrative into advertising in *The Great Loan
Land*. Whereas Turner had reflected on the closing of the frontier, Fryer
told British investors American land was a wide-open proposition. "Look
beyond the limits of Europe," he exhorted, "to find real security." In doing
so, Fryer offset any passing mentions of violence or social tension with assessments of social stability. "Judge Lynch" may have ruled parts of the
United States in 1887, according to Fryer, but "whether its citizens are white
men, black men, yellow men, or red men, republican or democrat, protec-
tionists or free-traders, they are all intensely loyal to the Constitution under
which they live."[57] Investors could be secure in the knowledge that U.S. land
was a stable investment, because no one wanted to upend the very institutions and laws that protected private property. For Jarvis, Conklin, and
Fryer, the promise of the American frontier lay not in the potential for
egalitarian opportunity but in the opportunities for British businessman
to extract profit from the land.

Fryer peppered his essay with comparisons between British and American land. Liberal U.S. property laws, in particular, stood out for him. Selling property in the United States was as easy as selling a horse, Fryer wrote.
Consequently, people owned property by purchasing it rather than inher-
iting it, which predisposed them, according to Fryer, to selling if the price
was right. Easy property transfer, an abundance of fertile western land, and
a robust market for resale allowed Fryer to conclude that the price of land
was steadily increasing—good news for British investors in mortgages, who

had become accustomed in recent years to seeing the value of British land plateau or decline.[58] In *The Great Loan Land* Fryer distilled how people, property, and value, if viewed together in certain ways, could serve as the basis for profit.

In organizing its business ventures around white population growth, the Jarvis-Conklin Mortgage Trust did not limit itself to rural areas. They branched out into waterworks and utilities in Bear River and other localities, transportation in their home base of Kansas City, and municipal bonds throughout Oregon, California, Missouri, and Texas. They also purchased property on the peripheries of fast-growing cities such as Chicago and Cleveland. All these choices had in common a presumption about settler colonialism as growth, whether focused on the land itself, resources, or financial instruments.

Throughout 1887 Fryer circulated *The Great Loan Land* among his associates while continuing to raise capital for the Jarvis-Conklin Mortgage Trust. The next year saw Fryer, Jarvis, and Conklin begin a new company to further increase their British business. On May 8, 1888, Fryer, Jacob Bright, and three other men assumed the directorship of the newly incorporated Lands Trust Company. This was the company in which Emma Dixon bought shares. Its prospectus advertised itself as a land speculation venture in the United States and British colonies. It also assured any potential investors in the company that they could count on the local knowledge and experience of the Lands Trust's American managers, Jarvis and Conklin.

Like the Jarvis-Conklin Mortgage Trust, the Lands Trust relied on settler colonialism as a main driver of profit. Investors likely learned about the company by reading its nationally advertised prospectus. In it, the company promised to "purchase lands in those more newly settled parts of the United States, or in the Colonies, where from the influx of population they are rapidly enhancing in value."[59] Those who requested shareholder applications also received from Fryer a copy of a report that summarized *The Great Loan Land*.[60] In it, Fryer elaborated on how the Lands Trust would select land to purchase. Farm, city, and suburban lands all held potential. All types fell into one of three categories. The first category were lands already held at speculative prices; the company would not consider these. The second category were lands that could be obtained very cheaply but which might be inadequate due to poor climate or "the absence of an emigrant population in the district." The last and best category of lands, according to Fryer, were those "in the very track of emigration." The Lands Trust would focus on acquiring these lands, spread out over a wide area to minimize risk. It would issue securities against some of this land rather than reselling it. In those instances, anyone working the land or building homes on it would "improve the security."

The Lands Trust struck a chord among members of the British public; they oversubscribed to all five hundred thousand shares at one pound each within three months.[61] Four hundred and six people purchased shares. From music professors to ministers to mustard manufacturers, a wide cross-section of society from all corners of the British Isles put their hard-earned money into the Lands Trust Company. It is debatable how much the shareholders knew or wanted to know about the daily activities of the company. What they most likely did know, however, were the contents of the newspaper advertisement, the prospectus, and Fryer's report. Spread across class, geographical, and other social lines, the disparate group of British investors were united by their endorsement of the company's stated aim of investing in the path of white settlement.

Some investors had close ties to both the Lands Trust Company and the Jarvis-Conklin Mortgage Trust, since the two were closely linked. Eli Sheldon was a case in point. The Lands Trust set up offices in London and shared the address 95 Gresham Street with Jarvis-Conklin Mortgage Trust. Jarvis and Conklin owned the most shares of stock, after Fryer. Sheldon was the general manager for the Jarvis-Conklin Mortgage Trust Company in the United States. He was such a valued member of the Jarvis-Conklin Mortgage Trust that the company named a small tract it purchased on the periphery of Chicago Sheldon Heights. Sheldon later moved London to become general manager of their British operation. He served in the role at the same time that he was listed as a founding member of the Lands Trust Company.[62]

When Sheldon and his wife May French-Sheldon relocated to London, they moved into a townhouse where they played host to members of London society. In the process of amassing social connections, they came to count among their friends wealthy explorers such as Henry Morton Stanley, who mapped the Congo River Basin for King Leopold II and served as U.S. delegate to the Berlin Conference. From these visits the Sheldons developed interests in Africa. Eli Sheldon used $50,000 from money he made from both the Jarvis-Conklin Mortgage Trust and Lands Trust companies to fund his wife's treks through eastern Africa. French-Sheldon, who adopted the names "White Queen" and "Bebe Bwana," published accounts of her travels including a book, *From Sultan to Sultan: Adventures Among the Masai and Other Tribes of East Africa.*[63] Based on the book, French-Sheldon gained notoriety as an authority on African peoples. Sheldon's employment and French-Sheldon's work shaped their imperial imagination and helped defined their social, cultural, and economic lives.

Sheldon maintained close direct ties with both the Lands Trust Company and the Jarvis-Conklin Mortgage Trust, but investors in the former also came from businesses that worked with the Lands Trust Company, like employees from the two banks authorized to conduct Lands Trust business. Still other investors shared the same address as the company's brokers or had nearby addresses in the heart of London's financial sector. For these bankers and financiers, the Lands Trust Company was one of many businesses with which they dealt. It is likely that they also did business with other companies engaged in similar activities around the world.

The majority of the four hundred investors who found the newspaper advertisements about white settlement persuasive had no prior connections to the Lands Trust Company. The Lands Trust officers sought shareholders from all corners of Britain and Ireland. They published their prospectus in newspapers in Ireland, Scotland, Wales, and throughout England. The greatest number of shareholders were concentrated in and around London and Manchester. These cities were two of Britain's largest population centers and the locations with the most personal and business connections to the company. The three holders of the most shares lived in London,

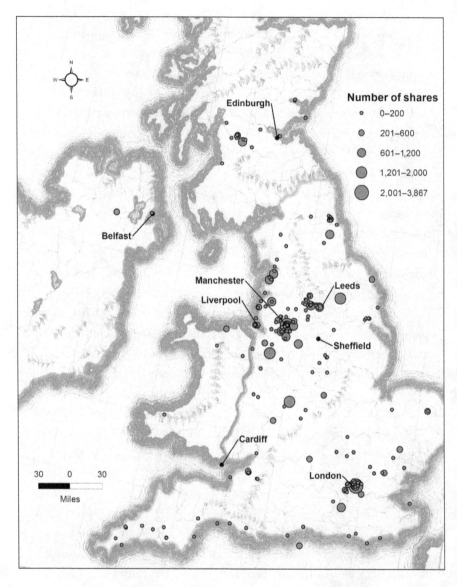

FIGURE 1.1 Geographic distribution of Lands Trust Company shareholders. The size of each bubble corresponds to the number of shares of common stock owned in 1892.

(Prepared by Stacy Bogan, Harvard University Center for Geographic Analysis)

Birmingham, and just outside Manchester in Cheshire, respectively. Small shareholders lived in all corners of the British Isles, from the Shetland Islands to the Isle of Wight and from Skibbereen, Ireland, to Norwich near the North Sea.

Investors listed 133 unique occupations. They ranged across every major category of work, with shareholders in labor, clerical, administrative, service, religious, and professional positions. They also covered a wide set of social strata within single sectors. Banking-related occupations encompassed bankers, accountants, and tellers. Both corn dealers and corn millers likewise bought stock. Machinists invested along with company presidents, and doctors along with drapers.[64] Legal changes in the nineteenth century enabled more people from a wider variety of classes to invest money to produce income. Lands Trust shareholders reflected that increasing variety.

Even so, the occupational diversity of Lands Trust shareholders had limits. Some occupations had only a little representation while others appeared disproportionately. Even the seemingly exceptional cases hint at networks based on employment, religion, and kin. Only one domestic worker—a butler—could be counted among the hundreds of shareholders. Many shareholders, especially those from around Lancashire near Manchester, worked in textile-related jobs. Twenty-one investors identified as spinners, drapers, clothiers, tailors, bleachers, or wool combers. They were joined by one sailmaker and a yarn salesman and merchants who specialized in textile products.[65] Lancashire mills, like those run by the Bright family, operated hierarchies of pay and prestige that were reproduced in terms of who could afford to invest in the Lands Trust Company. Cotton spinners, the "aristocrats" of mill workers, occupied the top of that hierarchy and were also the most represented mill employees among the Lands Trust shareholders.[66] Meanwhile, no piecers, who made considerably less, bought shares.

Shared religious ties shaped investor decisions. Though the exact number remains unclear, Quakers were heavily represented among Lands Trust investors.[67] The Society of Friends encouraged its members to invest in the company. It republished *The Great Loan Land* because it "so well and

37

completely answers most of the questions that an English investor asks concerning the merits and security of American Land Mortgages."[68] The handful of investors who lived in the United States were Quakers located near the Jarvis-Conklin Mortgage Trust offices in New York and Philadelphia. Not all investors belonged to the Society of Friends, however. Clergy from at least two different Protestant denominations also bought shares.[69]

Women as well as men financed the Lands Trust Company. British investors connected overseas investment, especially in land, to gendered modes of accumulating capital. In the face of the relative democratization of financial life in Britain, ways of seeing distant lands and people became a battleground for defining what constituted respectable British femininity. This was due, in part, to the fact that overseas and colonial investment had long been a sector of the British economy in which women disproportionately participated, since at least the eighteenth century.[70] In the late nineteenth century, legal changes to women's property rights led to an increase in British women investing. Banks and companies began to offer services tailored toward women, and investment advice literature was aimed at them. Yet, these agents—including brokers and financial writers—characterized financial risk taking as unfeminine.[71] As a result, agents channeled women's investments into what they considered to be more conservative and reliable sectors. Overseas land, bonds, and utilities fell into this category of low-risk and safe enough to be appropriately "feminine." By the 1890s two major trends emerged: women investors increased to 16 percent of all British shareholders, and 83 percent of them invested in firms that dealt primarily in overseas or empire assets.[72]

Women, however, frequently broke out of their expected role as low-risk investors and drew the attention of local observers.[73] Women accounted for 15 percent of shareholders and owned 8 percent of shares of the Lands Trust Company.[74] The Lands Trust Company only partly fit the recommended profile of a safe investment for women. While it was an investment based primarily on overseas and colonial assets with a focus on land, the company's practice of land speculation carried a higher risk. The company's founding documents also stated its intention to invest in land securities such as mortgages. Mortgages carried more risk than land ownership. The decisions by women to invest in the Lands Trust Company thus reveal the more varied risks that women took in juxtaposition to societal norms.

It is possible that women played an even greater role in supporting the Lands Trust Company than can be assessed by stock subscriptions alone. Twenty-five of the sixty women shareholders were related to other Lands Trust shareholders. Yet, their presence was often masked by the ways British companies reported shareholders by occupation. Such was the case with John MacKenzie Wilson, a Northumberland minister who jointly purchased thirty shares for thirty pounds with Anna Aikman Cunningham Wilson, identified by occupation as "his wife."[75] As a minister's wife, she likely performed church-related duties. Most women were listed by marital status. The widows who owned stock may have turned to investment to supplement their income, in combination with other survival strategies.[76]

Women also had other securities options such as purchasing debentures, or shares of debt, which carried lower risk than stock but did not give them voting power in a company. The Lands Trust issued debentures, but the records of debt holders did not survive.[77] Whether through stocks or debentures, women's choices to invest in companies such as the Lands Trust Company marked a key process by which British society developed new ways of thinking about individuals, risk, and the relationship between Britain and the world.[78]

BALTIMORE GROWTH

The exact reasons why the Lands Trust Company selected Baltimore are unknown, but its patterns of growth mirrored those of other areas where the company held investments, areas deeply structured by race and class.[79] The breakups of country estates north of the city in Baltimore County were connected to larger processes of change. In 1874 the owner of the Woodlawn estate, Hiram Woods, sold it to real estate dealers Richard and Laura Lee Capron. The Caprons made their living following a long-standing practice in Baltimore in which they purchased and then resold area property, initiating strings of transactions occurring over several days where property changed hands multiple times.[80]

The Caprons focused on two areas of the city that were currently attracting affluent white residents. One was northern central Baltimore. This corridor of growth had long been home to Baltimore's wealthiest and oldest white families. Through the 1870s and into the 1880s residents of these neighborhoods continued to move north, expanding the upper-class district from its stronghold of Mount Vernon into newly built three-story row houses on Mount Royal, North Avenue, and west to Eutaw Place. Their new spacious row houses resembled those of Mount Vernon, whose leafy square dated to the 1830s. The other area of the Caprons' focus tracked west along North Avenue into Baltimore County to country estates whose landowners began to sell them off piecemeal.

Locally based builders with limited capital reserves leased these small pieces of land from the property owners, usually borrowing from the ground rent, an annual rent owed to the landowner. This ground rent, derived from an English practice refined by eighteenth-century Baltimoreans, functioned as a form of credit for builders.[81] Landowners leased a lot for ninety-nine years to a builder who erected several houses and sold the lots and ground quickly in order to turn a profit before the annual payment was due.[82] This required turnover in as little as a few months. Even Baltimore's largest subdividers who broke up country estates funded their operations through ground rents and faced the attendant pressure to make profits quickly. The ground rent system was an enduring business model but also a short-term one, where the quickest work yielded the most profit.

The ground rent model was also a highly adaptable one that gave rise to Baltimore's iconic streetscape dominated by row houses. The row house was a building form that could easily be varied in size, and its facades could be constructed in the latest styles. Architectural historian Mary Ellen Hayward notes that landowners with ground rent rights preferred to have many houses built on their land to make the most of ground rent payments. As a result, builders opted to construct connected houses on uniform lots. There was, moreover, a direct relationship between Baltimore's street pattern and ground rents: to maximize the number of people paying ground rent, early Baltimore landowners laid out a mix of wider and narrow streets through their parcels.[83] Larger houses fronted main streets while smaller ones lined the alleys between them. Whether rich or poor, homeowner or renter, Baltimoreans in the nineteenth century likely lived in a row house in close proximity to people of different races and classes.

By the 1880s Baltimore had been rapidly growing for the three decades. The city's municipal boundaries, however, had remained unchanged since 1817. A new area that locals dubbed "the Belt" ringed the city in Baltimore County. The Belt was home to forty thousand people in three distinct sections. Its eastern portion consisted of residents who worked dirty and often dangerous industrial jobs in nearby slaughterhouses, distilleries, breweries, and refineries. The northern and western sections of the Belt saw a boom in a more varied population of Baltimoreans who could to live further away—and further uphill—from the harbor.

The emergence of the Belt gave rise to a decades-long fight over annexation. Recurrent debates centered on expenditures on infrastructure and services. Baltimore County did not provide services or infrastructure to the Belt. Pro-annexation Belt residents decried the injustice of serving as the otherwise rural county's main revenue base only to see their tax dollars redistributed by county commissioners to distant constituents. Baltimore City was already providing fire services just over the border and did not get reimbursed. Pro-annexation Belt residents also pointed out that the Belt would benefit from Baltimore City's superior sanitary infrastructure. Opponents of annexation inverted the argument; the Belt would require massive municipal expenditures. It was, they argued, full of polluted wells and silted farm ponds. The higher elevations of the north and western sections would also require massive changes to the city's water supply in order for water to be delivered.[84]

Political tensions came to a head in 1888 when each section of the Belt voted on annexation by Baltimore City. Richard Capron was a prominent supporter of annexation.[85] His pro-growth dealings also shaped his civic life; he helped found the Citizens' Improvement Association to advocate for better-developed roads in the northern section of the new annex, which would have improved access to his holdings. Campaigning by Belt residents paid off; the northern and western sections voted in favor of annexation. The industrial working-class east rejected annexation, though by a slimmer margin than predicted due to discontent with local health and sanitary conditions.

Annexation tripled the city's land area and shifted the city line two and a half miles north, from North Avenue to Cold Spring Lane.[86] The Baltimore City line now reached the southern border of Cross Keys, Woodlawn, and Oakland. This newly annexed northern section of the Belt, like the western section, still lacked the paved roads, infrastructure, or population density that would make it recognizably part of the country's sixth most populous city. Annexation produced a dramatic boom in land speculation, as many expected the value of any land near the new border to increase in value.[87] That would be even more likely if Baltimore City delivered the services and improved roads that Belt residents anticipated.

THE ROLAND PARK COMPANY

Edward Bouton arrived in Baltimore in 1891 to helm the latest real estate venture financed by the Lands Trust Company, the Roland Park Company. Bouton first became involved in development in Kansas in the 1870s after passing the bar exam and then deciding not to practice law. He subsequently established a home base in Kansas City, Missouri, where he met the three people responsible for creating his new job. The first, Charles Grasty, was a Kansas City newspaper owner who financed real estate speculation in Missouri. Grasty knew the other two Kansas City residents, Jarvis and Conklin. In 1888 and 1889 Bouton superintended the construction of four houses on their behalf in the new and affluent Hyde Park and Kenwood neighborhoods.[88] Jarvis, Conklin, and Bouton all built their own homes nearby and became neighbors. They developed a friendly relationship that mixed business and personal interests; the Jarvis-Conklin Mortgage Trust even negotiated a mortgage for Bouton's mother, which it placed with the

Quaker-run Yorkshire Investment and American Mortgage Company Limited.[89]

By 1890, the Kansas City land boom that initially made Hyde Park seem promising had tapered off. Meanwhile, the northern section of the Baltimore Belt matched the criteria that Fryer and the Lands Trust Company required: more than other sections of the Belt, its population was overwhelmingly native-born and white. More crucially, if Baltimore's growth pattern from previous years continued, not only would the Belt be in the path of affluent white settlement but so, too, would the areas immediately beyond it. The timing was fortuitous; Grasty had moved to Baltimore to purchase the *Baltimore News* and run the weekly southern-oriented business journal the *Manufacturer's Record*. It is unclear who first learned about the Caprons, the owners of the Woodlawn estate, but Grasty, Jarvis, Conklin, and Bouton were all in touch with the Caprons by January 1891. The Kansas City group had in mind the demographic profile of Hyde Park: affluent white Protestants, some of whom were newcomers to the city.[90]

Beginning that January, the Caprons began to purchase the country estates near Woodlawn in a prearranged deal with the founders of the Roland Park Company. The biggest tract they purchased was the Harper family estate, Oakland. Laura Lee Capron, whose sole name appeared on the deeds, then sold Jarvis and Conklin 55 percent stakes in the land throughout May and June. At this point, the Caprons, Jarvis, and Conklin assumed they had acquired a solid block of land spanning the entire top of the hill before it dipped down to Cross Keys in the Jones Falls Valley. It would be several years before they discovered the existence of the Moonier lot in the middle of their plot.

Seven months later, on July 30, Richard Capron joined four other signatories in incorporating the Roland Park Company. The original signatories included Bouton, Conklin, and two nearby Baltimore County landowners, Michael Jenkins and banker Douglas H. Thomas, who was a director of several Baltimore financial institutions that made loans to the Roland Park Company.[91] Jarvis and Grasty did not sign the incorporation paperwork, but they did join the five signatories in subscribing to company stock by the time the Roland Park Company held its first meeting later that day.

During the meeting Jarvis and Conklin "offered" to sell their land to the company in exchange for stock. They included in the deal their 55 percent interest in a tract of land Bouton had purchased in early May. Through the transaction, the Roland Park Company officially took hold of the property and began to develop the land. Meanwhile, Jarvis and Conklin came to own—on paper—7,527 of the company's 10,000 shares valued at a total of $752,700. In actuality, they managed these shares on behalf of the Lands Trust Company.[92]

The company's shareholder structure differentiated it from other real estate enterprises in Baltimore. Spousal relations formed a visible component of Baltimore's real estate speculation in the late nineteenth century that was common enough that it went unremarked in recordings of real estate transactions, court records, and the social pages of newspapers. Unlike her husband, Laura Lee Capron never assumed a formal position in the organization despite contributing land to the company's initial holdings. Whereas British women played a large role in financing Roland Park through the Lands Trust Company, only men filled the ranks of local investors and company officers. The Roland Park Company relied on local as well as British capital, but the Lands Trust retained the vast majority of shares.

In comparison to the existing system of housing development, the Roland Park Company's shareholder structure extended the timescale for returns. With the large amount of capital secured through shareholders, the Lands Trust Company was able to commit to a multiyear investment. The Roland Park Company also had enough capital to purchase land outright and vacate the annual ground rent. This meant it was able to avoid the yearly payments that motivated local builders to maintain a short turnover time. Moreover, the Lands Trust Company could provide steady injections of cash and loans to the Roland Park Company.[93]

The location of the Roland Park Company property marked another departure from local practices, in which builders developed land adjacent to already existing built-up blocks and "extended patterns more than they created new ones."[94] By contrast, the Roland Park Company leapfrogged built-up sections of Baltimore, developing land that was somewhat separated from the city. This distance proved crucial to the company's ability to market this land as a suburb, distinct from the existing urban landscape and yet connected to it.

CONCLUSION

The founding of the Roland Park Company linked Baltimore to a transnational network of capital spanning four continents. This network drew together far-flung actors under the logics of racial capitalism. In accordance with these logics, and beholden to distant investors for the long term, Roland Park Company officers began to experiment with different ways to segregate the new planned community 3,628 miles from the London offices where accountants issued Emma Dixon a dividend. In doing so, they made use of Dixon's and others' investments to transform the hill and valley just north of the new Baltimore City line into a planned development unlike others that came before it.

The newly acquired land's proximity to both the city and Cross Keys would shape the initial development decisions of the Roland Park Company. The Moonier family's half acre lay in the middle of the company's acquisition at the top of the hill. Cross Keys bordered the company's holdings to the west. The picnic grove, the dance hall, and the Jones Falls swimming spot all ringed the edges of the former country estates. Roland Park may have been the result of investors thinking about empty land and white settlement, but the reality was that Roland Park would develop cheek and jowl alongside a thriving African American community.

2

INFRASTRUCTURE

I n an 1891 letter to Alfred Fryer, Roland Park Company general manager Edward Bouton hoped "that there will not be any objections from
the authorities here, to our conducting our sewage into Jones's Falls.
Insomuch as down in the City the river is used as an open sewer, they ought
not to object to our doing it to the limited extent that our needs will demand."[1] To Bouton, resolving the issue of where sewage would go was one
of the most important infrastructural decisions to make about planning
Roland Park. Laying pipes would not be easy nor would it be cheap, but waste
had to go somewhere, just as water had to be piped in, sidewalks laid, and
lighting supplied. Moreover, any infrastructure needed to be maintained
and periodically updated in accordance with financial, political, and technological considerations.

With British investors watching from a distance, it fell to Bouton to solve
the puzzles of how to make Roland Park function. But that was not
enough—he also had to ensure its long-term profitability. This meant not
only planning the built environment but also experimenting with what
Seth Rockman calls "the submerged architecture—material, legal, and
ideological"—that would allow Roland Park to be "plausible in the first

place."[2] Over its first two decades, the Roland Park Company embarked on three interrelated projects: planning the built environment, advertising the new subdivision, and establishing the rules and relationships that would govern it. Taken together, the Roland Park Company was beginning an ambitious experiment with regard to how to lay out the infrastructure of one of the earliest planned segregated suburbs in the United States.

Under Bouton's hand and investor oversight, planning, advertising, and rulemaking came to center on the same key principle: nuisance. Nuisances, in contemporary understanding, were things that potentially created disease or otherwise impinged on well-being.[3] Thinking about nuisances was a way of thinking about people and property together. Planners and engineers, along with those in emerging medical and social science fields, deemed certain bodies and spaces as pathological dangers. They conflated sick people with unhealthy spaces and uses of those spaces. Nuisances comprised part of a broader discourse about health, hygiene, and the environment in the nineteenth century city. Nuisances were also a legal category that municipalities used in regulating, for example, where slaughterhouses or asylums could operate.[4]

Nuisance laws and nuisance discourse served as flexible state tools to manage people, police mobility, and regulate the terms of who could own property and where. There is ample evidence that nuisance law was drafted and enforced with race and nationality in mind. Its impact on the construction of difference, however, could vary. On one hand, it could collapse distinctions of citizenship, birthplace, and class into flattened categories such as "black." But nuisance laws could also sharpen differences. Some of Baltimore's earliest nuisance debates were about the presence of Haitians bathing in the Jones Falls. As the United States expanded west and overseas throughout the nineteenth century, regulating nuisances became a way to delimit citizenship and justify tactics of imperial population management.[5]

The Roland Park Company adapted nuisance law to suburban infrastructure by spearheading the use of restrictive covenants as a form of community-wide control. These nuisance laws went hand in hand with some of the earliest recorded racially restrictive covenants in the United

States. Historian Nayan Shah notes that "the rationale of nuisance law underwrote the cultural logic of residential covenants."[6] Until the 1890s, the few communities entirely covered by covenants comprised a handful of the wealthiest communities in the country. The Roland Park Company targeted a different demographic, namely Baltimore's affluent professional classes.

While restrictive covenants are some of the most well-known infrastructure of housing segregation, their origins as a form of suburban subdivision control remain murky. Much attention has been paid to the 1920s, when the spread of covenants coincided with the explosion of similar affluent planned suburbs across the United States. Omitted from that chronology is their experimental origins, as covenants were implemented by one developer at a time beginning in the 1890s. This tentative early usage changed markedly in later decades when both developers and homeowners in built-up areas hoped to emulate prestigious locales by adopting covenants for widely disparate neighborhoods.[7] Looking at how the Roland Park Company took steps toward creating restrictive covenants opens up new possibilities for tracing their origins, analyzing their logic, and understanding how they complemented other infrastructures of segregated suburbs.

The history of nuisances and racial restrictions mirrored the Roland Park Company itself—refracting racial hierarchies through imperial projects. The precursors to Roland Park's covenants included nuisance laws against Chinese-owned businesses in California, on the basis that Chinese people were inherently unclean and immoral.[8] In this case, the covenants targeted Chinese renters as well as Mexican and Punjabi property owners and were subject to court rulings concerning both international treaties and Reconstruction-era civil rights cases.[9] These legal precedents became known to the Roland Park Company when officials sought to specifically ban African Americans from Roland Park. But the chief person company officials turned to for advice was its sanitary engineer, whom it hired to design a sewer system. The engineer had gained experience working for the federal government in both the Caribbean and American cities. He would, company officials hoped, know whom to contact for examples of how to treat sewage and sanitary concerns in covenants.

So central were sewers to the creation of segregated suburbs that their environmental, social, and political ramifications spilled far beyond the boundaries of Roland Park to impact Baltimore City as a whole. To expand Roland Park after a decade in business, the company entered into negotiations with the newly formed Baltimore City Sewerage Commission to deviate from its master plan, which was designed to first serve areas most in need, including areas where disease, stench, and contaminated water were a part of daily life. Instead, the commission prioritized Roland Park houses, some of which were in Baltimore County. This episode elicited a set of questions similar to those raised during the 1888 annexation of the Belt: Who should access municipal infrastructure? Who would pay for it? What—and whom—would municipal government prioritize when considering future growth? These debates constituted some of the Roland Park Company's first forays into forging formal relationships with government officials. Their negotiations over sewers shifted Baltimore's political economy toward large developers.

The first two decades of planning Roland Park were full of experimentation, where the company worked out what types of tactics would be effective. In the process, they discarded alternatives. This was the case with the company's marketing. After initial sales proved disappointing, British investors demanded a change in advertising themes to center on fears of disease and health. The Roland Park Company consequently played on whites' fears that dirty and diseased racial others were gaining enough political capital and social mobility to start moving next door. Roland Park, they promised, could be kept healthy—employing a conflation of race, class, and disease that worked to their advantage. Roland Park, a planned suburb, was a better, healthier place to live because of the company's careful planning and guarantee of social homogeneity. The company thus wedded its quest for profits to classing diseased bodies and dirty streets as quintessentially urban.

RESTRICTIVE COVENANTS

As previously mentioned, the Roland Park Company's initial experiments had the backing of British finance. British investment made possible the creation of development companies with far more capital and potentially bigger projects than had been undertaken in older sections of many American cities. The larger scope of the projects meant that firms like the Roland Park Company faced a longer timescale for making a return on investment. Unlike the typical builders of Baltimore's row houses with short turnover time and limited capital, Roland Park Company general manager Edward Bouton sought methods to guarantee returns year after year.

Shortly after the founding of the Roland Park Company on July 30, 1891, Bouton began the daily operations of subdividing, planning, and selling the land in Roland Park. Though it held both the former Oakland and Woodlawn estates, the company opted to first focus all its efforts on the latter. This initial effort, Plat One, consisted of one hundred acres. Shareholders were prepared for the company to not turn a profit in 1891 as Plat One lots were not yet ready for sale. Because the Roland Park Company had Lands Trust capital from other enterprises, it was able to operate even when unprofitable. With a development scheme they knew would be realized slowly over time, financial backers remained committed to a multiyear investment, holding out for the possibility of long-term profits. British investors floated loans to the company with capital from its other investments, secured on the company's property; the largest loan was $65,000.[10] The Roland Park Company, unlike most local builders or individual property owners, had those resources.

This financial cushion also gave Bouton time to gather ideas about how to adopt restrictive covenants, which he took over two years to finalize. It is unclear how Bouton learned about restrictive covenants or when the Roland Park Company decided to use them. At least one developer advertised them in Kansas City when Jarvis, Conklin, and Bouton built houses and resided in Hyde Park, but they still were highly uncommon.[11] So, too, was the way Bouton considered using them. Covenants enumerated the rules in the contract a homebuyer signed to purchase property. The Roland Park Company used the type of agreement known as a deed restriction, where rules were inserted directly into the property's deed. By the early nineteenth century, a handful of American builders began to impose restrictions on individual or small groups of lots, often with a short expiration

FIGURE 2.1 Plat One of Roland Park.

(Courtesy of the Johns Hopkins University Sheridan Libraries)

date that allowed builders to make a profit and move on. It was much rarer for restrictions to cover an entire subdivision, and those that did comprised a handful of the wealthiest planned communities in the country.[12] If each lot in Roland Park contained a similar set of restrictions, it could function as a type of community-wide control for Baltimore's professional classes.

Bouton took the better part of two years to make inquiries, which, from the start, connected the final product to concerns about health. First, in September 1891 he asked the sanitary engineer hired to design Roland Park's sewers, George Waring, for "detailed suggestions" on how to treat sewers and cesspools in the deeds.[13] Waring replied with a "memorandum of points" with the proper "legal phraseology" to be included. He also advised Bouton to write to three people with ties to wealthy planned communities with restrictions: the mayor of West Orange, New Jersey, which was home to

Llewellyn Park; the manager of Wayne, Pennsylvania; and a lawyer from Tuxedo Park, New York. Finally, he suggested that Bouton obtain copies of a single lot with deed restrictions in Sudbrook, a summer community in Baltimore County then under construction. Bouton followed Waring's recommendations.[14]

These earlier restrictive covenants were influenced by nuisance legislation crafted in response to sanitary issues in the nineteenth century. Over the course of the nineteenth century, nuisance law became the chief tools by which municipal governments expanded state capacity and regulated property.[15] Baltimore City's early laws set fines for animal obstructions, the presence of pigs in the street, and the dumping of manure.[16] By the time of the 1888 annexation, Baltimore's nuisance laws restricted certain industries to the east of the city, establishing the industrial and working-class character of the eastern section of the Belt. Baltimore was not unique in this regard; throughout the country, government officials, increasingly aided by newly professionalized planners and engineers, marked spaces and uses as dangers to public health.[17]

Waring's career mirrored this trajectory. He engineered the drainage system for Memphis after the newly created National Board of Health sent him there to end the city's yellow fever epidemic—which had led to the passage of city nuisance laws. After stints around the world, Waring selected healthy campsites near Havana, Cuba, during the Spanish-American War for incoming American troops. There Waring's job was to, as one of his colleagues put it, "make clean and wholesome a city which has so frequently transmitted yellow fever to our shores."[18]

Bouton sought not only to create restrictions but to restrict African American ownership and residence in Roland Park. This reflected Bouton's particular understanding of how race worked in Baltimore. None of the deed restrictions Bouton received from the people Waring had recommended contained racial restrictions. He also surmised that a racial restriction might rest on shakier legal ground than other types of restrictions. In 1893 he asked company lawyers whether it was permissible. He did not ask about the legality of deed restrictions in general or of nuisances; instead, he inquired whether he could insert a restriction into Roland Park's deeds that banned African Americans from both purchasing property and living in its homes.

The lawyers called it a novel question they had not considered before, further indicating that Bouton was bringing a new legal instrument to Baltimore. After researching the matter, both lawyers—one a future appeals court judge and the other president of the Maryland Bar Association—answered that it was unequivocally illegal. Citing case law, they argued that it was illegal to make the buying and selling of property inconvenient. Prohibiting African Americans from purchasing property constituted an inconvenience, which was greatly compounded because of Maryland's sizeable black population. A restriction against African Americans would also be an "embarrassment" because they comprised the "whole class of people" for whom the Fourteenth Amendment of the U.S. Constitution was ratified. The attorneys acknowledged that legal precedent expressly limited the amendment's reach to state actions and not private contracts, but "the significance" of the amendment and its promise of equal civil rights for blacks and whites "was too great to be overlooked." Besides, they concluded, the U.S. Supreme Court ruled in *Barbier v. Connolly* (1884) that "all citizens" had the same right to acquire property.[19]

Referencing *Barbier v. Connolly* complicated the way Bouton and the attorneys conceived of Roland Park's racial restriction as a black-white binary. Bouton had inquired only about banning African Americans, and the attorneys' response largely hinged on this rather than on racial restrictions in general. Yet, *Barbier* applied more broadly. Like *Yick Wo v. Hopkins* (1885), it pertained to a San Francisco nuisance law intended to shut down Chinese-run laundries.[20] Curiously, the lawyers did not cite a court case from less than a year before that directly pertained to racially restrictive covenants, *Gandolfo v. Hartman* (1892).[21] *Gandolfo* revolved around the legality of a racial restriction against Chinese renters on a lot in San Buena Ventura, California. It was struck down on two grounds: the Fourteenth Amendment and an 1880 treaty between the United States and China.[22]

The final Plat One deed restrictions contained eight provisions. Many served both an aesthetic and socioeconomic function. For instance, houses constructed on lots had to cost a minimum amount penciled in by the company. Likewise, lots could only be used for residential purposes, precluding owners from deriving multiple forms of income from their property. Residents also paid a maintenance fee for Roland Park's sewers, street repair, and lighting, proportional to the amount of property they owned. Any outbuildings such as stables had to be set back a specified amount per lot, which varied depending on the lot's location. Bouton pulled the provision that only one house was permitted per lot from Waring's sources, again excluding flexible income-generating rental arrangements.[23]

Other provisions also reflected Waring's influence; the deed restrictions' longest and most detailed set of clauses delineated what constituted nuisances. They prohibited cesspools, privy vaults, the keeping of swine, and any use "which shall by noxious or dangerous to health."[24] The deeds also specifically banned hospitals, asylums, and factories, pairing places for the sick and disabled with industrial hazards, a combination found in Baltimore City nuisance ordinances.[25] Ultimately, Bouton opted not to include a racial restriction.

PLAT ONE PHYSICAL INFRASTRUCTURE

As Bouton weighed restrictions, he juggled the daily tasks of developing Roland Park's physical infrastructure. As part of its planning efforts, the company spent large outlays of capital for sewer, water, and electric systems as well as a network of paved roads intended to increase the value of its lots.[26] At this time, it was still rare for a developer to construct infrastructure without the help of the government; infrastructural systems were intricate works that required money, labor, and political will. Once again, the Lands Trust support and its long-term financial considerations shaped Roland Park's development.

Plat One covered a relatively flat one hundred acres on the eastern portion of the company tract, bounded by the Stony Run stream on the east, Cold Spring Lane on the south, and a small eighteen-year-old neighborhood called Evergreen on the southeast. Jarvis and Conklin brought in a landscape architect, George Kessler, to plan the streets. The German-born Kessler, like Bouton, had become acquainted with Jarvis and Conklin in Kansas City. He brought to the project an initial design that met Bouton's call for "a first-class suburb." Kessler agreed with Bouton and hoped to see Roland Park "developed into a great city."[27] Kessler's response reflected the lack of a rigid distinction between suburban and urban spaces.

Kessler laid out five curvilinear east-west streets intersecting six parallel north-south streets, each named after an investor, such as Fryer, Capron, and Sheldon Avenues. All had broad, tree-lined sidewalks. Lots backed directly against existing Evergreen properties. Kessler did not opt to connect Roland Park's streets with those of predominantly white Evergreen, but he created no boundaries between Roland Park and the older community of narrow brick and frame houses. Residents along the border of both neighborhoods would look directly onto each other's lots. Work proceeded over the course of 1891 and 1892.

Meanwhile, the company's sewer system took shape under the direction of Waring. A system of pipes emptied, by gravity, into two disposal fields on the periphery of Roland Park, where workers used rakes to spread the waste over layers of gravel. The sewage filtered through layers of sand and soil underneath to separate out solids before emptying into the Jones Falls at Cross Keys or the Stony Run stream by Evergreen. A series of underground flush tanks forced water through the pipes twice a day.[28]

The company's sewers raised concerns among Evergreen residents, who went before the Baltimore County commissioners to complain that the company sewage disposal field near Evergreen was "not only disagreeable but unhealthy." The commissioners dismissed the complaints, but Bouton worried that Evergreen residents could still take the company to court alleging it violated the very nuisance laws that informed Roland Park deed restrictions.[29] Bouton predicted a stream of lawsuits from residents motivated by a "universal spirit of antagonism which a poorer class or settlement will have against a better class." At the end of 1898 the company identified the Evergreen resident they thought would have the strongest claim against the company and paid him $500. Bouton hoped settling with him would "break the backbone of litigation."[30] Waring installed screens by the disposal field to improve its filtration process and overall appearance.[31] Both strategies proved ineffective.

Evergreen resident Charles Hull took the company to court seeking damages relating to the disposal field. Hull had sold land to the Roland Park Company for the eastern disposal field in 1892 but charged that the sewage harmed his health and rendered his remaining property valueless. Twice a day, pipes discharged the waste from Plat One and it was spread out over the field, to be dried and filtered through layers of soil and gravel. Hull alleged that each time this occurred, a "horrible, sickening, loathsome and disease breeding stench" arose and drifted over the area anytime the wind blew. The courts affirmed the company's right to operate the disposal fields, even if they created an "alleged nuisance."[32] Following the verdict, the company gradually reengineered the sewage system to shift more of the sewage disposal from the site near Evergreen west to the one near Cross Keys.

ADVERTISING

After a year and a half of preparing Plat One, the company opened its lots for sale in 1893. The timing could not have been worse, as the United States plunged into a severe economic depression. Few could buy a house even if they wanted to. Sales were so poor, in fact, that the trickle of prospective buyers began asking about rumors that the Roland Park Company could not pay its contractors, which raised the possibility that the company's creditors could seize the property to settle the debt.[33]

Bouton perceived an additional reason why Roland Park's lots were not selling: Baltimoreans did not understand the planned suburb. His suspicious were confirmed when the company tried to mortgage several of its lots to meet payroll. Much to Bouton's frustration, local bankers did not consider the property secure. Bouton blamed their decision on "the extreme backwardness among Baltimoreans," who, in his view, failed to recognize the value of property in planned suburbs. Bouton considered it necessary to educate Baltimoreans to "want more than brick walls and cobbled streets" or even the most upscale Baltimore row house.[34]

British investors also grew impatient. Jarvis and Conklin relayed a message to Bouton: raise the company's profile through better promotions. In response, Bouton reevaluated the company's advertising strategies. The company's earliest ads had emphasized Roland Park's proximity to Baltimore City. "Roland Park is almost within a stone's throw with the present city limits," read one ad. "In Roland Park you can shake hands with your city friend and open your own door with the other hand."[35] As part of the mandated retooling, Bouton decided to drop ads that highlighted Roland Park's proximity to the city.

Instead, at the urging of investors, Bouton changed tactics to emphasize the contrast between Roland Park and Baltimore City. From London, Alfred Fryer suggested the specific difference to accentuate: healthiness. Why not, he wrote, use the company's sewer system to distinguish Roland Park from Baltimore City, where people largely relied on cesspools? In one of several letters written over a course of months, Fryer encouraged the company to incorporate into its marketing "a brief, pungent article solely on the subject of 'Drainage.'"[36]

Fryer directed the Roland Park Company to advertise sewers at a time when the biggest Lands Trust Company investors were as interested in municipal sanitation and water infrastructure as they were in land. Leaving the Concretor behind in Antigua, Fryer had invented the Destructor, an influential early garbage incinerator patented in 1874. His engineering firm, Manlove, Alliott and Fryer, obtained a contract with the London municipal government for its use on a wharf on the southern bank of the Thames, part of an enormous new waterfront space first used for sewage disposal and later as the main receiving point for all of London's trash.[37] The firm would subsequently appear in directories as specializing in sugar machinery and refuse disposal. Bright, too, in the early 1890s focused his capital on his home city, as a director of the Manchester Ship Canal Company.[38] Set to become the largest river navigation canal in the world, the Manchester Ship Canal would allow ships from the Irish Sea, and the Atlantic Ocean beyond, direct access to the city.

With the help of the Lands Trust Company, beauty and safety were added to health as qualities Bouton used to define the planned suburb in contrast to the city. Advertisers had emphasized health, safety, and the beauty of land long before the 1890s, especially healthfulness and beauty, but seldom did they do two things: refer to those qualities as characteristics of suburban space and position the suburb in opposition to the city. Before 1890, in articles and classifieds, "suburb" usually appeared in the plural and denoted little more than a periphery. It applied to almost any type of property on the outskirts of a city. In Baltimore this included row houses and farms for sale.[39] The few exceptions Waring cited were for the very wealthy, and they all drew on the nineteenth-century romantic tradition of harnessing the picturesque of an imagined European past spearheaded by Andrew Jackson Downing, whose 1841 book on British country estates made him an influential tastemaker.[40]

The Roland Park Company was uniquely positioned to exploit public health and safety issues playing out in the public sphere by advertising that they could build their own infrastructure. Fryer's suggestion proved particularly appropriate for marketing to Baltimoreans, who increasingly complained about the city's sewage problem. An editor at the *Baltimore News* described the effect of sewage emptying into the harbor as "a 2000-horse-power smell that lays limburger cheese in the shade."[41] The lack of adequate sanitary infrastructure contributed to periodic outbreaks of cholera and typhus as the effluent from the growing city's leaky cesspools flowed into the Jones Falls or through open gutters downhill toward the harbor. Pragmatically, Roland Park's potential buyers, most of whom lived closer to downtown, could more easily envision existing problems in the city than imagine a planned subdivision.

The three most common features of Roland Park's advertising—air, water, and waste—all had potent sensory analogs: the smell of sewage in Baltimore's harbor, the soot from its factories, and rotting piles of garbage semihidden in its alleys. Roland Park's sewage had "no unhealthful effect" like that of the cesspools that predominated in Baltimore City. Roland Park's "pure water" would "never become contaminated" because the company owned the adjacent land and could keep the soil clean.[42] The headline of an article about Roland Park in the *Baltimore Daily News* blared, "SUBURBAN DEVELOPMENTS: How Baltimore Is Forging to the Front. Roland Park Suburb. Magnificent Improvement by Foreign Capital. The Addition to Be Provided with Pure Water and Scientific Sewerage— Progressive Policy of the Company." The newspaper was owned by Charles Grasty, a Roland Park Company investor for whom a Plat One street was named.[43]

Ads also began to allude to diseased people and the dangers of social heterogeneity. African Americans, immigrants, and poor whites bore the brunt of the fatalities from local epidemics because they tended to be concentrated in the lowest elevations of the city, which also had the laxest enforcement of existing health codes. These environmental disparities gave rise to and reinforced wealthy white Baltimoreans' views that associated these groups with disease, making them what the Roland Park Company euphemistically termed "undesirable neighbors." Undesirable neighbors were more likely to be disease vectors, based on their class, race, or place of birth. "In buying a home," went one ad from 1895, "a location should be chosen which is protected from unhealthful surroundings and undesirable neighbors."[44]

The focus on disease signaled that Roland Park was a domestic safe haven for even the most vulnerable members of the household, while Baltimore City was depicted as a place of disorder, sickness, and loss. On one occasion in 1894 the company's publicist wanted to rush a particular ad into print to "make everybody thoroughly believe that there is some reliability in the reported dangers of typhoid fever and other troubles."[45] The company relied on local popular knowledge that typhoid was especially lethal for children. Attempting to conjure a parent's worst nightmare, the publicist considered adopting the theme of "sewers" and "deaths of children."[46] Playing on fears of waterborne typhoid in the city, prospective homebuyers could sample Roland Park's water at the company's office or, should they choose to visit, at the company's springhouse itself on the site of the former Cross Keys water source.[47]

As a result of these and other measures, sales improved. Tourists and sightseers began to take the streetcar to get a glimpse of Roland Park. Bouton became optimistic given that Baltimoreans "had not heard of suburban living."[48] By the end of the decade 1,697 people lived in Plat One.

PLAT TWO AND CROSS KEYS

With the change in the company's fortunes, the company began plans to subdivide the Oakland tract, adjacent to Cross Keys. Plat Two's terrain was more varied than Plat One. Replete with deep ravines, sharp dips and rises, and an old rock quarry, it required more creative street planning and posed more challenges for laying infrastructure. The company hired the Olmsted Brothers landscape architecture firm in November 1897 to begin work on Plat Two. The firm already had a prominent reputation. Its founder, Frederick Law Olmsted Sr., had designed New York's Central Park and Riverside, Illinois and had begun work on Sudbrook, Maryland, though the project slowly progressed throughout the 1890s without ever coming to full fruition. While Kessler laid out Plat One, Olmsted and his sons, Frederick Law Olmsted Jr. and John Charles Olmsted, were planning the monumental White City at the Columbian Exposition in Chicago. The two brothers took over the firm in the 1890s as their father's health declined. Commissions included municipal parks, real estate developments, and university campuses.[49]

The Olmsteds and Bouton worked together closely to refine the details of Plat Two, as the Olmsteds insisted that all work be highly collaborative with their clients. As with Kessler's Plat One, the Olmsteds' plan emphasized the visual separation between Baltimore City and Roland Park. Like Bouton, the Olmsteds had a set of principles about what suburban space should be like, which they adapted to each place depending on local conditions and the needs of their client. These included curving streets named after local landscape features. Streets names, they advised Bouton, should "avoid citified designations such as street and avenue and use instead the word road."[50]

The result of their collaboration was a preliminary master plan for Plat Two. The plan advanced the precedent of disregard and outright contempt for the lives and property of people in Cross Keys. Whereas Kessler had called for weak borders between Roland Park and Evergreen, the Olmsted Brothers called for a hedge to ring the western edge of the plat where curving streets wound around the top of the steep hill that sloped down into the Jones Falls Valley. The hedge cut off sight lines toward the Cross Keys houses immediately below while still permitting sweeping views of the valley.

The Olmsted Brothers designed Plat Two to serve aesthetic, moral, and socioeconomic purposes. They laid out winding roads that encoded how residents should spend leisure time strolling on meandering paths and taking in the beauty of the surroundings. The Olmsted Brothers placed a premium on the value of beautiful views. In the tradition of Andrew Jackson Downing, they believed that creating a picturesque landscape would inspire moral uplift through the leisurely contemplation of nature. This conception of nature depended on the obfuscation of Cross Keys. It was not the first time the Olmsted firm had erased evidence of African American life in order to realize that vision; their father had done the same in designing New York's Central Park.[51]

With the black residents of Cross Keys obscured by the hedge, the brothers planned streets to intersect at triangles, which allowed them to add more trees and shrubs to highlight the area's "naturalistic beauty."[52] Bouton endorsed the plan strongly enough that he had the company purchase two houses from black residents of Cross Keys to move them away from the Roland Park property line.[53] In doing so he reinforced the fantasy of developing empty land, which had appealed to company investors and, once it was paired with healthiness, also to home buyers.

The company's Plat Two plans hit a snag, however, when Bouton discovered African Americans living in the middle of Roland Park property. The lot belonging to the Moonier family was completely surrounded by company property. The Olmsteds recommended to Bouton that the company purchase the property. Bouton agreed and requested two sets of

FIGURE 2.2 Roland Park streets planned by the Olmsted Brothers.

(Courtesy of the Johns Hopkins University Sheridan Libraries)

plans, one reflecting the scenario in which the company acquired the lot and another in which "the objectionable features of their ownership of the property would be reduced to a minimum" in the event the company was not able to acquire the land. The Olmsteds supplied the alternate plan a week later. In it, the property's only means of access was through a back alley.

Bouton next contacted O. Parker Baker, a lawyer who was a member of a white family that owned land in Cross Keys and employed the sixty-five-year-old heir Louisa Moonier as a live-in servant.[54] Bouton paid Baker to "conduct some outside investigations, to find out exactly who the owners are, and what their several interests are in the land."[55] Baker identified the twelve heirs with an interest in the property, all of whom lived in Cross Keys and Washington, D.C.

Baker was unprepared to have to negotiate on price. "Had a meeting on Monday night with the colored people," who were "demanding more money," he reported to Bouton. During the meeting, he had "almost secured" everybody's signature on a contract of sale when a husband and wife, Dennis and Clara Fenton, disputed the value of the land in question, saying the Roland Park Company had undervalued it by 50 percent. Eight more heirs joined with the Fentons in naming a price of $2,000 rather than $1,000, to be divided by the twelve.[56]

Bouton responded by informing Baker that the surveyor and company indeed had made an error. Whereas they initially thought the Moonier property totaled one acre, it was only half an acre. Therefore, the initial offer of $1,000 for the property actually reflected a value of $2,000 per acre. The Fentons and the Roland Park Company disputed the size of the property. The Fentons continued to claim the land was one acre while the company said half an acre based on what "had been used and occupied." With neither side able to settle the acreage, the Fentons countered by asking for a rate of $3,000 per acre, which would still net $1,500 for the half, a 50 percent gain from the company's offer. Baker stood up in the meeting and said any more money was "out of the question." He then threatened to go to court and open a partition and sale proceeding, which would force a sale of the interests held by the ten heirs who had refused the initial offer. By the end

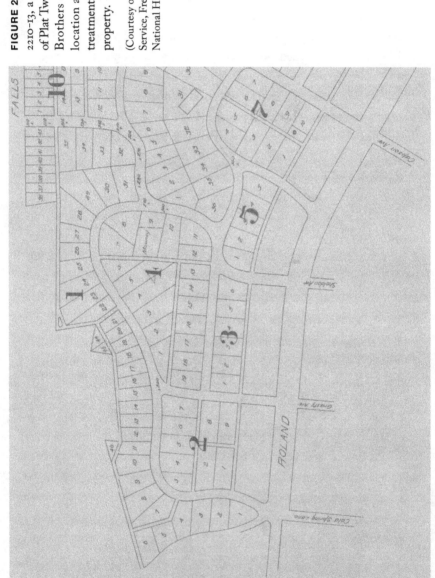

FIGURE 2.3 Olmsted Plan 2210-13, a preliminary plan of Plat Two by the Olmsted Brothers showing the location and proposed treatment of the Moonier property.

(Courtesy of the National Park Service, Frederick Law Olmsted National Historic Site)

of the meeting, the remaining heirs, including the Fentons, offered to sign the contract for a rate of $1,800 per acre. The matter of acreage size was left unresolved. Baker had hired a title company, which found the 1818 transfer of a half acre to Solomon Moonier but nothing after. Subsequent generations of Mooniers could have plausibly expanded the property to one acre, especially given the common practice in Cross Keys of making additions to homes. However, the subsequent paucity of records reflected the precarity of African American claims to property in the nineteenth century. [57]

Even with the signed contract, Bouton refused the offer, calling it "ridiculous" and opting to open the partitioning proceeding in court rather than negotiate the price. A partitioning proceeding would remove the negotiating power of the Fentons. Unbeknownst to the Fentons, however, bringing them to court would serve another purpose for the company. Baker had falsely assumed that because the Mooniers were black, they never held title to the property. Bouton then sought to have a title guarantee company insure the title in order to gain a clear legal claim to the land once the company purchased it. The agents of the title company, however, objected "to taking the title from the descendants of a colored man long since deceased" based on a standard sales contract. They would insure the title only if the Roland Park Company initiated a court proceeding in which the Mooniers "proved their pedigree" by tracing their lineage back to Solomon Moonier and establishing that the land "devolved" to them. It was in Bouton's interest, therefore, to bring the Mooniers to court.[58]

The Fentons hired a lawyer who suggested a final figure of $800 to be split among them and the other eight heirs who refused the initial offer. Of this number, each person received $100 for each one-twelfth stake in the property. The two heirs who had signed the earlier contract, by contrast, received $78.34 for their shares.[59] Baker informed the Fentons they should sign the blank deed and contract of sale he prepared, but that the company would delay paying them until after the court proceedings, where they would have to establish their "pedigree" on record. The Fentons refused. Baker then arranged to pay them before the court proceedings because he could unofficially establish pedigree quickly on his own. Bouton agreed to the plan the next day. The whole ordeal lasted seven months from the discovery that the Mooniers' land lay in the center of Plat Two.[60]

Bouton framed his decision to the British investors as a win: the cost of the Moonier land, comprising "a little less than an acre," including court fees and expenses, totaled $1,400. In contrast, the company had paid $1,500 an acre for Plat One land in 1891. The cost of the land purchase was therefore "about the same" as previous costs. The figure also included payment of $190 to Baker, whose earnings totaled more than any of the Mooniers received for their shares.[61] From the outset, Bouton characterized dealings with the Mooniers as "tedious."[62] Rather than approaching negotiations as a matter of business to be worked out, Bouton worked within a legal system that discounted blacks' claims to property and negotiated in bad faith.

By October 1899, only one matter remained. The Mooniers had used part of the lot for the family graveyard. Now that the Roland Park Company was going to subdivide the land, Bouton saw the graveyard as "a sore place in the midst of our holdings."[63] Bouton once again contacted Baker, who notified family members they had six months to remove the bodies. "If they are not moved within a short time," he stated, the Roland Park Company would do it.[64] It is unclear who ultimately disinterred and relocated the bodies that generations of Mooniers had buried over the span of ninety years. Bouton, however, looked forward to finally being able to subdivide and sell the Moonier land. The new owners, he said, would "not be objectionable."[65]

Even after the Mooniers were dispensed with, the existence of Cross Keys remained objectionable and threatening as far as the company was concerned. When Roland Park was still under development, a dog bit a white child living in Plat Two, exposing the boy to rabies. The boy and his family lived on Hillside Road, the only Roland Park street to directly intersect with Cross Keys on Falls Road. H. R. Mayo Thom and his wife contacted the Roland Park Company offices several times over the next week to discuss what measures needed to be taken in response.[66] Apparently with the approval of the company, Thom and another man armed themselves with shotguns and descended the hill. The subsequent newspaper coverage of what happened next described "a fusillade of shots and wild sounds."[67] The men killed every dog they saw, stopping only when Cross

Keys residents hid the remaining dogs inside their homes. One month later the company secretary and treasurer, Richard Marchant Jr., attended a meeting of the Roland Park Civic League, a volunteer neighborhood organization that served as a liaison between residents and the company. He suggested that the civic league form a committee on dogs in order to "suppress as far as possible" any further cases of rabies in Roland Park. Marchant recommended that Thom chair the committee and praised how he had worked together with the company.

The company's incorporation of antiblack violence into the operating apparatus of Roland Park mirrored the increasing incidents of violent dispossession of black property in areas throughout the country.[68] The sanctioning of the dog culling, like the bad-faith negotiations of the Mooniers' land, was merely one part of a pattern of actions the company took to define the social and economic relationships they considered crucial for Roland Park's success. Healthiness, including controlling black lives and property, was, after all, one of Roland Park's most valuable commodities. Thom had aided the Roland Park Company in this respect because doing so helped to assure current and future white residents that the company would deliver on the promises of the planned suburb free of nuisances.

While on one hand, controlling black bodies and property was seen as key to creating a healthy community, on the other hand, African American labor proved one of the key means by which white residents maintained clean, sanitary homes. In time, the company came to treat Cross Keys and Evergreen as crucial pools of labor for Roland Park. The Roland Park Company created a hierarchy of jobs for men based on race, employing white Evergreen residents as firemen and policemen as well as grounds crew foremen. Cross Keys residents worked in Roland Park as mechanics, groundskeepers, cooks, and servants.

Day employment in Roland Park became a family affair. Cross Keys resident Gert West began working as a cook in Roland Park at age eleven. "My grandmother cooked for the Slagles in the big house," she remembered, "and my father and uncle were their chauffeurs."[69] When she got older she began walking up the hill on a dirt path to work at two more Roland Park houses.[70] Cross Keys women also took in washing to do at home. Taking in washing enabled women to have more control over their own labor and time than if they lived with their employers. The company, however, made doing laundry in Cross Keys more difficult when it built a springhouse on the site of the primary Cross Keys water source, cutting off access to residents and partially destroying a second recreation spot popular among Cross Keys residents.[71]

The discourse on racial and class norms went both ways. Roland Park residents may have brought certain ideas about interracial and interclass interactions with them when they moved in, but the Roland Park Company likewise participated in establishing racialized labor norms that governed daily life. The company provided advice to residents about how to employ a black labor force. Company officials suggested, for instance, that residents hire local African American men to cut their grass because they could be paid less than white men.[72] In another case, an incoming resident argued that it was in the company's interest to pay for the construction of a separate bathroom for his black servant because in the event the house was sold in the future, it was a "fact" that the next residents would also require one.[73] The company obliged.

Indeed, Roland Park homes were unviable without domestic labor. Defying the literature that held that nuclear families formed the core of planned suburbs, early Roland Park households often were large because they consisted of a variety of family arrangements.[74] Frank Zimmerman was a typical Roland Park resident. He bought a lot in Plat One using money he made as a superintendent at the Boston-based John Hancock Life Insurance Company.[75] Zimmerman lived in the house with his mother, four siblings, their spouses, an aunt, and a nephew, all of whom were born in Maryland, like the majority of Plat One residents. One of his brothers clerked at the same life insurance company, while Zimmerman's brother-in-law Albert Stroble sold real estate. None of the women worked a wage-earning job. Eighty percent of Plat One's households employed at least one live-in servant. Of these households, 54 percent employed only blacks, 28 percent only whites, and 18 percent hired black and white workers.[76] In terms of people rather than households, African Americans constituted 62 percent of all live-in labor. It was not until the first decade of the twentieth century that newer sections of Roland Park began to consist primarily of nuclear families of parents and children.[77] Even then, households tended to employ one to four servants, 53 percent of whom were African American. As was typical in the United States, women composed the vast majority of the live-in labor who performed chores ranging from scrubbing floors to gardening.[78] Black women formed the largest group (51 percent), followed by white women, black men, and white men, respectively. Most of the women were listed in the 1900 census simply as "servant," though some were identified as nurses, cooks, and seamstresses. Even as Roland Park demographics shifted toward more affluent buyers and more nuclear families, reliance on domestic labor remained consistent.

NEW CAPITAL, NEW SPACES, NEW NETWORKS

As the Roland Park Company experimented with how to develop and maintain its subdivision, it also created new spaces that reconfigured Baltimore's social, political, and financial networks to the benefit of the company. The results further narrowed the definition of what constituted a planned suburb. One of those spaces at the center of Roland Park life was the country club. Bouton and the Olmsteds placed a premium on greenery, but Roland Park lacked any parks. Instead, it had a country club that attracted Baltimore's most powerful citizens. Extending down the hill and along both sides of Falls Road, the Baltimore Country Club was situated on part of the former Oakland estate, just north of Plat Two and Cross Keys.

The Baltimore Country Club was one of the first places the company used to create social and political networks that would be advantageous to its business. Like other country clubs, it arose out of a longer genealogy of male social clubs that proliferated in nineteenth-century cities.[79] Bouton joined the Baltimore social clubs that were home to the city's affluent white Christians—the clubs were often segregated by race and religion—when he moved to Baltimore to run the Roland Park Company. He then rummaged through the membership rolls to fill the Baltimore Country Club with lawyers, politicians, and bankers. Social clubs were often located in built-up sections of the city. Country clubs, by contrast, had ample room for outdoor activities. At the country club members including Baltimore City mayors could meet for a meal or hash out deals over a game of golf. Bouton, an active member and avid golfer, often dined at the club and struck up correspondence with its members. Once at the club, its president, Decoursey Thom, the brother of dog committee member H. R. Mayo Thom, advertised Roland Park homes for sale.

The country club, like the planned suburb in general, remained an unfamiliar type of space in Baltimore in the 1890s. As a result, Bouton worked to construct the two in relation to each other. Bouton used the Baltimore Country Club to talk with members about what he called "suburban living."[80] The route from the Roland Park streetcar stop to the club became the company's showpiece street. Club Road consisted of thematically uniform Tudor Revival homes on half-acre lots. Bouton carefully selected buyers from the ranks of the country club for half of the Club Road houses and encouraged them to nominate the rest. This would ensure that those concerned about privacy would have "acceptable neighbors," while the company would gain "unpaid sales agents."[81] The country club and Club Road constituted didactic spaces where the company could shape Roland Park's social and political networks.

The country club also provided the Lands Trust Company with a potential pool of local investors. In 1898 Lands Trust directors considered the possibility that it held too many shares in the Roland Park Company. It sent a request to Bouton to try to sell Roland Park Company shares to country club members and new Plat Two residents.[82] It is unclear whether Bouton successfully followed through. Lands Trust shareholder doubts continued to multiply in 1899 and 1900, and the company became less willing to grant Bouton's frequent requests for more money to fund further Roland Park expansions. As a result, Bouton began conversations about the Lands Trust Company selling its stake.[83]

The Lands Trust Company directors decided to end their involvement in 1903. The Roland Park Company required more daily oversight and financial support than the company's directors wanted to maintain. A British representative of the Lands Trust Company told Bouton that although investors considered Roland Park to be one of its "best assets" (the Roland Park Company paid dividends of $45 per share), it had become difficult "to be in as close touch and sympathy" with the daily requirements of developing Roland Park as it would be for Americans, with whom Bouton could "readily discuss and plan at any time." The Lands Trust board encouraged Bouton to pursue a Baltimore-based reorganization of the Roland Park Company in order to buy out the Lands Trust's shares. Bouton's reputation as a general manager was good and real estate conditions were favorable enough in Baltimore that they could secure any price they set. Getting a local group together would, they predicted, enable the new iteration of the company to easily form relationships with Maryland financial institutions and continue into the future.[84]

Bouton looked to his social clubs for his new collaborators to reorganize the Roland Park Company. As he did with the country club, Bouton mixed his social networks and business networks; by 1903 he was listed in Baltimore's annual social register blue book, as was the Baltimore Country Club itself. Bouton reached out to members of the Maryland Club and another institution where he held membership: Baltimore County's Elk Ridge Hunt Club, a former fox-hunting club that had evolved into a country club and social hub for former country estate owners and city businessmen.[85]

New investors came from the ranks of these and other elite social clubs. One investor, the president of the Baltimore Trust and Guarantee Company, became a member of the Baltimore Country Club's board of governors. Another, one of Baltimore's wealthiest and most well-known businessmen at the time, Robert Garrett, owned some of the area's last country estates, just beyond the city line. He, too, became a member of the country club's board.[86] By the start of 1904 the Roland Park Company could count seventeen investors, including Bouton. Eleven were based in the Baltimore area. Of these, seven were members of the Maryland Club and four were members of both the Maryland Club and Elk Ridge. The remaining six investors, who lived elsewhere, consisted of Jarvis and Conklin, a relative of Conklin's, a relative of Bouton, and an associate of Jarvis, Conklin, and Bouton from Kansas City.

After the Roland Park Company's reorganization, Bouton continued pursuing the priorities he had previously developed under the Lands Trust Company. Bouton, now company president, worked with the Olmsteds to change the street names of Plat One to bring them into thematic alignment with the later plats. Gone were the likes of Fryer, Capron, and Sheldon Avenues, to be replaced by Woodlawn, Oakdale, and Upland Roads.

ROLAND PARK AND THE BIRTH OF BALTIMORE'S SEWER SYSTEM

The Roland Park Company's dichotomy of city and suburb hinged on Baltimore City lacking its own sewer system. That changed while Roland Park was still being developed, and with it so did Roland Park's relationship to the city. On February 7, 1904, a fire swept east across downtown Baltimore. By the time it was extinguished the next day, it had leveled Baltimore's central business district. The fire created a rare moment of political unity. Politicians with a history of disagreement believed Baltimore had a chance to rebuild its downtown to be bigger and more technologically competitive than ever before. They included some of Maryland's most prominent politicians, who saw an update of the city's infrastructure as the linchpin in any rebuilding plan. Baltimore, they pointed out, was the largest city in the United States that lacked a comprehensive sewer system.

Prior calls for a sewage system had stalled in the state legislature. This time, however, the state allowed Baltimore City to hold a referendum. Voters decided whether to allow the city to issue $10 million in bonds to create a municipal sewer system, with repayments over seventy-five years, the heaviest of which were scheduled for the 1910s. Senator Isidor Rayner declared, "[If] these loans are rejected we cut loose from every progressive city in the Union and proclaim . . . that we do not propose to take a single step that will improve our environment or promote our success." The measure passed with 60 percent of the vote.[87] Baltimore would finally get a comprehensive sewage system.

Rayner's appeal was accurate—Baltimore City indeed lagged behind cities of similar size—but paying for a system with bonds was hardly par for the course. Instead, many cities relied on special assessment to pay for infrastructure. The Milwaukee and Detroit sewer systems were completely paid for by special assessment, a process in which property owners of a neighborhood paid for a service proportionally to the value of their property. Chicago financed its sewage system by bonds before switching to special assessment after a major annexation in 1889, when property owners in its new wards had to pay for extensions of the system into their areas. In all three cases, this led to unequal distribution of services. Baltimore itself was no stranger to special assessments for much of the nineteenth century.[88]

To begin the process, the mayor appointed a five-person sewerage commission composed of businessmen and sanitary engineers, with the mayor acting as member ex officio. Despite a promising start buoyed by the referendum's large margin of victory, the Baltimore Sewerage Commission quickly encountered obstacles. Shortly after forming in 1905, its members could not locate the old records and maps of the previous, unsuccessful sewerage commissions of the late nineteenth century.[89] The incident marked the first of many delays the commission faced due to missing, incomplete, or inaccurate records.

Recent changes in city government also posed obstacles. Seven years prior to the creation of the Sewerage Commission, a new charter reorganized Baltimore's government along functional lines with bureaucrats rather than politicians in prominent positions. Like so many similar attempts throughout American cities at the turn of the century, it was an effort to break machine politics and the resulting patronage system where the criteria for municipal jobs was, first and foremost, political loyalty. At the same time, the mayor also gained more power over the city council. The new charter shifted power away from the local Democratic machine, which had suffered electoral defeats in 1895, and gave new institutionalized advantages to the city's wealthy citizens, as was often the case during Progressive-Era reforms.[90] In fact, it was the wealthiest sections of the city that most strongly supported the sewage loan referendum.[91] The machine made subsequent electoral gains, but the criteria for Baltimore City positions were now likely to include some type of expert qualification.

The Sewerage Commission itself was a mixture of machine politics and the turn toward expertise, with its politicians and sanitary engineers. The limited extent of municipal transformations meant that few procedures existed for the engineers planning the sewer system to coordinate with the six other city departments—some of which were also new—to perform work necessary to construct the system. As a result, the Sewerage Commission engineers met with frustration and further delays.

The chief engineer, Calvin Hendrick, oversaw daily operations and helped draft preliminary plans for the system. Hendrick found his attempts to create a scientifically informed rational master plan for the sewage system repeatedly stymied by inaccurate data as well as by members of other city departments. There was rarely a report from Hendrick that did not contain the phrase "considerable expense." On one occasion he wrote that in seeking information from various city departments, "we have found the records very incomplete. In many cases on opening up a street we find the actual conditions at variance with the record plans, which have caused us considerable expense in changing our construction." So frequently did Hendrick receive inaccurate information from other departments that he prefaced the commission's work with a disclaimer: "This information is gathered from various City Departments and corporations and placed on our contract drawings, with a note that we are in no way responsible for its accuracy."[92]

Members of other departments adopted an adversarial approach as they staked out their jurisdictions while coordinating with the Sewerage Commission. The City Engineer's Office, which oversaw street paving, butted heads with the Sewerage Commission on how to split expenses. The city engineer wrote to Mayor J. Barry Mahool that his office spent $15,000 in 1908 in "repaving and readjusting intersections" because the Sewerage Commission needed to lay drains. In the engineer's opinion, the money was "properly chargeable to the construction of sewers and not chargeable to the Repairs of Roads and Streets as it has been charged."[93] Meanwhile,

Hendrick continued to write anxiously about losing precious time to departmental coordination issues. The mayor called a series of meetings to resolve disputes between the two agencies, in which the minutiae of street paving became the grist by which municipal actors worked out how the city distributed and paid for public goods.

Frustrated city engineers began turning to sources outside city government to remedy their data shortages and avoid cooperating with their colleagues. The Roland Park Company became one of these. After over a decade and a half in business, the company had planning experience, information about northern Baltimore's land and resources. Through their work they had compiled a repository of soil samples, maps, and comprehensive topographical surveys of northern Baltimore, all privately paid for—and precisely the type of records Hendrick and others needed. Members of the Topographical Survey Commission—which supplied city agencies with data—borrowed supplies and maps from the company.[94] Chief Water Engineer Alfred M. Quick wrote to the company requesting information on the area because he did not trust the accuracy of information furnished by the Topographical Survey Commission.[95]

The company and the municipal government shared personnel as well as information and supplies. Both the city and the company sought people from the limited pool of professionals with planning and engineering credentials at a time when that training was still relatively rare. Hendrick consulted for the Roland Park Company as it was expanding its own sewer system at the same time he was leading similar efforts for Baltimore City.[96] Hendrick was not alone in moving between company and city payrolls. The company's landscape architects, the Olmsted Brothers, planned Baltimore's park system precisely as it planned another expansion of Roland Park in 1905.

Despite the Roland Park Company's business relationship with Hendrick, his initial plans did not prioritize the northern section of Baltimore City. The company was displeased with that decision because it potentially complicated the company's decision to expand yet again, crossing the city-county boundary line for the first time to subdivide land just inside the city's northernmost limits. However, the Sewerage Commission justified the

FIGURE 2.4 Roland Park houses under construction along the city-county line. These homes would be connected to Baltimore City sewers.

(Courtesy of the Johns Hopkins University Sheridan Libraries)

decision by noting that it considered both current and likely future patterns of density and population growth in determining which areas of the city would first receive sewers as part of its comprehensive plan. Hendrick stressed in annual reports of 1905 and 1906 that while the population of that section was increasing and the city opened more streets there every year, it did "not compare with the necessity and obligation to sewer the old portions of the City."[97] The population remained too sparse; further downtown, the higher density of people and homes had already been creating public health hazards.

In addition, completing sewers downtown would raise the property value of the city's more expensive land in the district that had burned, thus increasing potential tax assessments that could fund future system construction.

In northern Baltimore, by contrast, the streets remained too "scattered and disconnected" to adequately add new houses to the system, which by its nature necessitated connecting pipes to each other under existing streets. Furthermore, Hendrick considered northern Baltimore an "outlying district."[98] By all measures, in terms of public health, population density, property value, and actual engineering considerations, northern Baltimore would have to wait for municipal sewers if the Sewerage Commission stuck to its need-based master plan.

But the Roland Park Company did not want to wait to expand into northern Baltimore City; it wanted the city to lay out sewers for the company's new city section as soon as possible. Given the relatively sparse population in the north part of the city and the slow progress of construction, the company knew it would construct the houses well before the commission began work in the area. Suggesting a solution, company officials wrote to the Sewerage Commission proposing to fully lay out and pay for sewer pipes according to the commission's plans and have the city incorporate those pipes into the general system when it reached the area.[99] At that time, the municipal government would fully reimburse the Roland Park Company and pay "fair compensation" for taking private drains into the city system.[100] These terms formed the framework of an initial agreement between the city and the company. The parties still had to work out the specifics, however.

Those specifics included who would carry out the work. The city wanted to assign men to supervise the construction, and the company agreed. Shortly thereafter, a conflict arose over what types of plans the commission would supply for the company. Hendrick opposed designing the project. During a routine commission meeting, he stated, "If we prepare plans for the Roland Park Company, as requested, it will not be possible to refuse similar requests made by other property owners, and our engineering department would be unable to handle the large number of cases."[101] As a result, the commission supplied only general information on how it was constructing its system and some guidelines for the company to follow. This information was generic enough for Hendrick to feel comfortable supplying it as frequently as needed.[102] Even with the agreed-upon general information, the Roland Park Company benefited when its network of planners over-lapped with those of Baltimore City.

The Roland Park Company connected the new sewers it constructed to the existing company sewer system already in place for the company's Baltimore County sections. Hendrick warned the Sewerage Commission in 1909 that the Roland Park Company needed to make provisions to disconnect the new pipes from Baltimore County houses once they were incorporated into the city's system. This provision, however, did not become part of a formal agreement with the company.[103] The next year, Bouton requested permission for the company to drain both city and county houses with the new pipes. Hendrick again cautioned against setting a precedent of the city "undertaking the care of houses in the county, when there are numerous sections throughout the City demanding and needing drainage relief." Furthermore, the Sewerage Commission had doubts about the legality of servicing county sewage under the terms of its Enabling Act.[104]

At the end of 1910, in letters to the commission justifying its connections to county houses, Bouton stated that the pipes still belonged to the company, so jurisdiction was not an issue. More importantly, the city was not being reasonable by forcing the company to separate its "city interests" on one side of the city line from its adjacent "county interests" on the other side. After all, Roland Park as a whole had increased Baltimore City tax revenue and future construction promised additional benefits. In a sharp contrast to the theme of its advertising, the Roland Park Company sought to blur the boundaries between city and suburb in order to secure municipal resources. The Sewerage Commission dodged the problem by approving the connections on the basis that the sewer still belonged to the company. It did not comment on tax revenue.[105]

Despite the tensions, the city's relationship with the Roland Park Company was far more amenable than with other parties. Indeed, the city regularly favored the Roland Park Company. In the working-class immigrant neighborhoods of East Baltimore, the Sewerage Commission faced threats of over one hundred lawsuits for insufficient sewage. In response, it built a drain "to avoid further damages."[106] But it took the one hundred suits for the commission to act. No single suit merited a response, but en masse, petitioners created enough of an economic concern in a concentrated area that the commission took action. By contrast, the Sewerage Commission read out the Roland Park Company's requests for Sewerage Commission services at meetings and entered them into the official record. Hendrick responded promptly, and the commission decided on the merits of the company's requests. One request from the Roland Park Company garnered more action than the first ninety-nine need-based requests from the residents of East Baltimore.

In the end, the Sewerage Commission supplied the Roland Park Company with plans, labor, and supervision. It changed its geographic and need-based schedule at the request of the company that had lent it knowledge and supplies. The houses the new pipes served would otherwise have been hooked up to the Roland Park Company's nearby private sewage system, including houses in Baltimore County that fell outside the service area of the city sewer system. As a result, it added extra houses into the total number of residences the city's system would serve. The Sewerage Commission diverted its own budget to reimburse the Roland Park Company twice over: for the cost of the construction as well as the condemnation costs required to officially take control of the works that it supervised in the first place. The commission made the arrangement knowing that condemnation costs would be high because the appraised value of the land under which the pipes ran would increase due to the added infrastructure. Taxpayer-approved bond money thus flowed to the Roland Park Company and away from the areas of Baltimore City with high morbidity and mortality due to poor sanitary conditions.

Even though it made a big difference in Roland Park's underground infrastructure, by 1910 Roland Park's political borders mattered little visually as it crossed the city line. Instead, the company continued to plan Roland Park with the division of suburban and urban space in mind. This was the case when the company planned a pair of apartment buildings on their newly opened University Parkway, which linked Roland Park's southern section to Plat Two. It hired architect Edward L. Palmer Jr. for the job. Palmer suggested that the company pay close attention to the heights of the buildings. Anything taller than four stories, Palmer asserted, "would miss entirely the general character which would make [Tudor Arms] a fitting entrance to the development beyond, the idea being to attach these buildings to Roland Park and not to the City."[107] Palmer, along with Bouton and the Olmsteds, envisioned a gateway as a transition area from urban to suburban space. Roland Park itself would continue to be marketed as a unified district that looked, felt, and functioned according to the company's vision of a suburb. In effect, Bouton successfully accumulated the city's resources to bolster Roland Park's infrastructure below ground while reinforcing its boundaries above.

CONCLUSION

By 1910 the Roland Park Company's political gains and social networks had surpassed the Lands Trust Company's assurance to Bouton that a locally owned version of the company would succeed. Yet, few of the major figures who helped shaped the nature of Roland Park's success remained connected to the company. Fryer and Bright had both died before the turn of the century. Waring had died after contracting yellow fever in Cuba. Surviving associates continued their work around the world. Jarvis and Conklin had severed connections with the Lands Trust after declaring bankruptcy. They both remained shareholders in a personal capacity and friends with Bouton, but offered little input on company operations. Their business priorities became managing currency in Cuba for the U.S. government.[108] The Olmsteds grew the landscape architecture firm begun by their father and took on commissions in the U.S.-occupied Philippines and the Caribbean. Like others tied to the Lands Trust and Roland Park companies, business brought them to Cuba. There, on what was then known as the Isle of Pines, an island claimed by both Cuba and the United States, they worked with a New Jersey–based company to develop a settlement for Americans. The result was a planned community with a country club, an enclave that was the real estate version of what Waring achieved for U.S. troops in the Caribbean: a "clean and wholesome" space for Americans in a country they associated with contagious disease.[109]

Between 1891 and 1910 the Roland Park Company developed and expanded its eponymous subdivision. In the process, its daily street-level experiments in laying infrastructure, restricting access, and advertising led to Baltimore's new spatial and social geography in which people came to think of the "suburb" not simply as the periphery but as a planned space that could be controlled and kept safe from the threats of unhealthy and undesirable people. These tactics came in response to the long-term needs of British investors, but continued after the investors had moved on.

Planning Roland Park did not stop with the street layout or the advertising campaigns or the revisions to street names. The Roland Park Company performed the daily work of promoting those ideas and maintaining them, whether it was taking out an ad in the newspaper or facilitating its residents' vigilante violence in Cross Keys. From its restrictive covenants to its hedge and its country club, Roland Park was premised on conflating aesthetic and socioeconomic concerns. Company ads came to warn about "unhealthful surroundings and undesirable neighbors" plaguing city life. But at Roland Park, with the help of the company, residents could live peacefully, relying on African Americans as sources of labor. Retooling nineteenth-century precedents, Bouton found new ways to emphasize that certain people could be nuisances to be managed accordingly. These modes of management and thinking about people became baked into the very DNA of the planned suburb.

Over time, Roland Park gained a reputation as one of Baltimore's most desirable neighborhoods. What began with Plat One just north of the 1888 city line had expanded in all directions and now lay in both Baltimore City and Baltimore County. Yet the company marketed a unified space where the political border mattered less than the boundaries of the company's holdings. This was the result of two processes over two decades: carefully cultivating the image of what a planned suburb was and using its capital reserves and planning experiences as leverage to negotiate with municipal government. The spaces it built and the nascent networks the company helped configure enabled it to weather the exit of the Lands Trust

Company while continuing to grow, following a similar model developed with British capital. By 1910, at the close of the Roland Park Company's second decade, Bouton no longer doubted whether Baltimoreans understood the concept of the planned suburb. Instead, he was emboldened to incorporate refined and hardened exclusionary tactics into the company's next development. As he did, Baltimore City emerged at the center of a national debate on the politics of housing segregation.

3

BOUNDARIES

n June 1910, a black lawyer named W. Ashbie Hawkins crossed the residential color line three miles away from Roland Park to purchase a house on the 1800 block of McCulloh Street in the Eutaw Place neighborhood of Northwest Baltimore. Hawkins rented it out to his partner George W. F. McMechen, also African American, who moved in shortly afterward with his wife and children. At the time, Eutaw Place retained a decades-old reputation as the center of one of Baltimore's most prestigious neighborhoods. This made Hawkins's and McMechen's actions particularly egregious in the eyes of local white residents.

Residents of McCulloh Street and the surrounding streets quickly mobilized. They initially committed anonymous acts of violence, pelting the house with rocks, tarring the front steps, and throwing bricks through the windows.[1] Vigilantism was a common strategy whites used throughout the country to terrorize black newcomers into leaving, but the McMechens stayed.[2] Changing tactics, residents formed a neighborhood group that organized a successful campaign to secure the passage of the country's first comprehensive municipal residential segregation ordinance.[3]

The West Ordinance was drafted by Democratic city councilman Samuel West, whose house was close to McCulloh Street, and passed with every Democrat voting for it and every Republican against. The new law designated each city block as open to blacks or whites and set penalties for any Baltimorean who moved onto a block that did not match their perceived race. Mayor J. Barry Mahool signed it into law, explaining that it solved the interconnected problems of race mixing, health, and property values. African Americans, he said, "should be quarantined in isolated slums in order to reduce the incidence of civil disturbance, to prevent the spread of communicable disease into the nearby White neighborhoods, and to protect property values among the White majority."[4] Journalists from Boston to San Francisco picked up the story.[5] The *New York Times* put Baltimore's segregation ordinance in "a class of its own" for going "beyond" any existing Jim Crow laws on the books anywhere to separate people based on race.[6]

Lawmakers hoped to target upwardly mobile African Americans such as Hawkins and the McMechens. The timing of Jim Crow laws was due to increasing black upward mobility at the turn of the century. "Successful African Americans' lives," writes historian Glenda Gilmore, "provided a perpetual affront to whites. The black lawyer, doctor, preacher, or teacher represented someone out of his or her place."[7] Elizabeth Herbin-Triant likewise notes that the subsequent copycat ordinances were most likely to be found in cities where black property ownership had markedly increased since 1890.[8] Hawkins, a proud property owner, surmised this when he dismissed the Eutaw Place organizers as attention-seeking renters.[9] As the recent purchaser of a Eutaw Place row house, he knew that the neighborhood's elite reputation did not match trends; property values had begun to fall years before as former residents moved to Roland Park.[10] It was possible that Eutaw Place residents hoped to harden racial boundaries to try and preserve what was left of the area's status.

It is precisely by looking at the construction of boundaries that one can best see the movement of ideas about housing segregation. The white residents of Eutaw Place hoped to shore up racial boundaries, while the Roland Park Company, too, was hard at work hardening boundaries. Focusing on those boundaries reveals the multitude of ways that housing developers began to codify and successfully disseminate the practices of exclusion despite their very different local contexts. The results included a spread across the country of restrictive covenants, laws, development practices, and grassroots movements that owed their forms, in part, to what came out of Baltimore during the 1910s.

Within the changing context of Baltimore housing segregation, the Roland Park Company began its second development, Guilford. Whereas the company had started Roland Park unsure about its reception, it began Guilford assured of its likely success. Bouton and local investors were encouraged by Roland Park's reputation, but also by increased competition; other local builders had switched their business models to planned suburbs as a means of promoting exclusion. And though Bouton himself never seemed to talk about the ordinance, multiple links existed between its chief proponents and the company. In fact, the four people most responsible for shepherding the segregation ordinance through the city council had personal and financial connections to Bouton.[11]

As a result, the company refined its experiments; its physical boundaries would be more impermeable, its restrictive covenants stricter, the advertising strategies about healthy neighbors and healthy neighborhoods bolder. With Guilford, the Roland Park Company followed through on what Bouton had wanted since 1893: to ban African Americans by restrictive covenant. To do so, Bouton inserted a racial restriction into the company's existing nuisance clauses, cementing the pairing made earlier between black bodies and unhealthy uses of property. These restrictions likely became the earliest formal restrictions against African Americans in an American planned suburb.[12]

The segregation ordinance laid bare the many faces of racial capitalism in a single city. On one hand, residents of Eutaw Place clearly drew inspiration from Roland Park—where a number of former Eutaw Place residents had moved—in pushing for the segregation ordinance. On the other hand, Hawkins and McMechen, the targets of the segregation ordinance, also revealed themselves to be influenced by the ideas embodied in the development of the planned suburb. As more and more white Baltimoreans moved to Roland Park, the development became increasingly influential in shaping local housing politics, even for some of the people excluded from living there, who drew on its business model in their own dealings. Hawkins and McMechen were investors and attorneys for a planned black suburb, while local developers, black and white, emulated the Roland Park Company's marketing strategies to target prospective buyers. Meanwhile, as a result of the ordinance, rents quickly increased 20 percent in the parts of Baltimore the ordinance designated for African Americans.[13]

The legal history of the segregation ordinance and of early twentieth-century housing segregation in general is well documented but insufficient to understand the law's afterlife. The ordinance immediately came under legal scrutiny, which was led by Hawkins and McMechen themselves as attorneys with the newly organized Baltimore branch of the National Association for the Advancement of Colored People (NAACP). Here, Hawkins and McMechen replicated a pattern exhibited by other black capitalists elsewhere in the country, who used the profits from their ventures to fund civil rights activism.[14] The fact that Hawkins made money as a landlord in segregated West Baltimore and both he and McMechen made money from planned black suburban developments did not, in their view, negate their commitment to fighting the hardening of Jim Crow laws in Maryland. Indeed, the passage of the segregation ordinance prompted the NAACP to make combating housing segregation one of its chief goals.[15] Each time the ordinance was struck down, city lawmakers passed a new version, which the NAACP would fight in the courts. Despite the dubious legality of the ordinance, it became an international model for segregating housing for seven years before being declared unconstitutional by the U.S. Supreme Court, which made a ruling in the case of a copycat ordinance in Louisville in 1917.[16] Even then, Baltimore City itself remained a model of segregation thanks to the ways segregated housing practices were and continued to be disseminated.

The segregation ordinance once again thrust questions of urban growth into the spotlight. Baltimore's population growth, a consequence of African American migration and European immigration, raised issues over the course of the 1910s about the need for another annexation. Proponents of the ordinance incorporated its principles into a multipronged approach to

86

shape the city's racial geography. These alternated between trying to freeze demographic change, as the ordinance itself did, and creating flexible legislation that could legally enable segregation if the city's boundaries expanded. The renewed annexation talks and the future of Baltimore's racial geography brought together an assortment of developers and politicians. Bouton played a prominent role in all of this, due to the relationships he had previously formed with municipal government officials through the social and political networks forged over the previous two decades in the service of the Roland Park Company.

DEVELOPING GUILFORD

The Roland Park Company acquired the land for Guilford in 1911 in both Baltimore City and Baltimore County. Whereas Roland Park initially relied on capital from British investors, Guilford was financed by Baltimoreans with whom Bouton had prior connections. Chief among them was Robert Garrett, with whom Bouton served on the Baltimore Country Club board of directors. Garrett had independently joined a venture called the Guilford Park Company that was interested in buying a tract of land near Roland Park. After the Guilford Park Company stalled, the Roland Park Company purchased it and brought Garrett and three employees of his investment firm, Robert Garrett and Sons, onto the Roland Park Company board of directors. Several of the Roland Park Company's lawyers, who also belonged to the Baltimore Country Club, facilitated the merger. The corporate consolidation reunited the Roland Park Company with the Olmsted Brothers, who had been drawing up plans for Guilford before the defunct Guilford Park Company was unable to pay them.[17]

The tract consisted of 336 acres of meadows, woodlands, pasture, a man-made boating lake, and a fifty-room mansion that, like Oakland and Woodlawn, had been built by a Confederate sympathizer.[18] Its last owners were the Abell family, who owned the *Baltimore Sun* before Roland Park investor Charles Grasty. The tract was bounded by Charles Street on the west and Cold Spring Lane to the north. A boulevard built by the Roland Park Company called University Parkway served as its southern border. On the east, Guilford bordered the built-up areas of Waverly and Govans. Both areas were composed of a mix of native-born whites, immigrants, and African Americans.

Guilford's restrictive covenants followed those of Roland Park, but went further. The company expanded the nuisance clause considerably, with longer enumerations of fairly similar types of establishments. Whereas residents of Plat One of Roland Park could not operate a factory or saloon, Guilford residents could not run a brewery, distillery, or malthouse, a jail or penitentiary, or a cemetery or graveyard. The company compiled the list with the intent of banning "any noxious, dangerous, or offensive thing, trade, or business or use of the property whatsoever."[19]

In another crucial change, the Roland Park Company inserted a racial restriction into Guilford's covenants that explicitly prohibited blacks from occupying Guilford property, with the exception of domestic servants. It read:

> At no time shall the land included in said tract of any part thereof, of any building erected thereon, be occupied by any negro or person of negro extraction. This prohibition, however, is not intended to include the occupancy by a negro domestic servant or other person while employed in or about the premises by the owner or occupant of any land included in said tract.[20]

The restriction appeared in the expanded nuisance clause between bans on livestock and on producing excess smoke.

At the turn of the century, Baltimore's rapid industrial development drew both poor immigrants and black migrants in search of jobs. As Maryland established formally segregated facilities with the rise of Jim Crow, Baltimore's voters narrowly rejected disenfranchisement, which became par for the course deeper in the South.[21] Unable to stymie formal black political power, legislators turned to nuisance laws and public health campaigns, both of which harnessed police power to regulate neighborhood life. In fact, a Baltimore City nuisance ordinance passed in 1908 contained a detailed enumeration similar to that in Guilford's later nuisance clause.

Bouton never established in his own words why the company, after twenty years, prohibited African Americans by restrictive covenant. No surviving evidence indicates that blacks tried to purchase homes or live in Roland Park prior to Guilford's opening. The most likely explanation is that a racial restriction was a measure the company could claim as a competitive advantage over newer local planned suburbs. An additional explanation lies in the company's intent to create a subdivision that was, on the whole, targeted to wealthier homebuyers than those in Roland Park, especially in Plat One. They therefore signaled that Guilford would be even more restricted than Roland Park, heightening its cachet. The city's residential segregation ordinance put neighborhood segregation at the forefront of priorities for potential Guilford homebuyers. It would be a selling point that continued the company's marketing practice of conflating race, health, and property, a conflation the company perpetuated by listing the presence of black bodies as a nuisance akin to the presence of animals.

There remains ambiguity about how many people reviewed the Guilford clause—containing one of the country's first racial subdivision restrictions—before it was presented to inquiring homebuyers. Bouton workshopped drafts with company officials, whose interoffice communications included comments on nuisances but not the racial restriction.[22] Company officials did, however, see the final version. Attorneys—different attorneys than in 1893—never raised an issue. The company also changed the relationship between deeds and the restrictions. For Roland Park, the company wrote the restrictions directly into each individual house deed. For Guilford, the company compiled the official list as a separate document called "the agreement" that accompanied deeds. Only the deeds were filed in Baltimore County and Baltimore City land record offices, where they met no objections.[23] Nevertheless, the agreement then became a binding legal instrument along with the deed.

Restrictions were only one tool that the Roland Park Company sharpened in developing Guilford. Along its borders, the company used a series of physical boundaries to separate Guilford from working-class, mixed-race

FIGURE 3.1 View of York Road from Guilford during construction. The stretch opposite Guilford supported a variety of building types and uses catering to the racially and socioeconomically diverse residents of Waverly and Govans.

(Courtesy of the Johns Hopkins University Sheridan Libraries)

Waverly and Govans. Nowhere was the border sharper than along York Road and Greenmount Avenue, a single street with two names that ran from just east of downtown Baltimore all the way north to York, Pennsylvania. York and Greenmount comprised the entire one-mile eastern edge of Guilford.

To further separate Guilford from the brick row houses, wooden dwellings, and businesses, which constituted a majority of the structures along the adjacent stretch of York Road and Greenmount Avenue, the Olmsteds helped the company create a series of streets which terminated just before or at York Road. These streets did not cross York and Greenmount to connect to neighborhoods on the other side. Likewise, the company opted not to run any of the older streets of Wavery and Govans into Guilford. The

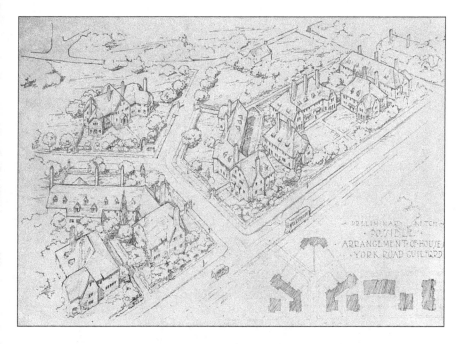

FIGURE 3.2 Plans for Guilford at the intersection of Bretton Place and York Road. Attached houses are set back from York Road with entrances fronting away from it. Note the ornamental gatepost.

(Courtesy of the Johns Hopkins University Sheridan Libraries)

overall effect created a long stretch of Guilford cut off from the east at York Road. This strategy enabled the company to use York and Greenmount to "separate it in a distinct manner from the adjacent land."[24] These boundaries ostensibly contributed to the Roland Park Company district's overall look but also reinforced a racially and socioeconomically homogenous environment.

The company also situated what Bouton called "smaller, cheaper" houses around Guilford's border with Waverly and Govans. Clusters of thematic attached housing called Bretton Place and York Courts, which garnered accolades for their architectural innovation, either faced inward or were set back from York Road and Greenmount Avenue behind a picket fence and

FIGURE 3.3 Laborers build Guilford's gates.

(Courtesy of the Johns Hopkins University Sheridan Libraries)

a shared green space. These homes obscured Guilford's view of Waverly and Govans and, according to Bouton, protected the "integrity" of the new planned suburb. The company put these lots up for sale at half the price of Guilford's next cheapest homes.[25] The small connected homes functioned as a de facto wall that prevented residents of the larger showpiece houses of Guilford's interior from seeing "eyesores" in the mixed-race, mixed-use Waverly and Govans.[26]

At Guilford's northernmost section the company elaborated on the hedge it had planted at Cross Keys by building a fourteen-foot-high stone wall. The buildings across from the wall were a storage facility for York and Greenmount streetcars, six stores, a garage, six detached dwellings, and a block of row houses. The stretch had more commercial activity than the rest of Greenmount and York fronting Guilford, but it largely consisted of the same mix of uses. The wall cut off sight lines to both the neighborhood across York Road and its inhabitants.

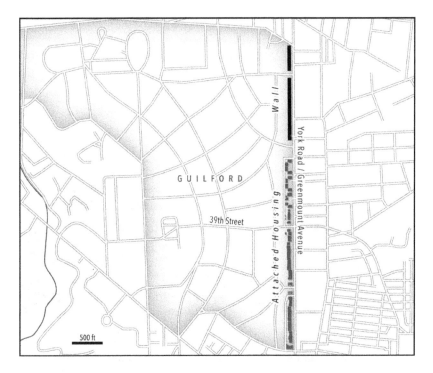

FIGURE 3.4 The total effect of Guilford's York Road boundaries.

(Prepared by Tanya Buckingham, University of Wisconsin Cartography Lab)

With the attached houses, lack of through streets, and wall, the Roland Park Company created a continuous set of boundaries that cut off Guilford from Waverly and Govans. At its entrances the company erected a series of uniform gateposts, which, like the wall, were built using black labor under white supervision. The gateposts gestured toward English estates in the Downing tradition. The purely ornamental gateposts—without actual gates to prevent access—also heightened the visual message that a single developer created Guilford and controlled the space, and served as a warning to outsiders.

The company reinforced this distinction in its marketing materials for potential Guilford residents. The company released a booklet to advertise Guilford shortly after it opened in 1913. Half of it was devoted to

FIGURE 3.5 Sign at the entrance to Guilford advertising "A Thousand Acres of Restricted Land." The Roland Park Company adopted this as its slogan.

(Courtesy of the Johns Hopkins University Sheridan Libraries)

enumerating restrictions. It opened with the heading "Guilford in the Roland Park–Guilford District, A Thousand Acres of Restricted Land," words repeated on a large sign at Guilford's entrance. It continued to highlight restrictions by informing readers that "to no other question involved in Guilford has more thought and consideration been given." It then listed some of the "more important covenants and restrictions" in the booklet. The first featured a portion of the nuisance clause, including the racial restriction.[27]

Guilford's racial restriction would make future enforcement of the Baltimore City segregation ordinance a nonissue for Guilford residents. This was a good thing for the company, because from the day of its passage, the ordinance faced legal challenges that were still winding their way through the courts when Guilford opened. A racial restriction offered a different mode of enforcement that bypassed the ordinance entirely. Even without the issues of the ordinance's legality, an awkward issue of its application to Guilford would have potentially presented a problem for the Roland Park Company, because Guilford straddled the jurisdictions of Baltimore City and Baltimore County. Only the subdivision's southern two-thirds were under the ordinance's purview. Guilford's race restriction rendered political jurisdiction moot and, along with its borders, created a unified space with an added layer of legal protection that even elite white city neighborhoods like Eutaw Place lacked.

SPREADING SEGREGATION

By 1913 the company had begun to disseminate its practices and helped give rise to a cohort of like-minded suburban developers and city planners. The distinction between developers and planners remained blurry at best because members of both groups faced shared infrastructural tasks such as laying out streets, paving, and sanitation. The overlapping interests facilitated the spread of exclusionary practices between developers and municipal governments. Personnel moved between ostensibly public and private projects in the same location. They also traveled widely. Noted British planner Thomas Adams was one of many to request a copy of the Roland Park Company's covenants. Famed planner and landscape architect John Nolen requested a copy of a Roland Park deed, crossed out the company's name in pencil, and replaced "Maryland" with "Florida" as he created a plan for the city of Clearwater. A real estate developer in Charlottesville, Virginia, liked Roland Park's deed restrictions so much that he requested them twice so he could show his associates copies.[28]

Among this growing informal network, Jesse Clyde Nichols, of Kansas City, forged a close personal and professional connection with Edward Bouton after Nichols visited Roland Park on a fact-seeking trip. He often cited the company's work as inspiration for his Country Club District. Not only did Nichols base the Country Club District's restrictive covenants on those of the Roland Park Company, he also erected a sign at its entrance advertising a thousand acres of restricted land.[29]

Nichols and Bouton shared a narrative about how they came to value planning and restrictions and worked to ensure that homebuyers would, too. They told and retold versions of this transformation in letters and through talks, baking it into the nascent professional identity of planners and developers through its widespread dissemination. In response to an enquiry from a city planner about the Roland Park Company's restrictions, Bouton claimed Baltimoreans did not know what restrictive convenants were before the arrival of the company. Understandably, they had initially expressed concern about having limitations placed on their use of property. Now, he said, Baltimoreans realized their value.[30] Nichols told a similar tale to a group of developers in 1912. "In the early time," he said, "I was afraid to suggest building restrictions, now I cannot sell a lot without them." To Nichols, restrictions went hand in hand with the built environment. In the same talk, he continued, "I used to feel the road must be the shortest route between two points; now the longer I can make it with curves . . . the more it appeals in a home district."[31] These practices, both of which he saw in Roland Park, were, thanks to him, becoming increasingly accepted and popular in Kansas City. Those who met Bouton or Nichols or corresponded with them likewise subsequently requested copies of their restrictions.[32]

It was in the 1910s that these informal correspondence networks, visits, and talks began to coalesce into the nascent professions of planning and real estate. Professional needs helped dictate the spread of the Roland Park Company's restrictive covenants to both developers and planners. A handful of planners who doubled as professors wrote to Bouton for copies to include in one of the country's earliest university courses on planning, at Columbia University. Nolen, too, taught classes.[33] These educators thereby ensured that the Roland Park Company's restrictive covenants became a cornerstone of training programs for future generations.[34]

Some of the most avid users of Roland Park Company restrictive covenants were none other than the Olmsted Brothers landscape architecture firm. The firm worked on at least twenty-three subdivisions with restrictive covenants prior to 1920.[35] An endorsement of restrictive covenants by the Olmsted Brothers carried a lot of weight. They, too, were leaders in professionalizing landscape architecture, one of the fields from which city planning emerged as a profession. The Olmsteds helped found the American Society of Landscape Architects in 1899, while they worked on Roland Park. John Charles Olmsted served as the society's first president.

John Nolen was the exception in lifting the entire Roland Park Company restrictive covenant; the vast majority of developers and planners who obtained restrictive covenants from the company adapted them to the perceived local racial hierarchies. In Baltimore, the Olmsteds, whose earliest tasks included advising Bouton on the Mooniers and Cross Keys views, operated under the assumption that the most salient racial distinctions for housing were those between people racialized as white and black. When Frederick Olmsted Jr. collaborated on Palos Verdes Estates in California, however, that subdivision's restrictive covenants prohibited African Americans as well as Asians and Mexicans, groups seldom mentioned by developers in Baltimore.[36]

Policies intended to promote housing segregation did not always reflect the diversity of local populations. Baltimore's black/white binary, enshrined into law with the segregation ordinance, clashed with how Baltimoreans were trying to encode racial hierarchies in other domains. Public education was an area that painted a different picture. Baltimore public schools were officially designated "white" or "colored." In 1913, the year Guilford opened, the city school board faced controversy after a principal refused to permit a Chinese student to enroll in an East Baltimore elementary school because he was "not white."[37] Previous attempts to enroll Chinese students garnered newspaper headlines such as "Is He White or Colored?"[38] Cities with different demographics went beyond the black/white binary in their approach to schooling. In contrast to Baltimore, San Francisco established a separate school for Chinese students and unsuccessfully tried to make it the only option for students of Japanese and Korean descent.[39]

The segregation ordinance was only one key piece of a national conversation about property and exclusion during the 1910s. Beginning in 1913, another part of that broader discourse began to circulate east and south. California's Alien Land Law initially targeted the property rights of Japanese immigrants, but it was subsequently adopted and enforced against a variety of Asian groups deemed ineligible for citizenship under federal law. Alien land laws and residential segregation ordinances rarely overlapped, except in New Orleans, which came under both a municipal segregation ordinance and a state-level alien land law. With two important exceptions— the U.S.-occupied Philippines and South Africa—the trajectory of Baltimore's segregation ordinance was primarily southward and westward, first to cities in Virginia, the Carolinas, and Georgia and then to St. Louis, Oklahoma City, and Louisville, Kentucky.

OLD AND NEW INFRASTRUCTURE

The segregation ordinance was just one way municipal government inscribed race and class into Baltimore's landscape. The unequal provision of infrastructure and municipal services was another. Sewers, for instance, continued to both further and generate inequality. While the Roland Park Company extended its sewer system with the help of the Balitmore Sewerage Commission, the commission bypassed African American homes. The percentage of houses that remained unconnected to the sewage system in the ward encompassing predominantly black West and Northwest Baltimore— west of Eutaw Place—stood twice as high as in any of the four poorest white wards. Houses that remained disconnected from the system tended to be rented out to black tenants in the narrow alleys between the main thoroughfares. There, landlords could count on chronic housing shortages to limit tenants' opportunities to move out of substandard housing.

Moreover, landlords who connected their buildings to the sewer system would see an increase in the assessed values of the property, increasing their taxes. Even if tenants wanted to seek remedy and redress through municipal agencies, they faced obstacles. Baltimore City held tenants, not landlords, responsible under its nuisance abatement ordinances. Landlords also bribed police to not enforce nuisance laws. Additionally, tenants faced municipal agencies already failing to equally service the alleys in West Baltimore, where the city's all-white Paving Commission paved only 333 of 2,100 alleys.[40]

Meanwhile, the Baltimore City Sewerage Commission provided resources that the Roland Park Company parlayed not only into physical infrastructure but also into an instrument of financial flexibility. As with the newer Baltimore City portions of Roland Park, the company built the city portions of Guilford's sewers under the supervision of the Baltimore City Sewerage Commission. The company issued bonds secured on Guilford's sewers, which still belonged to the company until such time as the city paid the company to incorporate them in its system. The owner-occupants of Guilford then paid to connect to the Roland Park Company's sewers. Sewers thus generated a steady revenue stream for the company, derived from the annual sewer rentals property owners paid. Failure to pay the rental fee resulted in a first lien on the property. Since the ratio of the rental charge to the value of the property was extremely low—ten cents per one hundred square feet—company officials likened the safety of the company bonds to "a class of revenues derived from public taxes" rather than bonds of "the highest class." Company officials did not market the bonds publicly, but instead used them as security for loans.[41] Unequal resource distribution between Roland Park Company subdivisions and elsewhere not only affected quality of life but also provided ways to generate capital.

In the midst of developing Guilford, the Roland Park Company could rely on residents to maintain Roland Park's infrastructure thanks to the success of years of its didactic approach to suburban living. In 1915 Roland Park faced a mosquito infestation. The company and residents blamed Cross Keys residents for keeping exposed stores of water that created a breeding ground. The company had destroyed the spring that had served as a local water source and built its sewage disposal field near the Jones Falls. In the following years it had also extended Roland Park's water and sewer infrastructure to neighboring white communities and subsequently began charging annual rental fees as Roland Park became fully built out.[42] The new pipes ran underneath Cross Keys and periodically contaminated residents' wells along the hillside. Cross Keys residents began to store rainwater as their main source of water. As it was told in the company-sponsored resident magazine, the *Roland Park Review*, residents entered Cross Keys to train "incredulous darkeys" how to eliminate standing water by using "mosquito-proof rain barrels." Roland Park residents provided the barrels, according to the *Review*. "Cross Keys has joined in the march of progress" even though "it may have had improvement thrust upon it as the new barrels are a largess from Roland Park." The rain barrels became "prominent features in the Cross Keysan backyard landscape."[43] Roland Park residents offered the barrels as a technological solution—the so-called progress of the article—to the African Americans they viewed as health risks because their inherent lack of intelligence resulted in diseased homes.[44] The measure reinforced the power of white employers over black people, which guided the "education" about health and sanitary practices that Roland Park residents took it upon themselves to provide in Cross Keys.

The results were twofold. First, the barrels protected Roland Park residents from a perceived source of disease, following the pattern the company set when it identified Cross Keys as harboring a rabies threat and allowed Thom to shoot the dogs. Whereas that act of violence happened suddenly and left no physical imprint on the Cross Keys landscape, Roland Park's rain barrels now dotted the hillside. It also followed the company's pattern of modeling labor relationships between white residents and black workers. Residents regarded Cross Keys inhabitants as a labor force as much as a potential source of disease. The barrels standardized the ways Cross Keys women drew water in their homes to wash Roland Park's clothes. The Roland Park resident who wrote the *Review* article imagined the first wash day after the installation of the barrels as a "gala occasion." Where the author saw the personal failings of unhygienic people, however, he was actually observing the outcome of the Roland Park Company expropriating Cross Keys water sources and polluting the land.

Bouton had long feared that "sensational stories" could circulate among potential buyers if they had any reason to perceive Roland Park as unhealthy.[45] He had reason to be concerned. Former mayor J. Barry Mahool personally complained to Baltimore Country Club president Decoursey Thom about the mosquitoes that seemed to be growing in number at the club, adjacent to Roland Park, every summer.[46] Mosquitoes did not observe the company's carefully laid physical and social boundaries. It says much about the racial views of the company officials and residents that they assumed the pests originated in Cross Keys, like the rabid dog several years earlier, but it turned out that the source of mosquitoes was likely Bouton's own backyard pond.[47]

FORMING A MARKET IN BALTIMORE

Despite the fear of mosquitoes, Roland Park continued to attract residents. The Roland Park Company's successful marketing became the model for other developers, including African American developers. Such was the case with Cherry Heights, "a new suburb for colored people" developed by black political activist, author, and librarian Daniel A. P. Murray, whose twenty-four acres of land northeast of Baltimore City went on sale January 1, 1910.[48] Hawkins and McMechen helped finance it through the Cherry Heights Realty and Construction Company and served as company attorneys. The company paid for the land outright to permanently vacate ground rents. It is likely that Hawkins used money from the endeavor to buy his McCulloh Street house six months later, and assisted McMechen in renting it. Advertisements equated the beauty of "first class" Cherry Heights to that of Roland Park. Like Roland Park, Cherry Heights was advertised as offering "every facility of the most advanced suburban settlement" such as "good water" and a respectable class of residents.[49] At Cherry Heights, homeowners would be "happy and healthy." Cherry Heights Realty emulated the Roland Park Company's description of a desirable suburban subdivision in terms of social character, access to healthy infrastructure, and aesthetic value. Rather than strictly copying the language, however, Cherry Heights blended Roland Park's exclusivity with a different intellectual tradition based on ideas of property ownership and citizenship. The line

Announcement Extraordinary

A New Suburb for Colored People

CHERRY HEIGHTS

⌀ ON *The* BELAIR ROAD ⌀

..First General Sale, New Year's Day, Jan. 1, 1910...

THE CHERRY HEIGHTS REALTY AND CONSTRUCTION COMPANY has secured a twenty-four acre tract of land on the Belair Road and has subdivided the same into building lots of moderate size, is now engaged in grading streets through the same, and is ready to offer these splendid lots to the colored people of Baltimore at reasonable prices and on the most reasonable terms. Within 30 minutes of the centre of the City.

No Ground Rents...

Why spend the rest of your life fighting and fretting about Ground Rents when you can own your ground at Cherry Heights and live happy and healthy?

An Opportunity...

Once in a life-time you get an opportunity like this to buy choice lots. If you are wise you will investigate these lots at once, and if you knew their real value you would not lose a minute in getting on the ground.

First Class Settlement

This neighborhood is in the process of daily development and is inhabited by a thrifty class of people. Good water and every facility of the most advanced suburban settlement

Location

These lots fronting on the County thoroughfare, Fullerton Ave. are equal to ROLAND PARK in beauty. Come and see it yourself. There is no location so near the city that has ever been offered to our people. They can be bought on reasonable terms at very low prices for those who take the advantage to buy now. These lots will go up in prices double to what they are now.

Growth

Baltimore is growing and she is growing fast. Already her residential districts are crowded and her busy people are forced to seek places for homes in the suburbs. They are investing in lots for these homes outside, where they will have room for constructing homes of their own taste.

Ownership of Lands

OWNERSHIP OF LANDS makes you independent for life. First, establish your income of an ENHANCING VALUE. Lay this foundation close to the soil, and especially where values are sure to increase. Direct ownership of land is desired for three chief reasons. 1st, On account of natural resources as in timber or minerals. 2nd, On account of productivity under agriculture. 3rd, On account of suitability as a site for a home or a shop or some form of industrial or commercial activity. The land owned by THE CHERRY HEIGHTS REALTY AND CONSTRUCTION COMPANY presents a fine location as a home site. Nothing better can be found within a 5 cent carfare and so near a large city of 600,000 people.

Already a Suburb

This property of ours is already a suburb of Baltimore. Every car in the city transfers to the Belair Road car with a 5 cent carfare. This is why we have called it one of the most beautiful SUB-DIVISIONS that was ever offered or will ever be offered to our people. They are deprived of all opportunities for purchasing building lots where accessibility to the city is so convenient and inexpensive.

Don't Be Shoved Back

Why accept a lot with a 10 or 20 cent carfare when THE CHERRY HEIGHTS REALTY AND CONSTRUCTION COMPANY'S lots can be reached by a FIVE CENT CAR FARE. So we say to you, whatever you may have had in contemplation just come to CHERRY HEIGHTS and see these lots on our first general sale day, which will be on New Year's Day, January 1st 1910, from 10 A. M. to 4 P. M.

Investment

The most substantial New Year's investment will be a Lot at CHERRY HEIGHTS, forty by one hundred and fifty feet or six thousand square feet of land to each Lot.

TERMS

These Lots ranging in prices from $150.00 to $450.00 are just HALF THEIR ACTUAL VALUE. A small cash payment of $10 down and $1.25 per week. NO TAXES, NO INTEREST UNTIL LOTS ARE PAID FOR.

How to Get to Cherry Heights

Take any City Line and transfer to BELAIR ROAD CAR and ride to its terminus, and our representative will meet you. It is only two blocks from the cars.

Cherry Heights Realty & Construction Co., 17 E. Saratoga St.

Ernest J. Jones, President.   Hawkins & McMechen, Attorneys.

FIGURE 3.6 An advertisement for Cherry Heights that promises lots "equal to ROLAND PARK in beauty." Hawkins and McMechen are listed as attorneys for the development.

(Courtesy of the Afro-American Newspapers Archives and Research Center)

"Ownership of land makes you independent for life" articulated a long-held belief among many African Americans that property ownership was one's primary claim to citizenship and escape from the violence and exploitation of white supremacy, a refrain Hawkins used in public talks.[50] Cherry Heights embodied the contradictions of suburban development in the 1910s: black developers sought profit by marketing a homogenous suburb based, in part, on established segregated subdivisions. Both Cherry Heights and Roland Park existed in 1910 because of racial and class segregation. Suburbs, in turn, made it possible for a select few members of Baltimore's black elite, including Hawkins and McMechen, to buy property and move into a white neighborhood in the heart of Baltimore City.

Another such planned suburb opened on the other side of the Guilford wall in 1917. Wilson Park was the brainchild of Harry O. Wilson, a black banker and founder of an insurance business. Wilson amassed an estate worth $200,000 by lending money and selling land, making him one of Baltimore's wealthiest citizens.[51] Like many of the most successful black entrepreneurs throughout the country in the early twentieth century, he also profited from segregated housing as a landlord.[52] Real estate development was a logical next step as he was already a property owner with a network of potential investors.

Wilson purchased nineteen acres from a German immigrant to subdivide into two hundred lots. For six of the lots, Wilson brought in a team of black architects, builders, and contractors from North Carolina to build homes with "hot water, heat, electric lights" and "large front porches."[53] Wilson Park presented an alternative to even the nicest row houses where Baltimore's wealthiest African Americans lived. The advertisements for both Cherry Heights and Wilson Park mentioned Roland Park Company subdivisions. Prospective Wilson Park purchasers could live near "beautiful Guilford." Wilson Park's high elevation and good views served as selling points. It lay four hundred feet above sea level "overlooking Baltimore City." Wilson also obliquely referred to health with ads that assured that Wilson Park was not situated on any "low-land" or "marsh," thus affording a unique opportunity for property owners who historically had access only to some of the area's most hazardous land.[54]

Wilson Park lot prices started at $300 and lots with houses sold for $1,600—beyond the reach of most Baltimoreans of any race. Wilson authorized a handful of real estate brokers to sell parcels, which they advertised as "suburban property."[55] One of the brokers listed an address of 1800 McCulloh Street, the same block where the segregation ordinance fight began. The rest of the brokers who sold homes in Wilson Park, all of whom were African American, were located west of Eutaw Place. Hawkins later moved to Wilson Park as did Wilson.[56]

Wilson Park attracted more members of the city's black intellectual and social elite in 1917 after the prestigious and historically black Morgan College relocated from West Baltimore to the predominantly white Lauraville, one mile northeast of Wilson Park in Baltimore County. Residents of the largely white working-class Lauraville fought Morgan's move on the grounds that proximity to African Americans would lower property values. At the time, the neighborhood was comprised of a mix of small new subdivisions that barred blacks by restrictive covenants and many older owner-occupied houses that did not. Without blanket racial restrictions covering the land under consideration, Lauraville residents, like their counterparts living on unrestricted land throughout the country, began to mount more vociferous and at times even violent campaigns to achieve the same racial exclusion secured by restrictions.[57]

Morgan's white president tried to counter what had begun to pass as common sense among Baltimore's whites: that black institutions—and black residences—lowered property values. Engaging whites on the same market logic, he explained to a delegation from Lauraville that he had made inquiries in other cities and "property near colored colleges always increased in value." Lauraville residents countered that not only would the arrival of the college be disastrous to property values, but so too was the mere possibility that Morgan would use some of its acreage to develop a "scientifically sanitary" suburb to house its black faculty and staff.[58] This latter claim formed the basis for a lawsuit to prevent Morgan's relocation. The Maryland Court of Appeals conceded that black neighbors could depreciate property values, but that it lacked the jurisdiction to intervene in Morgan's relocation because the subdivision of land for a black residential neighborhood did not in itself constitute a public nuisance.[59] Morgan subsequently relocated to Lauraville and faculty members began to move into Wilson Park. White residents indeed saw Morgan facilitate the development of a second planned suburb for black faculty and staff. In contrast to its competitor Wilson Park, which lacked restrictive covenants, Morgan Park made use of them. It included provisions found in Roland Park Company deeds including one pertaining to the minimum cost of lots as well as a racial restriction—this one against whites.[60]

SEGREGATION AND GROWTH

Cherry Heights, Wilson Park, and Morgan Park, like part of Guilford, were situated in Baltimore County. Their development took place during a contentious push for Baltimore City to annex surrounding territory in the 1910s. Guilford lay in a new ring outside Baltimore City's post-1888 annexation. The new Belt contained Roland Park Company subdivisions along with areas east of York Road and Lauraville. To the west it contained restricted planned suburbs. Though affluent and residential in many of its sections, the new Belt was also dotted with small industrial concerns, farms, and the occasional remaining country estate along with row house construction both new and old.

Annexationists eyed the Belt for its potential contributions to the city's population and economic development. The Belt had grown in population since 1888. The other area they considered included portions of the harbor lying outside Baltimore City in Baltimore and Anne Arundel Counties. If Baltimore City could annex the Belt before the 1920 census, it would add significantly to the city's population, demonstrating that Baltimore could keep pace with its rival cities such as Pittsburgh, which had annexed territory right before the 1910 census and pushed Baltimore down the list of the biggest cities in the country. The harbor area also figured into efforts to attract capital. Rapid and unregulated development of the harbor along the shoreline outside municipal oversight potentially impeded the city-run port facilities so crucial to Baltimore's economic standing.[61] Annexing these adjacent areas was thus critical for the smooth running of the port.

By 1916, annexation had become one of the key issues informing city and county politics. Led by Mayor James Preston and the City-Wide Congress, a series of annexation bills reached the state legislature in Annapolis, only to suffer narrow defeats. However, when rival factions within Preston's Democratic Party tried to craft a replacement annexing only the harbor, Preston and his supporters cried foul, calling it a "counterfeit bill." As important as more control over the harbor was to the future of Baltimore City, the only measures annexationists supported included the Belt.[62]

As both a Belt resident and head of one of its biggest development firms, Bouton was courted by both anti-annexation and pro-annexation groups. Anti-annexationists pointed to the higher tax rates people paid in the city.[63] In response, Bouton reached out to lawyers to clarify the provisions of each iteration of the bill. Would a city ordinance prohibiting sports and games on Sunday apply to Baltimore Country Club activities in Roland Park? It might, they answered. Would the Roland Park Company retain the right to extend company sewers and water mains and derive income from that infrastructure if the Belt were annexed? Yes. In the end, Bouton sided with the pro-annexation forces in favor of "Greater Baltimore."[64]

One of the predominant themes of the annexation debates that appeared in newspapers and pamphlets—and in Bouton's private correspondence—centered on whether the county areas to be annexed received "the services they were entitled to" based on the taxes they paid. No one disputed that improvements in services would accompany annexation, but anti-annexationists doubted they would be worth future tax increases.[65] In recent years, Baltimore County property tax rates, historically much lower than those in the city, had been increasing in the border area. By 1916, the difference was small enough to be palatable to well-off businessmen like Bouton.[66] Furthermore, the Roland Park Company would be able to devolve services such as garbage pickup and road repair to Baltimore City and receive better fire and police protection. Potential tax increases remained unpopular for working-class and poorer residents, especially those in the dense areas just east of Baltimore City, but nevertheless they desired annexation to secure better services. At the same time, residents would not be subject to the periodic special assessments for local county services, nor would they have to pay an extra county toll for telephone service.[67]

Bouton's desire to see a Greater Baltimore did not stand in tension with the company's longtime advertising strategy of defining urban space as disorderly, unhealthy, and diverse. By 1916, the company's reputation as a suburb had been secured. Guilford and Roland Park were already split between Baltimore City and Baltimore County, but it made little difference for selling them as "first class suburbs." Regardless of political jurisdiction, the company would still refer to them as such, thanks to its creation of a unified space defined largely by its aesthetic qualities and the terms of sale, rather than by political boundaries. In terms of operations, it could still carry on its sewer rental operations until, as had already been agreed, Baltimore City paid the company to incorporate the sewers into the municipal system. Nor would annexation change the wall on York Road or the relationship between Roland Park, Guilford, Cross Keys, Evergreen, Waverly, or Govans.

Bouton joined a delegation to testify in Annapolis before the State Senate Judicial Proceedings Committee on February 22, 1916, where they framed annexation as an issue of needing growth to remain competitive. A quarter of the thirteen-person delegation consisted of Roland Park residents. At least three others, including Mahool, belonged to the same social clubs as Bouton.[68] Bouton testified that Baltimore City was "one of the great cities of this country engaged in a fierce struggle for commercial supremacy and commercial growth." Only once the "harbor and outlying districts" came under the management of a "single entity" could Baltimore—and even Maryland—compete with other places. On account of Baltimore "not being allowed to grow," the entire state suffered.[69]

Though Preston staunchly supported both the residential segregation ordinance and annexation, he and the white supporters of the Greater Baltimore League did not make residential segregation a plank of their pro-growth platform. The editorial board of the *Baltimore Afro-American* noted the omission and offered an explanation: "Segregation is in no way an issue in the present campaign," it wrote, because the segregation ordinance was simultaneously making its way to the U.S. Supreme Court.[70] Enough ambiguity remained, however, to prompt members of the Conference of the African Methodist Episcopal Church to adopt a resolution supporting annexation so long as "the area of race segregation" was not extended.[71] The editorial board, too, supported annexation, but used the issue to rally readers to exercise electoral power in the 1917 city council elections. "Have any colored men been called into consultation or placed on any committee that are to work for the annexation of more territory to Baltimore?" it asked. "We have not heard of any. Don't forget to vote on Tuesday."[72]

In the end, however, annexation benefited avowed segregationists such as Preston, with or without the residential segregation ordinance. The population of the proposed territory was predominantly white, and much of the land in the north and west had been developed with restrictive covenants. Baltimore, meanwhile, would stand to gain more white representation in municipal elections and more majority-white wards overall. Annexation for the sake of gaining more white voters in municipal elections continued as a rationale for annexations in other parts of the United States for decades to come.[73] Baltimore's black electorate was increasingly concentrated in a few wards.

Preston's administration blatantly used additional strategies to regulate Baltimore's racial geography. One of these was infrastructure projects. Between 1915 and 1918 the city condemned a black business and residential district near downtown in order to construct Preston Gardens, on the purported basis that it was a source of "communicable diseases."[74] The clearance area came within one block of the law offices of Hawkins and McMechen, who crafted legal arguments for three separate trials against the segregation ordinance amid the din of demolition. Hawkins worked in a building that also contained the law firms of other black lawyers, located at 21 East Saratoga Street. Displaced black law firms joined Hawkins and McMechen on East Saratoga Street, but by and large, demolition greatly reduced the size of the neighborhood and accelerated the consolidation of Baltimore's main black business district across town, west of Eutaw Place on Pennsylvania Avenue.[75]

As various factions debated municipal annexation, the fate of Baltimore's segregation ordinance indirectly came before the U.S. Supreme Court. The case, *Buchanan v. Warley*, tested the constitutionality of a similar ordinance from Louisville, Kentucky. Louisville and Baltimore shared similar conditions. In the nineteenth century, African Americans and whites lived in close proximity in dense neighborhoods. At the turn of the century, factors such as changing employment opportunities and a public transportation system enabled people to live further from the center, giving rise to a sorting further shaped by disenfranchisement, conversations about health, and a rapidly growing population.[76] The Louisville segregation ordinance had begun as a campaign by a white property owner who was convinced Louisville could avoid the mistakes that resulted in Baltimore's ordinances being repeatedly struck down. As in Baltimore, legal action was initiated by the NAACP.

As the suit wound its way through lower courts, both supporters and opponents watched in anticipation. Once it reached the U.S. Supreme Court it became clear that it would serve as the test case for all municipal segregation ordinances. The Baltimore City solicitor—an ardent annexationist—filed an amicus curiae brief in support of the ordinance. Hawkins filed an amicus brief against the ordinance on behalf of the Baltimore branch of the NAACP.[77] One of the defendant's arguments in favor of the ordinance reflected the emerging white consensus that blacks lowered property values when they moved into a neighborhood, which justified the use of police power to maintain segregation. On November 5, 1917, the court handed down its unanimous ruling: the residential segregation ordinance violated the Fourteenth Amendment because it illegitimately used the state's police power to prevent African Americans from buying, selling, and disposing of property.

The ultimate failure of the segregation ordinance in 1917 seemed to prove that housing segregation might not form an effective bulwark to contain the geographic extent of black political power. Mayor Preston turned his attention to finding new ways to legally implement racial residential segregation in Baltimore. In letters to concerned supporters of the segregation ordinance, he urged them to organize into neighborhood associations that could write and enforce community-wide racially restrictive covenants. He quickly formed the Committee on Segregation to promote covenants. Preston predicted that restrictive covenants would prevent racial mixing because as private contracts rather than government actions, they remained outside the purview of *Buchanan v. Warley*.[78] Hundreds of Baltimoreans followed his suggestions.[79] Annexation passed shortly after. Baltimore City gained 46.4 square miles, including the Belt and a stretch of harbor from Baltimore County and 5.6 square miles bordering the harbor from Anne Arundel County.[80]

NEXT STEPS

Preston remained committed to finding additional ways for the municipal government to limit black mobility. One idea he presented was segregation based on public health issues. Citing how blacks disproportionately suffered from tuberculosis, Preston suggested setting aside sections of the city for black people on the grounds they "constituted a permanent menace to the health of the white population." The plan would employ police power to compel African Americans to live only in the designated areas. Preston's own health commissioner publicly objected that the public health rationale would be indefensible because of the many African Americans who worked as domestics, washerwomen, cooks, and chauffeurs.[81] The plan went nowhere.

Preston also proposed land-use zoning, which would regulate the construction and use of every property in the newly enlarged city. Zoning was a process in which municipal officials carved the city into areas or "zones" and then designated permitted uses and construction guidelines for property in each type of zone. Various scholars have concluded that what seemed an ostensibly color-blind use of zoning had explicitly racist intent.[82] Zoning designated clusters of blocks "residential," which triggered a set of rules ensuring that only dwellings could be constructed. These buildings looked

FIGURE 3.7 One page of a Roland Park Company photo album of negative influences on Baltimore neighborhoods, including the mixture of residential and commercial uses. Three of the photos were taken in an early competitor, Walbrook, while the other three were in the vicinity of Eutaw Place.

(Courtesy of the Johns Hopkins University Sheridan Libraries)

different from the tall, bulky skyscrapers permitted in commercial zones and served different purposes than factories limited to industrial zones. Two of zoning's largest proponents in the 1910s were suburban developers and city planners.[83] Among the city planners who most strenuously advocated for the adoption of zoning were George B. Ford and Nolen, both of whom had requested Roland Park Company restrictions to use as models.

In Baltimore, use zoning made sense in the context of *Buchanan v. Warley.* The Supreme Court opinion actually validated the assumption that African Americans lowered property values while it upheld black property rights. The ordinance in question, the decision said, did not address the fact that "property may be acquired by undesirable white neighbors or put to disagreeable though lawful uses with like results."[84] In other words, if the segregation ordinance had been color-blind and used police power to prevent *anyone* from depreciating property through usage, it would not necessarily be in violation of the Constitution.[85] Preston employed color-blind language heavily indebted to the link between race and real estate in claiming the new zoning would "prevent the destruction of real estate values and insure quiet enjoyment of residences." Zoning would also keep Baltimore competitive with cities such as New York, which had adopted zoning laws in 1916.[86]

Before he could implement this new zoning in Baltimore, however, Preston was replaced. The Democrat lost a bid for a third term in the 1919 Democratic primary. Preston's successor, a Republican, William Broening, signed a zoning ordinance into effect on June 14, 1921. The twin causes of protecting whites' property values and attracting capital to Baltimore had crossed the political aisle. Broening appointed a zoning commission consisting of Bouton and a mix of businessmen and city employees. The men created a master plan dividing every part of the city into hierarchies of residential, commercial, or industrial areas, which each were further divided into subcategories. Much of the newly annexed northern and western sections, including vacant land, was set aside as "first residential." First residential precluded future construction of row houses or other attached dwellings. The south and southeastern sections of Baltimore, with large populations of blacks and immigrants, were zoned industrial. Even neighborhoods composed primarily of homes were zoned industrial if they were majority-black, depriving them of the height, use, and construction restrictions neighborhoods of similar appearance received. The values of residential property in industrial districts would suffer, as would the residents, because all noxious businesses would be concentrated near their homes. This move sapped value from black-owned property and made it more difficult for the African Americans who could afford to own property in Baltimore to buy a new home outside the new industrial areas. For black renters, who already faced a housing shortage that had them paying much higher rents than whites for comparable units, zoning exacerbated the shortage of potential locations for new multifamily dwellings. The landlords of any race who rented to African Americans were among those who stood to gain from zoning.

The Zoning Commission put the racial considerations of land-use zoning on full display, even as proponents couched land-use zoning in more color-blind terms. Certain residential neighborhoods that were predominantly native-born and white and otherwise would have been lumped in as industrial were instead carved out of the industrial zone and designated residential. Baltimore's Zoning Commission made these and other decisions on the basis of protecting the property values of what they deemed the most desirable restricted planned suburbs of the new northern and northwestern sections of Baltimore.[87] The Zoning Commission traced these new zones, based on hierarchies of race and property values, onto maps and filed them among Baltimore City's records, making the new hardened boundaries legally binding.

CONCLUSION

In the eleven years between 1910 and 1921, the Roland Park Company grew, profited from, and gained political power because of how it both responded to and furthered exclusionary housing development. Certain about Baltimore's reception of the planned suburb, the company made Guilford's boundaries its central feature. No longer did the company delineate its boundary by a tall hedge; it rendered it in brick and mortar with walls and gateposts. Stricter covenants included a racial restriction that put down in ink a ban Bouton long doubted was legally possible.

Guilford, with its hard boundaries, thrived in a context in which white developers began to create a consensus that guaranteed racial segregation could indeed be a major selling point of the planned suburb. The Roland Park Company's reputation grew to the point where it set the standards for newer developments in Baltimore. Nationally, the company answered inquiries about its deed restrictions. Developers and planners sought information, then incorporated company exclusionary practices into their own projects. As a result, the company's particular forms of segregation, such as the wording of its restrictive covenants, spread throughout the country, giving rise to a cohort of well-financed peer developers who considered particular forms of racial segregation integral to their business. In the aggregate, these networks also spread the notion that the planned suburb—as the company had narrowly defined it—made for inherently valuable property.

When the Supreme Court ruled against the use of racial zoning ordinances, restrictive covenants and land-use zoning filled the vacuum. With the latter based on restrictive covenants and with developers joining zoning commissions, the line between municipal law and development practice was blurred. Members of both parties embraced measures to exert control over racial geography while remaining mindful of doing it in ways that continued to attract capital to Baltimore. The 1920s would see both an explosion of zoning laws and restrictive covenants. It was also when developers would turn their informal networks into a coordinated national project to standardize exclusion.

4

STANDARDS

I n 1929, Roland Park Company Sales Manager Guy T. O. Hollyday gave
the following advice to members of the National Association of Real
Estate Boards (NAREB) in an article published in the *National Real
Estate Journal*: "To keep out people who have not learned to live decently
[we have] a sales policy against certain nationalities, such as the poorer
south Europeans whose presence in the district would depreciate values."[1]
Hollyday echoed the policies espoused by his boss, Roland Park Company
president Edward Bouton, that race, religion, and nationality affected
property values. Hollyday's article reflected an existing culture within
the company, one that viewed the Roland Park Company as the industry
leader and trendsetter. The Roland Park Company knew, in Hollyday's
words, how to "create and maintain a market."[2]

In order to understand the rise of NAREB and the Roland Park Company's place in it, it is crucial to look at the interplay between industry-wide
conversations about real estate and local practices of individual firms. This
multidirectional exchange enabled the Roland Park Company to make the
leap from constructing Baltimore's suburban real estate market to helping
to forge a national one. Though NAREB was founded in 1908, it was in

the 1920s that it achieved a robust organizational capacity amid a nationwide real estate boom. Whereas previously developers informally disseminated forms, advice, and plans, NAREB opened new communication channels to make information available to any member of the association. NAREB, in essence, made it possible for members to easily have large nationwide conversations about important issues such as valuing property.

Suburban developers like those in the Roland Park Company filled the association's leadership ranks from the outset. As a result, they played a disproportionate role in shaping NAREB's platform. During NAREB's formative years, suburban developers spearheaded a drive to transform the image of those in the real estate business from scam artists to reputable professionals. They worked to standardize practices and introduce a code of ethics that its members would be duty-bound to follow. If members adhered to the rules and paid their dues, they could call themselves Realtors with a capital R, a name NAREB trademarked. But the association's dissemination of textbooks and training courses did not prevent individual members from continuing to shape the industry. In a departure from some theories of professionalization, NAREB's central office regularly distributed materials based on its members' advice and experiences.[3] Ultimately, though, through the mechanisms of professionalization, NAREB encouraged members to emulate suburban developers.[4]

Members of NAREB tended to have little in common during the organization's first decade aside from the fact they were white men involved in real estate. NAREB initially banned African Americans from membership and rarely admitted women before the Second World War.[5] NAREB members came from different parts of the country and had disparate interests ranging from selling farm property to managing cooperative apartments in large cities. Developing shared ways of seeing people and property together became a crucial facet of Realtor identity. Scott Kurishige writes, "Developers and realtors sought to control not only the trade in bricks and mortar but also the trade in images of race, neighborhood, and community."[6] This was the case with public promotions by NAREB, such as early collaborations with the U.S. Department of Labor for the Own Your Own Home campaign.[7] It was also the case with regard to advertising by individual firms. Often overlooked, but just as critical to real estate, was the circulation of images that were not intended for the public. Seeing people and property together, for example, occurred in the literal sense as NAREB members came together to travel, organize tours, and fraternize. Whether discussing business, driving through cities, or singing songs together, Realtors used NAREB to rehearse ideas about people and real estate. Through this process they reinforced their standing as white, as men, and as real estate experts. This enabled them to develop a shared way of seeing that inflected the development of professional practice.

In terms of documents not intended for public view, none illustrate the daily practices of segregation better than the Roland Park Company's exclusion files. The company created a cache of office records to keep track of rejected buyers. Whereas the company used the public document of the restrictive covenant to bar African Americans, it vetted others whom salesmen initially thought were qualified to live in a Roland Park neighborhood. The exclusion files most clearly illustrate the Roland Park Company's inconsistencies and ambiguities that put it at odds with national conversations on standardizing real estate practices. The company used exclusion files when it came to excluding any homebuyers other than African Americans. In the files, salesmen documented how they investigated potential buyers and debated with supervisors the potential merits of candidates before rejecting them. The company began to use exclusion files after moving the investigative apparatus of employee credit checks in-house after the opening of Guilford. Their use greatly expanded in the 1920s when the company opened its third subdivision, Homeland. Of the fifty-six exclusion files that have survived in the company records, all but three were created after 1920.[8]

The exclusion files cast light on the constant interplay between local understandings about racial hierarchy, national conversations, and federal laws.[9] Natalia Molina argues that scholars often "miss how regionally constructed notions of race developed, circulated, and gradually percolated to the national level."[10] The exclusion files fill in a missing piece about the relationship between local and national segregation efforts, because Realtors' positions often depended on where they lived and how they understood racial hierarchies to be constituted in their localities. These ideas filtered up to the national level through Realtor participation in NAREB. As a result, national institution building both depended on and stood in tension with local practices of exclusion.

The give-and-take between local real estate firms and the national association shaped how questions of racial hierarchy and housing exclusion played out.[11] Despite NAREB's top-down attempts to codify directives about exclusion, suburban developers never reached a consensus on what exclusion looked like on the ground. This remained the case even as developers became NAREB leaders with a disproportionately large platform within NAREB to work their views into real estate standards.

FORGING A NATIONAL INSTITUTION

In the early twentieth century, the popular perception was that real estate developers were scam artists. Colorful descriptors such as "fly-by-nighters," "land butchers," "sharks," and "curbstoners" appeared in magazines and literature. These depictions lumped together developers with real estate brokers and just about anyone who conducted business related to real estate. With no barriers to entry and the promise of a living to be made, especially in rapidly growing cities, the numbers of brokers soared. Established developers and brokers needed to prove their trustworthiness to suspicious new customers, who doubted whether they could perform their jobs competently and in good faith. Over time, they began forming local real estate boards that charged membership fees and set rules about how to conduct business, with the intent of distinguishing themselves as a class of reputable real estate firms. The Baltimore board, founded in 1858, was the nation's oldest.[12]

In 1908 nineteen local boards met in Chicago to form NAREB. They aimed to scale up the gatekeeping and reputation building of local boards into a national enterprise. Doing so would also enable them to better exchange information and, in their words, exert a "combined influence upon matters affecting real estate interests."[13] Accordingly, the leaders of local boards quickly assumed top positions in the national association.[14] The group elected as its first president a developer from Detroit to lead in "the assumption of social responsibility by real estate men for good city planning and good community structure."[15] Large-scale suburban developers became leaders of NAREB, giving themselves strong voices in shaping the nascent association. This meant that planned suburbs and the practices of these developers stood the greatest chance of representing the best work in North American residential real estate.

The association's first president called for "real estate men" to be "classified among the so-called professions," citing contemporary organizations such as the American Bankers Association, though law, engineering, and medicine also were frequently evoked.[16] NAREB leadership laid out a professionalization project that encompassed four main objectives: create barriers to entry, establish norms and standards, generate and disseminate a body of knowledge, and fashion members as experts. Early efforts to create barriers to entry intersected with what would become another central facet of NAREB: influencing local, state, and national policy. NAREB combined these goals by sending members to their state legislatures to campaign for real estate licensing laws, thus restricting who could legally conduct business.[17]

To begin cultivating an image as experts, NAREB coined and trademarked the name "Realtor," which only members could legally use. Members sought to brand themselves and spread the term so as to "institutionalize the Realtor" with the general public, investors, and other businessmen. It was their hope that "people come to realize that this term [Realtor] distinguishes an entire class of men."[18] Unlike curbstoners, Realtors were to be seen as possessing "high ideals, business capacity, civic loyalty, national patriotism and broad all round manhood" by virtue of their NAREB membership.[19]

To adopt standards, a NAREB members approved a code of ethics in 1913. Its formal title, "Ethics of the Real Estate Profession," linked it to the Realtor professionalization drive.[20] Such codes of ethics typified professionalization at the turn of the century.[21] The NAREB code laid out "duties to

clients" concerning fair prices and transparency, such as inspecting a property before agreeing to sell it, and "duties to other brokers" about fair competition among NAREB members.[22] The code's provisions were generated
through discussions about the issues that most concerned members.

To form a body of knowledge, NAREB began publication of the
National Real Estate Journal, which subsequently covered issues from all
over the United States and Canada, reprinted speeches from events, and
contained editorials written by Realtors. Its writers treated developers of
planned suburbs like celebrities, presenting them as experts among experts.
One article, for instance, praised the developers of Bay City, Michigan, by
saying they "were almost in a class with Nichols, Bouton, Ninde, Thompson and other subdividers."[23] Such was the respect for this small group, including Edward Bouton, that the writer referred to them only by their last
names, expecting members to know them automatically. All of them—
Bouton; J. C. Nichols of Kansas City, Missouri; Lee Ninde of Fort Wayne,
Indiana; and King Thompson of Columbus, Ohio—developed large
planned tracts of upscale single-family homes. All used racially restrictive
covenants. Nichols, Bouton, and Ninde all chaired NAREB committees
and, when not chairing, served on them. Nichols and Bouton in particular
had become friends through sharing information about their businesses and
meeting at city planning conferences.[24]

In addition to playing active roles at NAREB, suburban developers also
participated in other nascent organizations. Historians have noted Bouton's
role in generating interest in city planning among Realtors, which led to
their participation in the National Conference of City Planning (NCCP),
an organization founded a year after NAREB and composed of planners
and housing reformers. As developers increasingly participated in the
NCCP, the organization shifted to focus on how municipal planning could
benefit planned suburbs.[25] In turn, urban planning also guided the course
of NAREB. The association formed a city planning committee due to
developer interest in NCCP activity.

During their first decade of activity, neither NAREB nor the NCCP
replaced the informal networks through which developers disseminated
practices. To meet these needs, a group of suburban developers formed a

separate and more informally organized group called the Developers of High-Class Residential Property in 1917. The Developers of High-Class Residential Property was comprised of Bouton, Nichols, Ninde, Thompson, and a handful of others who specialized in planned suburbs around the United States. In many ways, the group functioned as a transition between the informal networks of earlier decades and the institutionalized communication channels of NAREB that would be more fully realized in the 1920s. NAREB brought these members together as most were also part of the association's City Planning Committee.[26] Many of the members, however, knew each other from prior interactions. In addition to Bouton and Nichols, Bouton and John Demarest of New York had been former business partners during Bouton's brief stint as general manager of the Sage Foundation's planned suburb, Forest Hills Gardens.

Rather than frame their goal as a project of standardization, which was championed in NAREB, the Conference of Developers of High-Class Residential Property aimed to provide a source of knowledge as members shared their experiences through annual candid conversations and mailed questionnaires. Significantly, none of the group's members were in direct competition. Conversations covered a wide range of daily problems and business procedures. One year's meeting included over two dozen topics, including restrictive covenants and labor practices, which had long been central concerns of the Roland Park Company.

The topic of restrictions attracted Indianapolis developer Emerson Chaille to the group. Chaille hoped the annual meeting would help him decide how to use restrictive covenants and set house prices since, as he pointed out, the developers at the meeting had also begun using restrictions they had adapted from others. The matter was urgent for Chaille. He had already invested in land several miles from the city center and he did not have local models to look at because nothing like "the highest grade subdivision" had "ever been thought of in Indianapolis."[27]

On the subject of restrictions and house prices, attendees took turns saying whether they included minimum cost restrictions in their deeds. Minimum cost restrictions served as both a barrier to entry for buyers and a measure of quality control on the house a resident would commission. All attendees except one did, though they clarified that it was not a uniform figure per subdivision but varied depending on the block. King Thompson of Columbus, Ohio, believed that a minimum cost should be inserted into restrictions as a signal to the public about the nature of the subdivision. Demarest concurred that "restrictions are unquestionably one of your best-selling assets, if they are properly presented." A discussion ensued about how to determine the base price, especially in light of soaring building costs nationwide. The one developer who had not included the restriction expressed particular concern over deciding on a figure because he was determined to adopt a minimum cost restriction on a future development. Bouton suggested he could avoid the matter completely and adopt the method the Roland Park Company used for Guilford, where it included in restrictive covenants the right to approve all house plans.[28]

Bouton then raised the question of whether residents attempted to violate the restriction and build homes for less. Nichols recounted several incidents. Two others claimed it happened only in the parts of their subdivisions where homes were the cheapest. Here, Bouton reiterated that the Roland Park Company avoided such incidents because it exercised approval over all plans. In actuality, the Roland Park Company staff noted several cases in which owners might have violated the restrictions along the eastern edge of Guilford, precisely the location of Guilford's cheapest homes.[29]

At the 1919 conference developers voiced concerns over the future of domestic labor in their suburbs. This became a question about racial hierarchy. Everyone agreed that it had become increasingly difficult over the 1910s for residents to find servants.[30] Thompson wanted advice on improving servant conditions that would make it easier to live in his subdivision's large houses. Some members of the conference responded that they had begun to simplify house layouts and stock houses with more conveniences to require less housework overall.[31] Others tried to create better ventilated attics and basements, the likely quarters for live-in servants, to make accommodations more attractive to potential employees. Nichols, Demarest, and Chaille were exploring the possibility of bringing movie theaters near their developments because cheap leisure activities could make working in the area more enticing. Thompson was considering ways to shorten the hours his residents might need servants. The root of "the servant problem," as he saw it, was that residents treated their servants "like slaves." Improved hours might even entice "white girls" into service, he reasoned, by reducing "the stigma attached to it" due to the fact that the majority of live-in servants were black women. At the very least, he concluded, they would be more likely to take up day labor, though probably not live-in labor.[32]

Hugh Prather responded that he already had a ready source of black domestic labor that was meeting the needs of his company's Dallas suburb, Highland Park. Before his team laid out Highland Park, it first subdivided seven and a half acres of land to sell to twenty-five black families to form what Prather called a "servants' addition." Named Booker T. Washington Addition, the servant residences were separated from Highland Park proper by a "high railroad embankment" and surrounded by tracks.[33] The land, he added, "never could have been used for any other purpose." Prather called the families "a pretty good class" because residents owned property and built a church. Prather's company constructed a small school. Nichols interrupted to ask if Booker T. Washington Addition had only houses, a church, and a school. Prather replied that nothing else was necessary. "It makes them satisfied there in Highland Park to have some place to go at night and visit," he said. "They have some place to go and walk up and down the railroad tracks and streets, as Negroes like to do."[34] Prather did not mention that Highland Park's reputation as a sundown town meant that black residents were unlikely to move about at night safely.[35] Prather used his example of Booker T. Washington Addition to illustrate why he, unlike his colleagues, did not need to take measures to better labor conditions in order to retain a workforce.[36]

Bouton agreed that "establishing a community which will furnish servants is something which might be done by all of us." He did not bring up Cross Keys, which predated Roland Park by decades. Rather, he discussed his idea to "establish a Polish community"—Christian Poles, he clarified, because he "understood they were very cleanly and made good servants." His perception of Poles as clean stood in contrast to how the company treated the black residents of Cross Keys, and their land itself, as health threats. Bouton went so far as to make inquiries about the possibility, but "ran up against the immigration laws." He turned to Prather and suggested he could "probably do that" instead of relying on the black residents of Booker T. Washington Addition. Prather replied, "We could."[37]

A NATIONAL FORUM ON LOCAL BUSINESS

Bouton's experience with immigration laws as an obstacle to his plan to re-cruit Polish labor was indicative of the times. Immigration policy became a contentious issue among Realtors in the late 1910s and early 1920s, as Con-gress considered a slate of comprehensive immigration bills that had the potential to severely restrict or ban immigrants based on national origin. NAREB provided a centralized forum for debate. Anti-immigration Real-tors framed their opposition in two ways, namely through labor issues and race science such as eugenics, both of which found an audience through popular books. Realtors who spoke at meetings and published pieces in the *National Real Estate Journal* often began their remarks by introducing them-selves as employers. As employers, they could play a role in preventing immigrants from driving down the "good living wage" commanded by "American artisans."[38] Eugenicists believed that the most biologically and intellectually superior people hailed from the Protestant countries of north-west Europe. Many voiced concerns that the growth of other populations endangered white civilization. In order to preserve their own survival, they called for action to ensure the continued domination of Protestants from northwest Europe over other races. One anti-immigration Realtor, who de-clared his home state of California to be on the brink of Japanese "invasion," implored fellow Realtors to help "to save our land to the white race, to preserve our social and economic standards, to exclude an alien race whose God is not our God, whose standards are not ours, who is debarred from American citizenship." Calling the Japanese aliens, he warned that if more immigrants arrived, they would tip the balance of social and economic power in the state.[39] Another said that "different races should be kept apart."[40] This last statement, made by a Jewish Realtor and son of a Mississippi sugar planter, applied to native-born Americans and immigrants alike.[41]

Pro-immigration Realtors also framed their views in terms of labor. Some of the association's most outspoken members in favor of open immigration came from agricultural areas and wanted to attract immigrants to remedy farm labor shortages. Rural Realtors from Michigan, Idaho, Montana, Minnesota, and South Dakota wrote pro-immigration pieces in the *National Real Estate Journal*.[42] Michigan Realtors viewed immigration as necessary for rural settlement. Even so, the pro-immigrant Realtors, like the anti-immigrant Realtors, considered only immigrants from northwest Europe to be desirable, following the eugenics hierarchy that prized "Nordic stock" as physically and intellectually superior.

Tensions between the two camps boiled over at the 1923 NAREB midwinter meeting when delegates interrupted a Michigan Realtor advocating for lax immigration controls and forced him from the stage. The *National Real Estate Journal* recapped the incident with the headline "Oppose Further Immigration."[43] Subsequently, a Chicago Realtor called on colleagues to compromise. Both sides, he reasoned, had "extremists of belief and resultant propaganda."[44] Still, Realtors continued to have open disagreements.

In 1924, the Johnson-Reed Act ushered in federal comprehensive immigration laws in the United States.[45] It instituted a quota system that supplemented or strengthened existing legislation already targeting people of Asian descent. Its net effect permitted a continuation of European immigrants from northwest Europe, while severely limiting or outright banning immigration from most other parts of the world. The act carved out a large exception for the Western Hemisphere after lengthy congressional debates about Mexico and Mexican labor.

One of the long-term impacts of the Johnson-Reed Act was the federal construction of a white race whose ancestry provided the basis for their admission to the United States. In the short term, however, the quota system's unequal treatment of European groups continued to reflect widespread notions of which differences were questionable or suspect.[46]

Suburban developers remained largely quiet during NAREB immigration debates, but questions of racial hierarchy continued to inform their candid conversations at the Conference of Developers of High-Class Residential Property. These meetings discouraged any alternate views, as one developer after another broadly agreed about the merits of exclusion, and simultaneously provided a venue for working out the specific mechanics of how to discriminate.[47] For example, each year conference members voted on whether to sell to Jews (generally a resounding no) and then discussed their rationales. In 1919 Nichols met with disapproval when he said that his company had relaxed its policy on Jewish exclusion since the end of the First World War. He asked other attendees, "Can't anyone have a few kind words to say on my behalf?" to which Bouton responded, "I think it is a perfectly ghastly mistake."[48]

John Demarest feared losing control over his development if he began to sell to Jews. Whereas Nichols believed he and his salesmen could vet clients and make exceptions for certain Jews, and Prather occasionally sold to Jews, Demarest said, "When you open the door, it is gone."[49] Demarest articulated the idea that undesirable groups irreversibly lowered property values; the reputation of Forest Hills Gardens would be ruined. Moreover, developers believed they would lose the ability to strongly control their investment if they began to make exceptions. Bouton warned that residents would "stampede" from their homes if Jews moved in.[50] And who else but other Jews, or people Bouton considered even lower on the racial hierarchy, would want to fill the newly vacant homes?

Jews occupied a distinct place in these early theories of white flight. Demarest and Bouton espoused an ecological theory of succession in which Jews would rapidly drive out Christians, who would never return.[51] Thompson recognized how he was the beneficiary of people moving away from Jewish buyers. "I am profiting by them going into the East End section and crowding those people out," he added, "so I am getting the benefit of that."[52] At the same time, the position of Jews at the end of the 1910s was ambiguous;

they were sometimes viewed as a racial other and at other times as white enough to be dangerous infiltrators. Jewish affluence in places such as Kansas City, New York, Dallas, and Baltimore, in particular, created a consistent contradiction for members of the Conference of Developers of High-Class Residential Property, which never saw the need to vote on other groups such as blacks, who were already banned by restrictive covenant.

The members of the Developers of High-Class Residential Property tackled a broader question: Who should maintain the social order in and around the properties they developed? For Demarest, the answer was himself. Demarest told of how he once had a homeowner who insisted on selling his house to a Jew. Demarest threatened the homeowner by saying he would have a neighbor rent his house to an African American in retaliation, even violating the racially restrictive covenants of Forest Hills Gardens to do so. To Demarest, the social order tracked closely with what he considered the hierarchical relationship between people and property. He did not comment on whether the threat worked, but in his mind, no one could lower a property's value more than a black renter.

Unlike Demarest, others in the group joined Bouton to advocate for solutions based on ideas of white popular sovereignty. Bouton proposed that in order to be democratic, the developers poll residents about whether to make exceptions for certain people. He also insisted that the real test of whether Jews should be allowed would follow if a developer polled residents and got approval. The belief at Roland Park was that if a Jew moved in, on the very next day all the property around it might depreciate by as much as "thirty-three and a third percent," a figure no one explained.[53] The lone dissenting voice was Prather, who would not allow residents to vote because he, like Demarest, wanted to control each case. He also assumed that Highland Park residents would vote against their own interests to permit affluent Jews.[54]

Prather chimed in that if he had tried what Demarest did down in Dallas, the next morning "he would be hanging from a flag pole somewhere."[55] It is unclear whether Prather meant himself, the black tenant, or the landlord would be lynched, but either way, violence was guaranteed. Despite disagreement, the conversation centered on presumptions about how racial hierarchy informed the social order in their cities. As they characterized it, this hierarchy not only would make or break the long-term prospects of their business, but also carried risks of violence for anyone perceived to be transgressing it.

Assumptions such as Prather's indicate developers were aware that the actions of residents could, indeed, be a double-edged sword. The Roland Park Company vice president, who also attended the conference, informed the group that right before he left Baltimore there had been an issue where a resident had sold her property to someone who turned out to be Jewish. She wanted the company's advice on how to stop the sale, which he gave. The resident also shared the news with her neighbors, "three or four" of whom informed the vice president that if she could not stop the sale "they were going to wait on [the buyer] as a vigilance committee and tell him how strong they felt about it." These residents of a Roland Park Company development (it is unclear which) felt it acceptable and urgent enough to discuss exclusion frankly with the company, which had a history of both facilitating resident action in Cross Keys and setting the tone for racial-ized labor relationships. By telling the company, however, the residents were also ensuring that the Roland Park Company followed through on maintaining the exclusion it had long promised and which residents had come to consider as necessary.[56]

ORIGINS OF THE EXCLUSION FILES: CREDIT REPORTS AND THE FEMALE INVESTIGATOR

One issue that was not discussed by members of the Conference of Devel-opers of High-Class Residential Property was how the Roland Park Com-pany's own salesmen factored into the exclusion/inclusion process through the daily tracking of potential sales, a crucial part of company operations in which employees exercised discretion based on locally informed as-sumptions. The Roland Park Company's chief mechanism of documenting sales was actually an elaboration of an earlier vetting process adopted by the company: credit reports on its employees. In 1907 the Roland Park Company sought the services of the Union Credit Company, but it was not interested in credit checks per se. Rather, the company wanted to use the investigative services to determine the "general character," "habits and honesty," and "ability" of its staff.[57]

Initially, the company also used Union Credit to vet a handful of prospective buyers, with emphasis placed on investigating their finances and "extraction."[58] After Guilford opened, however, the company sought to establish its own in-house investigative arm to vet future customers. Bouton sent identical letters to two people, asking if they knew anyone suitable for "a little special work of investigation." One recipient was Roland Park resident, Johns Hopkins University provost, and former director of the Baltimore Country Club, Joseph Ames. The other was Lilian Welsh, a physician, instructor, and administrator at the Women's College of Baltimore. In the letter, Bouton explained that all prospective buyers had to submit references to the company. The investigator would contact the references. The duties of the investigator job, which would consist "almost entirely of interviews," meant the employee should meet certain criteria, including being a woman. Namely, Bouton sought "a woman, not too young, of good address, education, and above all, good judgment." Bouton also preferred that the woman be local, because it was part-time employment and he did not want the "responsibility" of ensuring she had other things to do.[59] For unknown reasons, the Roland Park Company dropped its attempt to hire an investigator shortly thereafter.

Bouton may have gotten the idea of hiring a woman from his brief stint working with Demarest, who employed a woman to follow up on the references of prospective purchasers. At the Conference for Developers of High-Class Residential Property, Demarest shared his thoughts on how the "female investigator" formed part of a good sales strategy. The woman, he said, "stimulates interest in the man whom she may go see as the reference or prospective purchaser." If a client knows the developer vetted all residents of a community, then he would "get a certain protection for his investment, a certain protection for his family." A professional and "conscientious" woman would impress those men with the tenor and nature of her investigations. Demarest called his female investigator "a walking advertisement" who generated new business when she interacted with a prospective buyer's coworkers or acquaintances "in a businesslike way." Even if the target of her investigation ultimately proved unsuitable, his coworker would know he was going to fulfill his duty as husband and father if he bought a house with that developer.[60] Even though Bouton did not hire an investigator, having one became another potential practice to be circulated among his network of suburban developers.

After Bouton shelved the idea of the female investigator for Roland Park, the company continued to seek out ways to establish an investigative system. Subsequently, the company created a new card system for tracking interactions between salesmen and consumers. This marked the first time the company kept the sales card of someone it decided *not* to sell to. Salesmen would follow leads of interested buyers who possessed the means to purchase a home. They wrote down brief summaries of their interactions with the client and added commentary. When they learned information that led them or their supervisors to terminate the sales process, the card was stamped "Exclusion File" and kept in a collection in the office.

An early card from 1916 detailed the interactions of Frank Carozza, a Baltimore-based general contractor from Govans. On July 1, Carozza inquired about lot prices in Guilford. He told the salesman he wanted to see the lots on his own, without a salesman, but would get in touch if he liked what he saw. Four days later, the sales manager made a follow-up phone call to Carozza at his office. Carozza was too busy to talk, but salesman George Simmons noted that "he has the appearance of being an intelligent rather high type of Italian."

For the next month, Simmons recorded whenever Carozza visited the company to talk about which lots to purchase. Then, on September 5, a different salesman recorded the following on Carozza's sales card: "Happened to see the children of Mr. Carozza's family in Govans on Monday and I really think they would be undesirable residents for Guilford; their dress and looks are very much of the Italian type and I am satisfied that neighbors would object to them."[61] The Carozza family did not notice the salesman on the street at the time. A week later, the company rejected Carozza's plans to buy lots and build houses in Guilford.

That marked the end of Carozza's transaction, but Simmons recorded one final interaction on the exclusion file a month later. This time *he* saw Carozza on the street. Carozza approached him. According to Simmons, Carozza "seemed to be wrought up about something. . . . Someone had told him the reason his plans were turned down was because he was Italian." Here, Simmons lied in response, telling him "I had been away and was not up to the situation but would find out about it and let him know." There was no follow-up noted. Company staff stamped "Exclusion File" on Carozza's card and retained it separate from other sales records.[62] Carozza's exclusion file became one more piece of a growing system of investigating, surveilling, and recording who could and could not buy property. The company focused its investigations on people like Carozza who may have passed as desirable white persons but ultimately proved to be not white enough.

Realtors often treated religion, national origin, and race as interchangeable for the purposes of establishing a racial hierarchy. According to historian Thomas Guglielmo, Americans were likely to classify Italians as a race in the 1910s and 1920s, rendering their place of birth less important than their overall ancestry. However, Italians were still considered white enough to be treated as potential homebuyers.[63] In this sense, the Roland Park Company conforms with what historians of race and immigration have detailed with regard to how individuals could be white for certain purposes and not others. This includes instances in which people tried to be recognized as white in order to secure access to full citizenship or took measures to avoid being classed as nonwhite or, in particular, black. In doing so, they recognized that access to the rights and privileges of citizenship was tied to a hierarchy of race.[64] The permutations and exceptions were many and they often varied by region, year, and circumstance, but the common thread running through such complexities was that different groups were defined and defined themselves in relation to others beyond a simple black/white binary when it came to buying and selling property.

THE HEYDAY OF THE EXCLUSION FILES

The Roland Park Company continued to grow its business operations in 1924 with a third subdivision north of Guilford called Homeland. The expansion of the company's business appears to have paved the way for the further implementation of the exclusion files, which joined physical boundaries and restrictive covenants in the company's growing toolbox of exclusionary instruments.

With the expansion of the exclusion files, salesmen discretion became both more nuanced and, at times, more ambiguous. Despite the heavy attention paid to ancestry, it was never the sole criteria for exclusion of whites. Rather, the exclusion files paint a more complicated picture of how developers excluded people on a daily basis, revealing how salesmen employed a flexible calculus to work out ambiguities on a case-by-case basis. Few exclusion files were more ambiguous than that of "Mrs. Mildred Wonneman." Ostensibly, the Roland Park Company salesman deemed her and her husband unacceptable homebuyers because they were both hairdressers. However, other details on the card that could have also been factors included the fact that Wonneman's business was located on Greenmount Avenue. The card also noted that she was "also known as Mrs. Bracket."[65] A combination of local geography, gender norms, and occupation contributed to her exclusion.

As these examples indicate, appearance and social networks played an important role in shaping company decisions. Both were the deciding factors in the sale of a house to George Boas and his wife, Simone Brangier Boas, in 1926. Five years earlier, Boas, born to Jewish parents, had accepted an invitation to join the Johns Hopkins University faculty.[66] Sales manager Guy T. O. Hollyday remained reluctant about the sale because the company had "a very strict rule against selling to Jews."[67] Rather than rejecting the sale outright, however, Hollyday wrote to long-time resident of Roland Park, former Baltimore Country Club board member, and Hopkins provost Joseph Ames. He asked Ames's opinion "as a resident and one personally acquainted with Dr. Boas" to help him determine whether he should

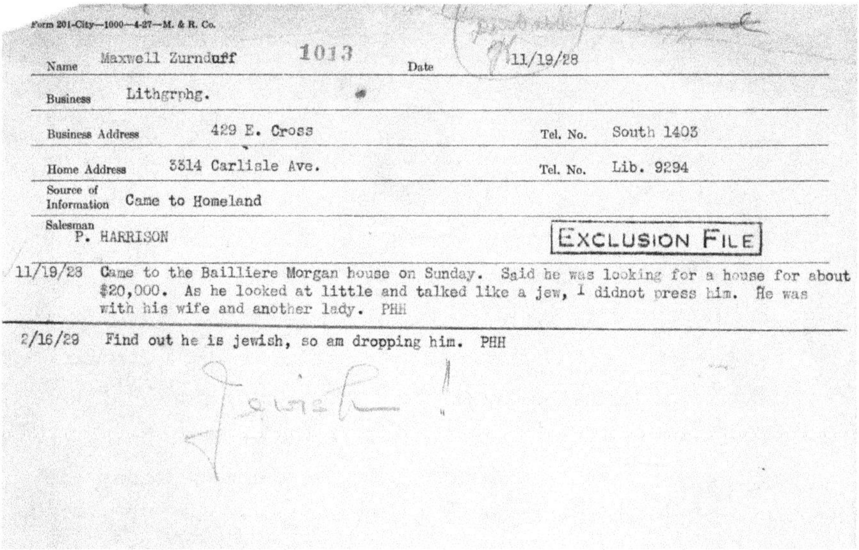

Form 201-City—1000—4-27—M. & R. Co.

| Name | Maxwell Zurnduff | 1013 | Date | 11/19/28 |

Business   Lithgrphg.

Business Address   429 E. Cross   Tel. No.   South 1403

Home Address   3314 Carlisle Ave.   Tel. No.   Lib. 9294

Source of Information   Came to Homeland

Salesman   P. HARRISON |EXCLUSION FILE|

11/19/28   Came to the Bailliere Morgan house on Sunday. Said he was looking for a house for about $20,000. As he looked at little and talked like a jew, I didnot press him. He was with his wife and another lady.   PHH

2/16/29   Find out he is jewish, so am dropping him.   PHH

FIGURE 4.1 A Roland Park Company exclusion file about a prospective buyer in Homeland. The salesman believed the buyer might be Jewish, investigated him, and stopped the sale.

(Courtesy of the Johns Hopkins University Sheridan Libraries)

make "an exception" to company policy.[68] Ames replied the same day with a glowing recommendation: "He and his wife are both delightful people. . . . The fact that he is a Jew has no bearing on the case. His associations are strictly among people whom you and I know."[69] Hollyday also reported that Boas did not "worship at any synagogue and has no Jewish religious associations being an Agnostic."[70] In this case, an exception was made for Boas because Ames judged him to have no Jewish acquaintances.

Just as one's network could insulate a potential homebuyer from the company's process of exclusion, as was the case with Boas, so could it expose potential homebuyers. The non-Jewish Diehls, for example, were excluded because "of Jewish influence."[71] Meanwhile, a salesman apologized to his superiors for reaching out to someone who turned out to be Jewish. "This person was on our mailing list, but was removed," he explained. "He is a Jew, but his wife is a gentile and they have gentile friends."[72]

Salesmen used the combination of networks and appearances to seek exceptions to general company practice. Boas and Brangier Boas would not be *visibly* Jewish in their dress, the company they kept, or in their daily lives. Hollyday, on Ames's word, would be able to control any risk Boas's Jewishness might present. In other cases company salesmen, as a general practice, did not sell to people with Italian surnames. Salesman John Mowbray judged Pietro Pipetone favorably, however, after visiting his place of employment and his home, phoning a reference who called him a "high class Italian," talking to an employee of the Italian consulate personally acquainted with Pipetone, and meeting Pipetone and his teenage son. The appearance of Pipetone and his teenage son, noted the salesman, impressed him.[73] However, Mowbray disqualified the family of M. T. Cavacos even though they were "neat and respectable" and had "a great deal of money" because when he met them he concluded they were "unquestionably Greeks."[74]

In addition to expanding the exclusion files, the opening of Homeland also afforded Bouton the opportunity to finally hire the "female investigator" he had sought a decade earlier. Edith McHenry fit Bouton's criteria; she was "not too young, of good address" and of good education.[75] McHenry was born into one of Baltimore's elite families, a descendant of a Revolutionary War general and Confederate soldiers. She split her early years between Baltimore and Boston, with summers in Europe. As a teenager, she became an avid golfer, including at Roland Park's Baltimore Country Club. She also was one of Baltimore City's first women to obtain a driver's license. By the time she joined the company, she was thirty-two, unmarried, and living alone in an apartment at the fashionable Geneva within walking distance of Guilford.[76]

McHenry joined the male sales staff in vetting prospective homebuyers. She was not a NAREB member, nor was she a saleswoman. Rather, the Roland Park Company employed McHenry as supervisor of personnel, an emerging and usually feminized sphere of the corporate workforce.[77] In this role, McHenry often stepped in to assist on exclusion file candidates in ways that reflected the gendered expectations of her job. Such was the case with her work on the exclusion file of Assistant City Solicitor William

Laukaitis. His post was a major one in the Baltimore City government and came after the Roland Park Company began to take municipal funds for its infrastructure. Nevertheless, the company was still willing to deny city employees access to its developments if they did not meet its terms. The salesman conducted a cursory investigation that included phoning people "to get Mr. Laukaitis's religion" and found he was not Jewish. Though he felt Laukaitis was "on the doubtless list in regard to respectability," the salesman asked McHenry "to call on his wife to see what she thinks of them." McHenry recorded the results of her home inspection on Laukaitis's exclusion file: "I do not think that Mr. Laukaitis or any of his tribe are desirable as residents of the District. They are foreign and not too hot! The men appear very nice but the women and their living quarters are something! Drop." Even though the domestic habits of the Laukatises were, as McHenry noted, unlikely to be visible to neighbors, the unconventional gender roles she observed, combined with a perceived foreignness of the "wrong" type, doomed the Laukaitis family's efforts to live in a Roland Park Company suburb.[78] The Laukaitises were born in the United States—he was born in Baltimore. They were of Lithuanian descent, and their address at 851 Hollins Street put them in the heart of Baltimore's Lithuanian community—facts the salesman did not acknowledge.

In making her assessment of the Laukaitises, McHenry echoed the assessment of other real estate professionals who determined that what happened *inside* a home was just as important as outward appearances when deciding who was included and excluded. As one Realtor put it in the *National Real Estate Journal,* "Citizenship has its basis in the home, and citizenship is what we want to impress on the foreigner. Our home life has made our country the greatest in the world."[79] Drawing on the authority granted her as a woman, McHenry judged the Laukaitises' home life as a marker that they were foreigners unable to assimilate to good, American standards. Her decision fit squarely into the NAREB immigration debate, even though Laukaitis and his wife were both American-born. Those who took the position that immigrants could assimilate looked to the home as a basis for proving the merit of the immigrant. McHenry did not detail what she found off-putting about the Laukaitis home, but she emphasized their "foreignness" and, by calling them "a tribe," paired foreignness with otherness and backwardness.[80]

In terms of the daily practices of exclusion, Realtors' understandings of local racial hierarchies mattered. Roland Park Company salesmen were prepared to be vigilant but flexible about European groups. They were, however, caught off guard by Bacon and Idella Chow.[81] Due to the proliferation of alien land laws during the 1920s in other states, Maryland afforded more opportunities for the Chows to own property than elsewhere. Bacon F. Chow was born in China, attended college and graduate school in the United States, and received a PhD from Harvard. He married the American-born Idella Tong, who accompanied him when he took a university position in China before moving back to the United States so he could take up another position.

The salesman M. Rodgers noted that the Chows were "Chinese" and then wrote about a day of typical home visits in which he took them to several houses across the company's developments.[82] Rodgers also penciled in a notation next to the typed notes that the Chows were "good buyers," because they were willing to spend $18,000. In addition to that, Chow was a biochemist about to begin work with the Johns Hopkins School of Public Health and Hygiene. Being new to Baltimore, however, they were unlikely to have the type of well-established social network through Johns Hopkins that had benefited Boas and Brangier Boas.

Two days after remarking on how the Chows were good leads, Rodgers consulted with a sales manager who "advised no further contact" because of "racial considerations." Idella Chow called the office two months later to say they were still looking, and the same salesman once again consulted a sales manager. Though he had been told to add the Chows to the exclusion files, Rodgers thought it was worth reopening the subject. The sales manager did not tell Rodgers to drop the file a second time. Instead, he went to the president of Guilford's neighborhood association to get a resident's opinion about selling to Chinese buyers. The president consulted with other members of the association and replied that "he, personally, would have no objection," but others residents were opposed to "a sale to such a person."

Only then did Rodgers move the Chows' card to the exclusion files. The Chows instead moved to Lauraville in Northeast Baltimore near Morgan Park.[83] The discretion the company used with the Chows and the ambiguity of their position in Baltimore's racial hierarchy stood in tension with NAREB's emphasis on standardization.

MOVING TOWARD STANDARDIZATION

The daily, inconsistent practices of local real estate companies stood at odds with the vision proponents of real estate professionalization wanted to project to the public. NAREB wanted its membership to be considered experts by the general public. To do this, it had to establish what expert knowledge consisted of and to what extent it could be standardized. Nichols became one of the most ardent supporters of making Realtors into experts through a social scientific approach. "Realology," he argued, "should be as much an established science as geology and zoology."[84]

By 1923, fifteen years after the organization's founding, NAREB had grown to over thirty-seven thousand members.[85] It had clear communication channels and various institutionalized apparatuses for disseminating information. That same year, NAREB formed a national educational committee, after isolated efforts by local boards to create course offerings.[86] The formation of the committee was in many ways in tune with the original promise of the organization as a source for disseminating best practices. From this drive came the Standard Course of Real Estate, developed, in part, by economist Richard Ely, whom NAREB named education director. Ely aimed to construct a course specifically to standardize real estate practice, provide uniform training, and professionalize real estate by giving it a curriculum developed through a rigorous scientific process. NAREB subsequently disseminated the curriculum to local boards and, shortly thereafter, to universities.[87]

Ely's participation in the drafting of the Standard Course lent ideas about real estate development a technocratic authority, though developers had already been putting them into practice. It did not hurt that Ely, like leading suburban developers, believed that the most valuable property was in socially restricted and aesthetically homogenous planned communities. NAREB's selection of Ely, the founder of the American Economic Association, evinces Realtor interest in modeling NAREB after existing professional organizations. Moreover, a partnership with the academic Ely and his Institute for Research in Land Economics and Public Utilities provided NAREB with a major source of credentialed knowledge. Ely's institute offered a model for how to package information such as digestible lectures, books, and articles, and sell its educational material.[88]

The introduction of the Standard Course did not replace other educational material NAREB printed and sold as textbooks. These textbooks were often composed of reprinted Realtor speeches. The Realtors who authored these pieces used their own local practices to offer nationally disseminated advice on subjects such as racially restrictive covenants.[89] An edition from 1923 encouraged readers to "give this subject of restrictions our very best thought" by linking it to a Realtor's "duty to properly anticipate the probable future, as well as the present, use of the specific piece of land." Restrictive covenants, and the long-term scale of decision making that informed their proliferation, had previously been the domain of developers of large-tract, planned suburbs such as Roland Park. Now, NAREB reconfigured what had been a key logic of planned suburbs as the obligation of *all* Realtors, regardless of the kind of real estate business they conducted. NAREB justified the inclusion of restrictive covenants in the textbook by evoking widespread concerns about black migration and European immigration, noting "each succeeding year brings with it a constant increase in population."[90]

Textbooks also served the function of settling legal questions about exclusion. The same textbook that linked restrictions to Realtor duty included a section titled "Court Approves 'Colored Person Clause,'" in which the author included a copy of his company's restrictive covenants. Despite the growth in restrictions in the 1920s, Realtors repeatedly raised concerns about what they perceived to be a legal gray area thanks to conflicting local and state court rulings. Textbooks reprinted portions of meetings where the

NAREB legal counsel assured Realtors that covenants were permissible.[91] This reference was in line with other NAREB publications, which periodically published articles on legal developments that facilitated Realtors' adopting restrictions and understanding their context. Realtors received some of these publications, such as the *National Real Estate Journal*, as part of their membership. Realtors purchased others, including the textbooks, with money that funded NAREB operations, including the reprinting of discussions endorsing housing segregation as an example of best practices nationwide. Even as its national apparatus became more robust in the 1920s, real estate professionalization continued to function as a multidirectional process in which members transmitted ideas that filtered up to the national association, which institutionalized them through various means and later repackaged and consolidated them, then filtered them back down to be adopted by other developers.[92]

By 1923, many in the association believed that NAREB had grown large enough to necessitate divisions. These were organized by Realtor specialities such as brokerage, farmland, and industrial property. Developers were gathered under a new division, Homebuilders and Subdividers, which chose as its symbol a single-family house surrounded by trees. The house would have fit in comfortably at Roland Park. The Homebuilders and Subdividers group also created its own structures. Developers contributed material from which the director, himself a developer, disseminated selections as examples of best practices for subdivision selling. By the following year, members had contributed enough samples to form a national library.[93] The Roland Park Company contributed copies of the *Roland Park Company's Magazine*. NAREB published an image of it alongside magazines from two members of the Developers of High-Class Residential Property as "attractive and interesting" examples Realtors could consider.[94] Developers throughout North America could request copies under the assumption that any of the materials were association-approved.

On one hand, the institutional structures such as the library made development more egalitarian: not only could companies big and small have a major resource to shape their development and sales strategies, but small firms could gain visibility by making their materials widely available to peers. On the other hand, the rise of NAREB made it easier for developers to emulate the practices of their most well-known peers. NAREB leaders had the ability to select for inclusion, categorize, and group submitted advertisements, potentially discarding those that did not meet with approval. In turn, the library shaped how developers would then locate and engage with the content.

In addition to its library, the Homebuilders and Subdividers Division also published in its *Idea Services* bulletin a booklet from the Metropolitan Life Insurance Company of New York called "Functions of the Sales Manager," which recommended that sales managers keep "prospect cards" containing information on prospective clients and the results of an attempted sale. Prospect cards were similar in form and purpose to the Roland Park Company's exclusion files, a tool the company had adopted from credit reporting companies. With the bulletin, NAREB endorsed adapting strategies from actuarial science to suburban development. By the mid-1920s, the national circulation of prospect cards among different professions created a demand for data-intensive files. Prospect cards served the twin purposes of improving office organization and facilitating exclusion.

Beginning around the same time, the Roland Park Company began to use a standard form for its exclusion files. Prior to the mid-1920s, the categories of information had differed from card to card. Each of the later, more standardized cards contained a form number and the year the form was bulk printed. This shift in card production indicated a growth in the market for such cards, which coincided with an increase in the dense links different professionalizing groups developers shared with each other. Companies that already practiced exclusion used such developments to refine their daily methods.[95] As Realtors adopted them, more of them gave talks about their file organization and the equipment they used.[96]

In concert with its growth during the 1920s, NAREB revised its code of ethics to codify the relationship between race and property value. The revised code's Article 34 prevented a Realtor from "introducing into a neighborhood a character of property or occupancy, members of any race or nationality, or any individual whose presence will clearly be detrimental to property values in that neighborhood."[97] Realtors deliberately worded the

FIGURE 4.2 An advertisement for a prospect files cabinet. The description reads, "Typical visible filing equipment for prospect files. Such equipment is easy to install and use and reveals facts quickly."

(Used with permission of the National Association of REALTORS® Library & Archives)

article broadly, giving wide-ranging discretionary powers to individual Realtors. Thus, Realtors became duty-bound to "exercise their social responsibility" by considering how people affected the surrounding area.

Members based the code, in part, on their understandings of how notable developers became successful. Whatever division members belonged to, they had likely been exposed to such ideas by NAREB leadership, which consisted of developers such as Nichols, who conducted sustained and vocal campaigns within the organization in support of standardizing real estate around developer practices. Realtors that followed the code of ethics thus used their powers to enhance local property values by fostering residential segregation.

ANNUAL CONVENTIONS

No event was more important for forging a Realtor identity than the annual convention, which NAREB's historian called "the central real estate school of the times quite as much as it was a forum and a means of collective action."[98] It was here that Realtors practiced ways of seeing people and property together. They did this by depicting what historian Philip Deloria calls their "broad cultural expectations" of people unlike themselves, resulting in an "act of domination" through which they could emphasize their own place at the forefront of American progress.

At conventions, Realtors had the option of attending a business session where they could, for example, hear about the benefits of restrictive covenants, before joining colleagues in another room where they sang songs from an official booklet containing selections such as "When Greek Meets Greek," which lampooned various European groups, or "Massa's in de Cold Cold Ground." Sung in dialect, the latter included lines such as "Mas-sa made de darkies love him / Cayse he was so kind."[99] During the 1928 convention organizers treated delegates to "a real genuine 'treat of thrills'" that included a blackface quartet, a watermelon-eating contest, and spirituals.[100] Following the 1922 convention in San Francisco, the *National Real Estate Journal* published comical drawings of its attendees. They included a cartoon of a Realtor dressed as a Native American "doing an Indian dance," with a dialog bubble containing broken English.[101]

These actions sat beside the image of Realtors as good citizens at the forefront of progress. In 1925, the Detroit Board, tasked with organizing

FIGURE 4.3 (*opposite*) The official poster for leisure program of 1928 annual convention of the National Association of Real Estate Boards featured extensive use of racist tropes, including blackface and one direct allusion to slavery with "the hottest Charleston team in captivity."

(Used with permission of the National Association of REALTORS® Library & Archives)

RAIN OR SHINE

A real genuine "treat of thrills" has been planned for the Annual Convention of the National Real Estate Boards. Stunts! My, oh my! Girls and boys and all such joys, and

Food and Drink a la Kentucky

(Catch as catch can)

Time; 5 to 9:30 P. M.
Place: State Fair Grounds.
Date: Wednesday, June 20th, 1928.

Here are some of the Entertainment Features

BUT! THERE WILL BE MANY MORE!

the annual NAREB convention, published an issue of the *Detroit Realtor* that featured cover art of a dignified white man in classical garb holding a car, surrounded by scenes celebrating Realtors' positive impact on Detroit. Rendered in expensive color ink, the art included a white family in front of a red and white suburban house with a large front yard; bustling, clean, contented white industrial workers; and the Detroit skyline, complete with belching black smokestacks. Though hardly representative of Detroit's housing, labor, and demography, the cover conveyed the industrious hard work and uplifting values of Realtors who embraced progress—or in this case, a car—to turn Detroit into a thriving metropolis. In this and their patriotic songs during the convention, Detroit Realtors demonstrated their good citizenship, constructed with racialized and gendered imagery, that reflected both their ideas about themselves and their aspirational values.

In May 1931, Baltimore hosted a NAREB convention. In many ways, it contained the typical slate of events that had proved successful in past years. Every NAREB member across North America received a promotional pamphlet advertising the convention's leisure activities, including regional and local tours put together by Hollyday as chair of the Sightseeing Committee. It promised a "general sightseeing trip around Baltimore" that included stops in Roland Park and "a real chummy trip around the Baltimore Harbor."[102] In selecting the sights for the tour, Hollyday crafted an image of the ideal Baltimore as white. Organizers did not shy away from depicting the class diversity of the city—factories and affluent suburbs were depicted side by side in the convention material and on itineraries, as they had been on the cover of the *Detroit Realtor*—but the tours also carefully avoided any predominantly black areas. The regional tour had a heavy emphasis on Civil War sights. A picture of the monument of confederate general Robert E. Lee graced the pamphlet Baltimore organizers sent out to participants. Next to the picture of the Lee statue, organizers highlighted Roland Park a second time. In an inset called "Homes," the Real Estate Board of Baltimore held up the Roland Park Company suburbs as the very symbol of Baltimore's progress on the national stage. "Although retaining the charm of old architecture," it read, "the note of Baltimore is distinctly modern. To the north is the Roland Park–Guilford–Homeland develop-

FIGURE 4.4 The cover of the *Detroit Realtor.*

(Used with permission of the National Association of REALTORS® Library & Archives) ment, considered the most distinguished in America."[103] After a day of convention activities, attendees were treated to a lawn party and concert with the theme "Night in Dixie Land." The program promised entertainment from "a number of darkies from 'Way Down Sou' in the Land ob Cotton.'" The following day, convention goers had the option of visiting two former plantations before stopping at Edward Bouton's house in Roland Park.[104]

Realtor I. Norwood Griscom captured the link between national professionalization and local Realtor activity in an impassioned convention speech. Beginning with the oft-repeated narrative of how NAREB elevated real estate practice into a profession, he reminded his audience that "several years ago, the job of selling Real Estate was considered more or less a joke," but "the real estate man of today is a builder due to the high ideals that have been placed before him by this great Association." These lofty principles obligated Realtors to "be conversant with the values and every fact pertaining to the growth and development of his city or community." Griscom tied the Realtor duty to be ethical to his duty to "the race that borne you on its mighty current from eternity to now," exhorting the Realtors in the room to embrace all the duties that came with being a professional. "Get this into your head," he exclaimed, "You are the men higher up! If you will be but this, from this minute you will grow and gather power." "You," he repeated, "you Realtors, are the men higher up!"[105] NAREB's *Idea Services* reprinted and mailed the speech to all members of the Homebuilders and Subdividers Division.

CONCLUSION

During the organization's first two decades, members of NAREB institutionalized the practices of suburban developers like the Roland Park Company by tethering those practices to its professionalization effort. As such, the project of professionalizing real estate involved debates about race and immigration, which provided Realtors with a standard way of seeing people and fraternizing. Taken together, these actions resulted in the emergence of a real estate industry that embraced exclusion from local boards all the way to the association's national offices.

In the 1929 article where Hollyday advised fellow NAREB members "to keep out people who have not learned to live decently" in order to "create and maintain a market," he articulated a notion of property value based on racial hierarchy. Without exclusion, developers assumed, white residents would resort to violence, or at least mass exodus, to preserve the benefits of their status. The particular images of violence they summoned—lynching and vigilantism, mob rule and policing neighborhood borders—were deployed against many people. But mob violence disproportionately affected African Americans, who as one historian noted, posed a "categorical threat to sound development," as far as white Realtors were concerned.[106]

Through NAREB, developers institutionalized and sold these assumptions as expert knowledge. On the ground, though, exclusion proved a murkier business. Notwithstanding a set of clear guidelines outlined in NAREB and other professional materials, salesmen continued to work out the details of exclusion based on fungible lines shaped by local contexts. Nevertheless, these contexts informed national conversations as a handful of suburban developers became NAREB leaders whose work set an example of what excellence looked like.

The stock market crash later that year plunged the country into the Great Depression. Real estate would be among the hardest hit areas of a devastated economy. Thanks to their professionalization efforts, NAREB members would be able to continue to characterize themselves as experts. When the federal government began to consider sweeping policies to salvage the housing sector, Realtors, and especially suburban developers, were poised to step in.

5

POLICIES

Realtors' push for professionalization began to pay real political dividends in the 1930s as the federal government increasingly turned to them as experts to aid in the crafting and implementation of housing policy. The National Association of Real Estate Boards (NAREB) used its leverage as the authority on real estate practice to become a powerful lobbying group in addition to a clearinghouse of personnel. Key association leaders formed working relationships with federal officials beginning on the first day of an agency's creation. As the New Deal state expanded in the 1930s, the "network-based reputation" of NAREB reinforced its legitimacy among federal officials, strengthening ties even when NAREB fiercely opposed certain policies.[1]

At the beginning of the 1930s, members of NAREB were still working out the most salient ideas about property value and the ways they could operationalize them in policy. The concept of neighborhood "rehabilitation" subsequently became a key component of housing debates during the era of the New Deal. As the decade advanced, rehabilitation took on shifting meanings in response to particular contexts. Throughout the 1930s Realtors defined rehabilitation, in its many potential forms, as a solution to "blight."

The notion of blight arose from ecological models put forward by social scientists in the late 1920s and adopted by planners, who regarded cities as natural resources akin to forests.[2] Under these terms, cities could decline as if infected by a disease. Because of the close relationship between planners, Realtors, and policymakers during the 1930s, members of all three groups adopted urban ecology as their dominant paradigm. Like "zoning," the term "blight" could be ostensibly color-blind. In practice, however, all three groups—planners, Realtors, and policymakers—considered the racial and class composition of a neighborhood an indicator of an area's health.[3] Specifically, these groups used the term "blight" to describe the movement of certain people such as African Americans into an area. Taking the metaphor of the human ecology model to its logical conclusion put a new spin on equating race with health. In the 1930s, city land was the forest, African American residents were the disease that infected trees, and their spread, like that of a disease, had to be controlled through expert application of planning and real estate knowledge.

Rehabilitation was comprised of more than ideas; it encompassed a set of economic tools.[4] Beginning in 1937, John Mowbray, the second president of the Roland Park Company, helmed a joint pilot study with municipal and federal agencies to rehabilitate Baltimore's Waverly neighborhood, with the goal of protecting it from blight. In particular, the project aimed to prevent property values from declining by empowering white property owners to keep the neighborhood white. Developers such as Mowbray were no strangers to the machinery of municipal governance; the Roland Park Company had worked to obtain city resources since its inception. However, by 1937 developer power had become so firmly established at the national level that Realtors like Mowbray were able to help forge a consensus within the New Deal state that tied property value to racial hierarchy. Using this logic, the federal government pursued a strategy of rehabilitation in which the only neighborhoods in need of protection were white neighborhoods. The Waverly pilot study presented an opportunity for those involved to jointly marshal capital, people, and legal measures to apply the long gestating ideas about desirable neighborhoods, with the blessing of the New Deal state.

Historians looking at other cities such as Chicago have assigned a disproportionately large role to academics for generating ideas about race, space, and neighborhood change that later found their way into federal policy in the 1930s.[5] While academics added precision to the vocabulary of city planning and helped to facilitate housing expertise, such as when they consulted with NAREB, it was the everyday business interests of residential developers that by and large informed the professionalization of the real estate industry in the 1920s. Those developers continued to inform NAREB policy stances, fill the ranks of NAREB leadership, and serve as federal consultants during the 1930s.

Looking at Realtors and the directions of New Deal housing implementation in Baltimore also challenges the notion of a neat separation between the federal government's approach to public housing on one hand and suburban development on the other.[6] In the 1930s the different agencies that managed public housing and mortgage lending carried out local endeavors in interconnected ways, due, in part, to mutual financial stakes and shared ideas about how race affected property value. Undoubtedly, the divide between public housing programs and mortgage lending programs deeply shaped political possibilities in subsequent decades by structuring relationships between people and the state and, closely related to that, public perception and popular culture.[7] In Baltimore, the Housing Authority of Baltimore City (HABC) and its parent, the United States Housing Authority (USHA), were the major stakeholders in the Waverly project along with the two most well-known mortgage agencies, the Home Owners' Loan Corporation (HOLC), which refinanced mortgages according to its risk-rating system and appraisals standards, and the Federal Housing Administration (FHA), which insured mortgages made by lenders who followed its guidelines. Even Baltimore's nascent public housing program facilitated buying and selling property between the HOLC and the housing authority. Instead of assuming a neat division between real estate interests and public housing advocates, it is more useful to see how "the New Deal State spent its money" and to track the people who spent it, as this reveals the overlapping logics and institutional connections that shaped an unprecedented infusion of capital into metropolitan areas in the mid-twentieth century.[8]

Even today, some scholars continue to try absolve the HOLC of participating in the perpetuation of racist policies by claiming it was the FHA that had the bigger impact on New Deal housing policy, including redlining. Furthermore, some continue to debate whether redlining was racist. The case of the Waverly Project shows that racist logics were embedded in New Deal–era thought on housing from the beginning.[9] Even when race was not explicitly mentioned, federal appraisal standards were largely derived from restrictive covenants. The most well-circulated restrictions, including those of the Roland Park Company, had been conflating the social, economic, and physical characteristics of people and property since the 1890s in ways not limited to the specific clause mentioning race.[10] Moreover, policy stakeholders sought to protect white-owned and -occupied property using appraisal tactics. In line with the rationale behind covenants, the new coalition of Realtors and policymakers aimed to ensure long-term economic prosperity and status of white neighborhoods specifically.

During the 1930s, Realtors worked within the New Deal state to create a set of mechanisms for protecting white property investment.[11] In the process, both the HOLC and Realtors such as Mowbray revealed the ways their own economic fortunes were tied to keeping Waverly white. The project's sponsor, the HABC, owed its very existence to controlling the boundaries of Baltimore's neighborhoods. Realtors, then, helped shore up their own profits by codifying their ideas about whiteness and property into a new market created and supported by the federal government.

THE CREATION OF FEDERAL HOUSING POLICY

Two years after the stock market crash, with the economy in a state of collapse, Herbert Hoover convened the President's Conference on Home Building and Home Ownership to discuss ways to stem the damage. The conference itself did not represent a change in approach—as secretary of commerce in the 1920s, Hoover preferred to solve problems by calling an industry conference to coordinate different sectors and he counted on businesses to implement the results.[12] What emerged from it, however, was the general agreement that the federal government needed to enact its first peacetime housing policies.

The Hoover administration created two agencies to reverse the crisis in 1932: the Federal Home Loan Bank Board (FHLBB) and the Reconstruction Finance Corporation (RFC). NAREB cheered the former. Whereas the issue of federal involvement in home financing had split the association only a decade before, the Depression spurred NAREB to support this seemingly radical measure. With broad-based support from housing, banking, and finance groups, the FHLBB implemented and oversaw a system of regulated regional banks that lent money to member institutions, freeing up credit and stabilizing operations.[13] The creation of the RFC, however, alarmed NAREB leadership. The RFC made loans to locally organized limited-dividend corporations to construct low-income rental housing. The association's Housing Committee lodged a complaint to the corporation protesting the loans on two grounds. First, the RFC created uncompetitive access to finance. Second, it "discriminate[d] against private property" by facilitating housing in which tenants would rent apartments at lower rates than other area landlords offered.[14] The NAREB Housing Committee and Board of Directors did acknowledge the RFC's limited reach. Still, they complained that RFC housing would create more multifamily houses and apartment complexes in cities, increasing density. The best city planning, they said, should decrease density.[15]

In response, NAREB created a program of "neighborhood rehabilitation" to counter the RFC. NAREB secretary Herbert U. Nelson called on members to help states enact legislation that would create "neighborhood improvement or reconstruction districts." John Mowbray worked closely with Nelson to offer feedback and then disseminate it to NAREB members. Working together, Nelson and Mowbray crafted a model statute in which three-quarters of contiguous property owners could apply to access guaranteed municipal resources to create, implement, and enforce a master plan for their district. The federal government played no role in the proposal. Instead, NAREB sought solutions whereby state and municipal governments would facilitate the goals of local property owners. Cities would compel the remaining quarter to join by employing their power of eminent domain. The rehabilitation district would be financed using "district bonds, secured not only by the property of the district but by the faith and credit of the city as a whole."[16] Under the neighborhood rehabilitation statute, one group of property owners could initiate, plan, and drive a rehabilitation project that would be the financial responsibility of the entire municipality. Bonds would be tied to the appraised value of the properties.

Neither the FHLBB nor the RFC stemmed the tide of foreclosures and bank failures that swept the United States in the early 1930s. NAREB believed the FHLBB did not go far enough to free up credit for mortgage lending, nor did it put mortgage refinancing within easy enough reach of homeowners. Shortly after Franklin Roosevelt took office, the chairman of the Senate Banking Committee, alarmed at how institutions were pulling out of mortgage lending in his state, called on NAREB's central leadership to join the general counsel of the FHLBB in Washington to help draft legislation to increase the board's purview. The chairman and NAREB had already developed a working relationship after NAREB backed his plan to eliminate tax exemptions on securities.[17] Ultimately, the Senate Banking Committee solicited feedback from members of lending institutions as well. In June 1933, NAREB trumpeted what became known as the Home Owners' Loan Act. Reinforcing the act as a major legislative victory for the organization, the final version contained three provisions taken directly from NAREB's policy platforms.[18]

The act created the Home Owners' Loan Corporation within the FHLBB. With an initial appropriation of $200 million taken from the RFC, the HOLC purchased mortgages in danger of default and issued longer-term, lower-interest loans with equal monthly payments to be made over fifteen years. For the person paying the mortgage, the terms were likely to be much more affordable than any options previously available. The lender who held the delinquent mortgage holder received an influx of capital to continue its operations. In just three short years, the HOLC refinanced $3.1 billion in debt for over eight hundred thousand property owners.[19]

The HOLC did not just directly refinance the mortgages of homeowners. Its parent, the FHLBB, applied its appraisal standards to institutions within the federal banking system beginning in 1933. This included "member banks of the federal system, federal savings and loan institutions, regional banks that received federal bank insurance, and other federal agencies."[20] In addition, the FHLBB published HOLC appraisal forms to give private lenders access to them. Thus, the distinction was blurred between HOLC criteria and that of both other agencies and private lenders. In effect, this dissemination spread ideas about exclusion far and wide.[21]

NAREB literature formed the cornerstone of the HOLC's institutional culture.[22] Nelson reported to members that top NAREB officials, including himself, met regularly with government officials from the head of federal departments "down to the third assistant to the assistant office boy."[23] Administrators also encouraged federal workers to "subscribe to the *National Real Estate Journal* and the NAREB-affiliated *Journal of the American Institute of Real Estate Appraisers*."[24] Many well-placed NAREB members pulled double duty as government consultants, including the president of the NAREB appraisal institute, Philip Kniskern, who served as advisor to the HOLC.[25] Kniskern allowed all HOLC appraisers to attend NAREB conventions on paid time.[26]

To decide which mortgages to purchase, the HOLC created an infrastructure of appraisal and data collection to assess the risk it would assume.[27] The HOLC and NAREB worked together to draw up the "appraisal forms and regulations" HOLC appraisers used.[28] The FHLBB and NAREB both promoted the collaboration to their members. The final system arrived at by the HOLC included a form filled out by various HOLC personnel. HOLC appraisers had to fill in ninety-eight lines, a HOLC office worker another six, and a manager an additional five, concluding with "CORPO-RATION VALUE."[29] The HOLC adopted two core NAREB principles: first, the value of a single property affects all surrounding properties; and second, the characteristics of occupants affect value along with a property's physical characteristics. The forms included sections to describe the building and any improvements made on it. It also contained a section called "District" with a line for "Residents in Neighborhood." The appraiser had to fill in four lines recording the percentage of area residents who were "American," "Foreign," "Negro," and "Oriental." Because the HOLC wanted to determine the future of the neighborhood to protect any investment it made there, it also included two lines in the district section about trajectory: "Trends," where the appraiser could choose "Static," "Up," or "Down"; and "Transition," where the appraiser determined the rate at which a district was moving "To Business," "To Apartments," and "To Industry."[30]

The HOLC likewise embraced the NAREB assumption, initially established by developers including the Roland Park Company, that the most valuable type of residential property was a white-owned, white-occupied single-family house on a planned street. The HOLC incorporated this assumption into the trend and transition questions. If a district transitioned downward, it would be to a denser, more mixed-use, or more mixed-race character.[31] The idea echoed the words of suburban developer John Demarest, who warned his colleagues at the 1919 Conference for Developers of High-Class Residential Property, "When you open the door, it's gone."[32]

The HOLC used a separate appraisal process to construct "security maps." The HOLC used the security maps to decide where to issue loans. Recent examinations of both the individual loan forms and the neighborhood appraisals point to the HOLC exerting more labor and placing more emphasis on evaluating neighborhoods than on individual properties.[33] The maps divided over 230 major population centers into "areas." Each area received an identifying number and a grade that reflected the level of risk it posed for lending purposes. Security maps contained four risk grades corresponding to color. A, colored green, was the highest grade because neighborhoods carried the lowest risk; B (blue) and C (yellow) signaled increased risk; and D (red) had the lowest property values and highest lending risk. Each grade took into account future as well as present conditions.

These areas did not necessarily correspond to historical neighborhood borders. Rather, they were the creations of appraisers, who identified patterns across sections of a city. HOLC-designated areas could be large or small. They were often bounded by major roads, but in some cases they stretched and twisted to link different groups of streets in a manner akin to political gerrymandering. Other times, the groups of streets that composed an area were not contiguous at all. The HOLC then compiled "area descriptions," each of which was clearly marked at the top with the area's assigned number and the appraiser's letter grade.

The forms used to grade areas were significantly shorter than those for individual properties of mortgage applicants (15 and 109 lines, respectively), but they had a greatly expanded number of questions devoted to the social and racial traits of residents. The new forms retained the "trend" question but instead of "transition," the area descriptions contained a question about "infiltration," which specified "any threat of infiltration from foreign-born, negro, or lower grade population." Appraisers were to "indicate these by nationality and rate of infiltration like this: 'Negro-rapid.'" The area form combined questions about demographic patterns found on the individual property forms into the broad question on "Detrimental Influences," in which the HOLC instructed the appraiser to again mention "infiltration from lower grade population or different racial groups." Together, these forms served as the basis for grading the risk an area posed. Based on the answers, the HOLC would redline an area or ensure access to mortgages.[34]

The same summer that the Roosevelt administration created the HOLC, the new Housing Division of the Public Works Administration (PWA) took over RFC operations funding limited dividend rental housing. Despite its initial opposition to the RFC the previous year, NAREB came to see potential opportunities for the PWA to benefit Realtors. NAREB approved of limited dividend projects so long as Realtors sponsored them. In October 1933 a NAREB delegation composed of leading suburban developers traveled to Washington to lobby for both the PWA and RFC to issue direct loans to homebuilders. Though the delegation left empty-handed, NAREB took a pragmatic approach in trying to benefit from federal programs.[35]

The PWA fared only marginally better than the RFC in financing limited dividend housing. Whereas the RFC approved only two projects in its first thirteen months, the PWA green-lighted seven. All of them were geared toward white workers in the South, Midwest, and Northeast. Six were constructed on vacant land.[36] The PWA suspended the limited dividend program in February 1934 to focus on directly building and managing low-rent housing on land designated "slum clearance" sites.[37] NAREB opposed the change. It acknowledged the need for low-cost housing and saw large-scale construction of it as one of the best ways to generate jobs and stimulate the homebuilding industry, but called the new turn "destructive to private enterprise."[38] It wanted the PWA to return to helping businesses "develop low cost housing projects in the manner and locations required by local needs."[39] Nevertheless, the board of directors remained cautiously optimistic as agency staff changes brought in people who had not been responsible for the new direction of the PWA.

Shortly after the policy shift in 1934, NAREB became one of the chief lobbyists for the passage of the National Housing Act. Indeed, the association was so heavily involved in the development of the act that it was the only group to receive a dedicated conference room in the Senate during hearings for the bill.[40] NAREB president and Houston suburban developer Hugh Potter stayed in Washington for extended periods of time.[41] When not there he "continued close contact by wire and phone" with the committee steering the legislation.[42] By contrast, scholars have found that legislators allowed little input from "organized labor, housing reformers, civil rights activists, or interracial housing advocates."[43] Nelson happily told NAREB members that the final version of the National Housing Act "contained everything we had asked for."[44]

The act created the Federal Housing Administration (FHA) and tasked it with insuring loans from select private institutions. The FHA insured mortgages, home improvement loans, and developer-financed rental complexes. Lenders applied to the FHA to be eligible to issue federally backed loans. These lenders then followed the FHA underwriting guidelines that laid out the loan terms it would insure. NAREB immediately set to work developing a relationship with the FHA by inviting the agency's administrator and his executive assistant, a former Realtor, to speak at the annual NAREB convention a week after its founding.[45]

NAREB's lobbying efforts produced tangible results. One wide-ranging revision NAREB secured was the deletion of a provision from Title II of the act that would have required those seeking government-backed mortgage insurance to live in the property they owned.[46] Nelson explained to members that the association worked to eliminate the owner-occupancy requirement in order to "broaden the measure." Many homeowners, he continued, had to rent properties "due to reduced incomes" during the Great Depression.[47] NAREB framed its actions as protecting distressed individual property owners. In reality, the measure's erasure from the National Housing Act empowered absentee landlords, institutional investors, and corporations to avail themselves of federal mortgage insurance.

The creation of the FHA only further entrenched the ideas of developers into the new federally subsidized housing market. FHA officials issued insurance underwriting guidelines based on HOLC security maps and the widely circulated *Federal Home Loan Bank Review*, which contained samples of appraisal forms and nationwide lending data.[48] It also drew from the recommendations of the 1931 Subdivision Layout Committee of the President's Conference on Home Building.[49] The *Underwriting Manual* both endorsed restrictive covenants and modeled lending conditions on their clauses. Released in 1934, the manual contained a paragraph prohibiting "undesirable racial or nationality groups," business and commercial uses in residential areas, excess smoke, and nuisances. To a precise degree, these measures and their very order of enumeration mirrored the Roland Park Company's restrictive covenants, which grouped black occupancy under a nuisance clause before a restriction against smoke. The manual set forth a model covenant containing a racial restriction with wording nearly identical to that in the older covenants. The manual also called for restrictions on "types of structures, the use to which they are put, and racial occupancy." It made no distinction between racial segregation and other guidelines.[50]

Even seemingly neutral guidelines were often rooted in practices Realtors developed to promote exclusion. For instance, the FHA penalized households that kept livestock. Restrictive covenants often banned the keeping of livestock in subdivisions, including in Roland Park. In many cities such as Baltimore, black people were much more likely to keep livestock as an extra means of income or food subsistence.[51] Furthermore, the manual's attention to the "size, shape, and topography of the lot in relation to the size and shape of the dwelling" echoed earlier provisions in restrictive covenants for minimum lot setbacks and housing costs, both of which functioned as class restrictions. The FHA evaluated each property in relation to others, rewarding areas for their homogeneity.

The HOLC and the FHA consolidated support for the New Deal from both the existing white middle class and its aspirants, the latter of whom could now look to the federal government to support their dreams of securing upward mobility through homeownership. The Roosevelt administration and NAREB alike touted the program as a victory for families who owned and occupied their homes, even though other types of property owners also qualified. The FHA also proved a boon to suburban developers. Within its first year, the FHA financed 68.8 percent of all Roland Park Company business.[52] Meanwhile, the HOLC and the FHA earned strong rebukes from the black press, which suspected discriminatory practices. These criticisms intensified after a white FHA employee exposed to the head of the NAACP that the FHA required racially restrictive covenants for mortgage guarantees.[53]

In 1935 Mowbray was elected chairman of the NAREB Housing Committee. He and Nelson decided to revisit the 1932 model neighborhood rehabilitation statute. This time, however, they involved officials from the FHLBB, HOLC, FHA, and PWA.[54] Whereas the 1932 plan was a reaction against federal housing policy, for the 1935 plan NAREB worked with federal agencies to create locally implemented legislation based on shared principles about property value and neighborhood change.

The new statute focused on the relationship between blight and rehabilitation. Nelson penned an initial draft that did not distinguish between slums and blighted areas, or what was sometimes regarded as the final stage of decline once blight took hold.[55] Mowbray suggested that the model statute would be effective only if NAREB differentiated between slum areas and blighted areas and, by extension, slum clearance and neighborhood rehabilitation. The "only possible way to eliminate the kind of slum area I had in mind," he continued, "is to tear down the houses and replace them with modern ones."[56] Neighborhood rehabilitation was better suited for areas where "blight had not gone too far."[57] He drew from Baltimore as an example. "Our slum areas," he explained to the NAREB secretary, "are old houses once occupied by well-to-do families, now housing anywhere from three to twelve" black families renting out units.[58] These properties, he said, were owned by absentee landlords who would not want to invest money to modernize the buildings and perform necessary ongoing maintenance. Rehabilitation would generate opposition from absentee landlords, who would lose income.[59] Nelson agreed that under the conditions Mowbray described, rehabilitation would not work.[60] The secretary accepted Mowbray's point but did not consider absentee landlords to be "typical of most American cities."[61] They were.[62]

The end result was similar to the 1932 NAREB proposal in that it laid out ways for municipal governments to fund efforts by groups of property owners to replan neighborhoods, supply funds to renovate houses, and enforce stricter land-use controls through restrictive covenants and zoning changes.[63] "The general idea," Nelson told Mowbray, was "to give the owners in a blighted district power to do much of the same things good developers can now do through their deeds."[64] Mowbray introduced the statute with a speech at the 1935 annual NAREB convention that reiterated the point and explained that the statute would most benefit owner-occupiers of property, an uncontroversial and morally defensible stance that evoked images of nuclear families. "The standard of the dwellers of the neighborhood and their land," he said, were "truly the yardstick of value."[65] The statute, he continued, would enable property owners of good character to apply what "every subdivider knows."[66] NAREB members adopted a resolution approving the model statute.

BALTIMORE'S HOUSING POLITICS

The PWA did not build any complexes in Baltimore, though it did explore the possibility. In 1934 the State Advisory Board of the PWA formed a committee called the Joint Committee on Housing to identify uses for PWA funds.[67] The head of the committee was W. W. Emmart, a member of the Baltimore City Planning Commission and former architect of Roland Park houses. The committee found that Baltimore did not have "slum areas."

Instead, it contained a "ring of blight" near downtown that consisted of clusters of tax-delinquent property with long-standing maintenance issues.[68] It singled out predominantly black areas within the ring to be demolished and redeveloped with rental housing targeted at white suburbanites to entice them to move back to the central city. Redevelopment would "turn the outward growth of the city inward."[69] This made little sense for addressing the issues of current residents, who suffered the poor conditions that the committee's report detailed. However, the members of the committee concluded that the blight that characterized each site was a "problem of the Negro race."[70] The new residents, it said, would pay more into Baltimore City's tax coffers, benefitting all of Baltimore.

Despite previously concluding that Baltimore lacked slums, the report equated rehabilitation with a process of slum clearance. Emmart explained that "rehabilitation" referred to "restoring the taxable basis" of each neighborhood. It should not, he believed, consist of "building for slum dwellers."[71] Emmart submitted a lengthy design proposal for the replacement housing that also called for covering open rail yards, reorganizing downtown commercial blocks into arcades and squares, and building underground parking garages.[72] The plan met resistance from the Baltimore Urban League, which published a rejoinder that specifically addressed the idea of suburban whites moving into slum clearance sites.[73]

After the joint committee submitted its report, the state legislature created the Maryland Emergency Housing and Park Commission, which failed to successfully secure funding for proposed PWA rental projects in Baltimore. The plans for the projects were prepared with the help of a new architecture firm, Associated Architects of Baltimore, which was composed of members of the joint committee looking to secure contracts.[74] Various white state and city officials refused to cooperate with a mixed-race federal advisory board tasked with selecting housing sites for blacks. Black members of the commission, both men and women, reported that the white members excluded them from discussions.[75]

Baltimore's local real estate board opposed any PWA activity in Baltimore. Representing over eight hundred white developers, brokers, and real estate agents, it handed a resolution to Mayor Howard W. Jackson during a 1935 meeting, condemning any "home building business in Baltimore in competition with private enterprise" as "Un-American." The board warned that the federal program "will tend to destroy property values and investment in mortgage loans and make us a nation of tenants."[76] The letter was signed by Guy T. O. Hollyday, president of the real estate board and the former head of the Roland Park Company sales force who enforced the company's exclusion files.

The Jackson administration ultimately thwarted PWA projects that year by withholding land unless the PWA paid exorbitant prices.[77] It did so despite support for the PWA, including from the Baltimore Building Congress, which represented three hundred architects and members of the building and construction industries. At the 1935 meeting the Building Congress submitted a competing resolution in favor of PWA projects, which was backed by the Maryland Emergency Housing and Park Commission.[78] The mayor justified his administration's resistance to the PWA by saying he could not "permit" himself "to do an injustice to the real estate owners."[79]

Over the next two years, Jackson faced increasing pressure to create low-income public housing from an organized campaign mounted by a newly formed biracial, cross-class coalition, the Baltimore Citizens' Housing Committee. When new federal housing legislation looked imminent in 1937, he admitted Baltimore's need for a comprehensive housing policy to address "blighted areas." In May, he appointed a thirty-four-person committee of real estate developers, bankers, planning officials, and attorneys that included Emmart and Harry O. Wilson, the black banker and developer of Wilson Park. Jackson hoped the committee would find alternatives to the formation of a public housing program.[80] The committee conducted a survey but did not report the details to the public. It concluded that if the new federal legislation passed and Baltimore decided to consider creating a housing authority, the mayor should appoint other people to look into it, and pay them for the job.[81] The formation of the committee itself was an effective stalling tactic.

The Jackson administration's approach to public housing changed with the passage of the Wagner-Steagall Act, which led to the formation of the United States Housing Authority (USHA). The USHA devolved responsibility to each local housing authority to establish its own racial policy within a loose set of guidelines about retaining "neighborhood composition" that the agency did not enforce in Baltimore.[82] Mowbray and other Baltimore Realtors who had opposed the Baltimore PWA projects supported the creation of a federal authority whose primary job was to empower local policy and implementation. The USHA functioned as a funding conduit to local housing authorities while, at the same time, the government ceased to directly own or build rental housing. This calculated deployment of localism became a hallmark of New Deal political compromise.[83]

Later that year, Jackson formed a different exploratory committee to report on whether to create a Baltimore City housing authority. They unanimously voted in favor.[84] On December 13, 1937, Jackson signed a bill establishing the Housing Authority of Baltimore City (HABC). It had the power to select sites for public rental housing, decide on whether and how to segregate each complex, appraise property, and purchase or condemn property through eminent domain.[85]

In the same year, Baltimore became one of 230 cities for which the HOLC made a residential security map.[86] As in the other cities, map consultants assisted the HOLC appraisers. In the case of Baltimore, a number of the consultants had ties to the Roland Park Company. One, a brokerage company called Piper and Hill, operated in Homeland and Roland Park and had business ties to the Roland Park Company's attorneys. Another map consultant was the chief evaluator of the FHA, Paisley Lemmon, who was a former Roland Park Company employee. Two representatives from building and loan associations also consulted alongside a HOLC official based in nearby Towson, Maryland.[87] Rounding out the list were four businessmen, two of whom had strong connections to the Roland Park Company. Theophilus White was Mowbray's business partner for various enterprises and Guy T. O. Hollyday. One map consultant, a professor of economics and sociology at Goucher College, provided statistical analyses for the HABC.[88]

The Baltimore security map, like both Roland Park Company policies and city determinations of blight, correlated race with risk. Of Baltimore's twenty-two C-rated areas, African Americans lived in six, but always comprised under 10 percent of the population. African Americans lived in all of Baltimore's redlined D areas, generally making up over 20 percent over the population. Two B-rated areas just outside of Baltimore City limits had "small" percentages of blacks. In each of these cases, the appraiser qualified that the areas were "suburban" in character and had an otherwise "homogenous" population.[89] In other words, black residence was not automatic grounds for redlining, but the redlined neighborhoods contained Baltimore's largest concentrations of black people.

In general, HOLC maps reflected the subjectivity and geographic imagination of appraisers, though the very nature of their task was framed as an objective quantification of value based on conditions. In several instances, map consultants labeled as entirely white areas that in reality included black neighborhoods. For example, area B-10, which was rated blue and thus "still desirable," took in a swath of Northeast Baltimore City and County that included the upscale planned black suburbs of Morgan Park and Cherry Heights. The appraiser who completed the form described it as a "desirable residential section" containing a "substantial class of people," with no African Americans and a "mixture" of foreign-born residents. Wilson Park was in another blue area, B-8, which the same HOLC employee described as having no black residents. Cross Keys received a C grade, but its existence, too, went unacknowledged by the HOLC. The HOLC identified the "not very desirable area" as Hampden and Woodberry, two venerable mill villages, with an "infiltration of foreigners" and no black residents.[90] The failure of HOLC mapmakers to include black neighborhoods outside West and East Baltimore (where the majority of African Americans lived)—even relatively high-profile ones such as Morgan Park—is further reason why the HOLC maps should not be taken as an objective snapshot of local racial geography. At the same time, these maps had real material consequences for those living in the areas due to the connection between ratings and home financing.[91]

Elsewhere in Baltimore City and Baltimore County, only 8 percent of the graded areas received an A grade. The largest of these consisted of Roland Park Company developments. The HOLC even took the unusual step of awarding an A grade to a large, still-undeveloped tract of Roland Park Company land on the basis of the company's reputation. Roland Park above Cold Spring Lane received a B grade, however, because its houses were older.[92] B grades, usually reserved for areas the HOLC considered native-born white, did not hinder the ability of property owners to obtain credit. This left some of Roland Park's largest homes ranked lower than its attached and semidetached houses along University Parkway. The HOLC area description characterized University Parkway as part of a "single-family detached house" zone.

As the HOLC put together Baltimore's security map, the HABC selected sites for its first housing projects using older data. It relied primarily on the 1934 Joint Committee on Housing study.[93] Shortly after its founding in 1937, the HABC selected five sites outlined in the report. To further support the need for slum clearance in those locations, it gathered data on the status of recreational opportunities, zoning, property appraisals, schools, and transit options. In addition to these seemingly color-blind criteria, authority officials presented to the mayor a chart of black occupancy data from 1930 highlighting which sites were already predominantly black, and a density map from 1930 indicating the "future direction" of black movement in the city. It did not present data about other populations who faced housing discrimination in Baltimore, including immigrants and Jews. The use of the black demographic data, the attention to future patterns of black settlement, and the HABC reliance on the 1934 report all amounted to what historian Rhonda Williams describes as housing officials portraying "poverty, substandard housing, and disease as the natural conditions and inevitable consequences of African-American residency."[94] The HABC designated two sites for black occupancy and three for white occupancy. Four of the five sites, each several square blocks in size, had at least double the number of blacks to whites. The fifth site had about double the number of whites to blacks, but the area's black population was increasing.[95] If mapped onto the Baltimore security map, each site would fall in a redlined area close to downtown, further demonstrating the overlap between HOLC and HABC activities.

This overlap only deepened as the HABC moved from the planning to the implementation stage in developing public housing. Despite their different data and different missions, the HOLC and the HABC had to coordinate to conduct daily operations. Prior to the formation of the latter, the HOLC had issued mortgages in the areas now selected for public housing sites. It also owned property outright in cases where it had foreclosed on its mortgages. HOLC-owned homes constituted a small minority of properties. In the McCulloh Homes site, for instance, the HOLC owned only one property outright. But that does not reflect how many properties it had held at any time before that point. How many mortgages it held is even less clear, though it held at least two in an East Baltimore project area.[96] A HOLC presence, no matter how small, required the HABC to negotiate with it in order to acquire the property for public housing.

When a resident in a designated site held a HOLC mortgage, the housing authority first went to the resident and signed an option with them that contractually obligated the resident to sell the property to the housing authority rather than to any other party if the housing authority exercised the option at a later date. The authority's supervisor of appraisals—a white Realtor who had strongly opposed the PWA—then contacted the local head of the HOLC advisory division to work out a deal for purchasing the mortgages. Both the housing authority and the HOLC considered it in their interests to work out a deal quickly.[97] It cost the HABC money, manpower, and time to negotiate options with each property owner of a multiacre site. Meanwhile, residents in the selected sites were the HOLC mortgage holders most likely to be unable to make monthly payments. The HOLC was increasingly left owning property it did not want. Both agencies sought to prevent similar situations from occurring in the future.

ORIGINS OF THE WAVERLY PILOT STUDY

By 1938 the HOLC owned seventy thousand properties nationwide through foreclosure. These constituted liabilities that the agency found difficult to move off its books. Dealing with this "major problem" became a priority. The HOLC determined that almost all of the properties required some type of repair work before they could be resold. Until it found buyers, it employed local NAREB-affiliated brokers to rent out units on a month-to-month basis. The same brokers often acted as sales agents. The operation proved costly, especially when combined with repair loans it issued to property owners with HOLC mortgages. It "spent or directed the expenditure of approximately $120 million for the repair of more than 640,000 properties."[98]

One HOLC official with his eye on the mounting costs of managing foreclosures was Donald McNeal, who had moved from director of reconditioning at the HOLC to deputy general manager. During his time in the Reconditioning Division, McNeal oversaw renovation and repair loans made to homeowners with HOLC-financed mortgages. The FHLBB compared the HOLC Reconditioning Division to a private lending business. Both had "a practical interest in the security behind so large a percentage of the business on their books." Furthermore, both the HOLC and private lenders needed reconditioning "done efficiently and at the least expense." If carried out well, the FHLBB concluded in its official organ, "efficient reconditioning protects the institution's investment and ensures a satisfied borrower."[99] Though it was referring to the HOLC, the statement applied equally well to a building and loan enterprise. With its focus on property *investment*—and its role as property *owner*—the HOLC took a keen interest in current and future real estate values.

McNeal came up with the idea of conducting a demonstration on the usefulness of renovating and restoring an entire neighborhood's properties as a way to increase value, keep current owners in their homes, and prevent foreclosure of properties where owners held HOLC mortgages. He sought a pilot area where the HOLC had a concentrated presence. From his office in Washington, D.C., he selected Baltimore, which was close enough to Washington to allow for easy travel to the project site.[100]

McNeal approached Mowbray in July 1938. The two knew each other from their involvement in the 1935 NAREB neighborhood rehabilitation plan, and McNeal wanted a Baltimore NAREB member to direct the project. Mowbray proved the ideal choice.[101] Mowbray chaired the powerful NAREB Housing Committee and had served stints as president of the Real Estate Board of Baltimore. Most importantly to McNeal, Mowbray served as spokesman for NAREB neighborhood rehabilitation ideas.[102] Mowbray agreed to work on the pilot study in order to "put into practical effect some of the theories that our National Association [of Real Estate Boards] has advanced."[103] It was Mowbray who suggested the Waverly neighborhood for the pilot study.

The mission of the pilot study was to stop blight and protect the neighborhood by bolstering long-term property values. This would be accomplished by inventorying each property in the project site, collecting information about owners and occupants, opening lending channels for owners to improve their property, creating a master plan to reconfigure streets and landscape in order to create a unified and more valuable overall neighborhood, and incorporating a self-sustaining neighborhood group of property owners to implement the findings indefinitely. If successful, the HOLC would have an easier time reselling the properties it owned in Waverly, while at the same time saving Waverly from city or federal slum clearance. For NAREB, which closely monitored the study through Mowbray, it would be a chance to put into practice its model neighborhood rehabilitation plans.

Under the terms of the project, Waverly was a blighted area because its property values had declined, but it was not yet a slum. Mowbray and McNeal reasoned that Waverly was on track to become a slum because Baltimore's black population might move into it from the south and "seriously impair property values in the choice sections adjacent thereto."[104] Roland Park Company developments constituted much of those sections. Guilford bordered Waverly to the northwest and the Roland Park Company's new subdivision Northwood lay northeast. This was the undeveloped tract that had received a green A rating from the HOLC. The company was having trouble developing Northwood, which it began in 1930. Waverly, then, served as a beachhead for Baltimore's most affluent suburbs.

The project site also made sense based on HOLC holdings. The HOLC held 122 mortgages in the project area, or 7.5 percent of the project area's total of 1,610 properties, including five vacant homes. Of the 122 mortgages, 10 percent had been in default for twelve months or more. The HOLC had already been disproportionately investing in its housing stock in Baltimore compared to other locations.[105]

Mowbray and McNeal delineated an area running from the Olmsted-designed parkway of Thirty-Third Street north to Belgian Avenue, Forty-First and Forty-Second Streets, and from the Greenmount Avenue/York Road corridor on the west to Pen Lucy Avenue (now Argonne Drive) and Ellerslie Avenue on the east. A project report described it as a "selected residential area which, although not classified as a slum area, shows marked evidence of depreciation in usefulness and property values." For the moment, "at least, desirable neighbors are generally assured." South of Thirty-Third Street they saw "a fully developed slum which continuously menaces its social and economic integrity."[106] The slum area they referred to had also historically constituted part of Waverly. Waverly always had porous and dynamic borders, but the selected project site omitted even the Waverly post office and its town hall, both south of Thirty-Third Street. The existing streetscape features reinforced the borders of a newly defined Waverly. Thirty-Third Street on the site's southern end had a wide median. To the east was Municipal Stadium. Greenmount Avenue's commercial activity on its west side ceased shortly to the north of Thirty-Third Street where the border of Guilford along Greenmount and York was comprised of a distinctive set of dead-end residential streets, limited through streets, and a stone wall.

The HOLC did not consider the area south of Thirty-Third Street part of Waverly. It designated it D-6 and grouped it with a portion of the Remington neighborhood three-quarters of a mile to the west. The security map appraiser listed the buildings as being in predominantly poor condition. Residents consisted overwhelmingly of renters; rental demand remained fair while sales demand was poor. The one "favorable influence" of D-6 was its proximity to "desirable properties." The appraiser noted that no access to credit existed to purchase or construct homes. The HOLC recorded its demographics as "laborers" who were a mix of 35 percent foreign-born and 35 percent African American, with both populations increasing due to infiltration.[107]

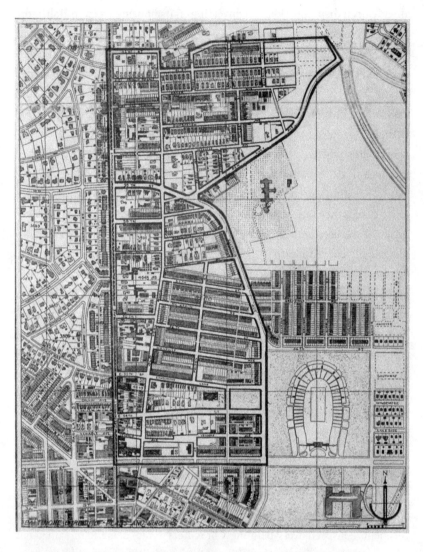

FIGURE 5.1 Map of the Waverly pilot project area. Note Guilford's treatment of York Road frontage along the project area's western border.

(Arthur Goodwillie, *Waverly: A Study in Neighborhood Conservation* [Washington, DC: Federal Home Loan Bank Board, 1940, 12])

The pilot site covered residential areas that the HOLC rated A, B, and C. A-2 consisted of a mixture of detached brick and frame homes and row houses no more than ten years old and listed no foreign-born or black population, no infiltration, and no "relief families." The HOLC appraiser described it as "a fairly new suburban area of homogenous character. Well planned development." Its population "type" consisted of a "substantial middle class." B-8, considered by HOLC appraiser's as a "good residential area" "holding up in value," was home to "a few" relief families but no foreign-born or black residents (despite the unacknowledged nearby presence of Wilson Park). C-9, which primarily hugged York Road/Greenmount Avenue, received low marks because of commercial activity.[108] Houses were on average thirty-five years old, the same as in D-6. In addition to other demographic differences between the D-6 and the project area, renters made up only 20 percent of the project site's occupants and the vast majority of housing stock consisted of single-family dwellings. Project officials also approved of the character of residents, noting that "considerable pride of ownership is apparent, social and cultural activities are established."[109]

In addition to altering the borders of Waverly, project officials further redefined the geography of Waverly in relation to the rest of the city. Early reports described the project area's southern boundary as "making contact with one of the downtown districts." That contact exposed it to "infiltration of sub-standard influences."[110] Waverly was situated between two and three miles north of the harbor, well removed from the central business district and adjacent areas. Nevertheless, officials placed it in the same imagined geography as predominantly black areas of East and West Baltimore. Whether or not the geographic description "downtown" fit the southern portion of Waverly, it functioned as a social and aesthetic descriptor that linked a working-class rental district to the other mixed-race D-rated areas closer to Baltimore's old center.

After their initial meeting in July 1938, Mowbray, McNeal, and a Baltimore-based HOLC administrator drew up a proposal to take to a sponsoring agency, the HABC. In the proposal, they mapped out a program to "secure" property values by preventing an at-risk area from further socioeconomic or demographic change.[111] HABC sponsored the program

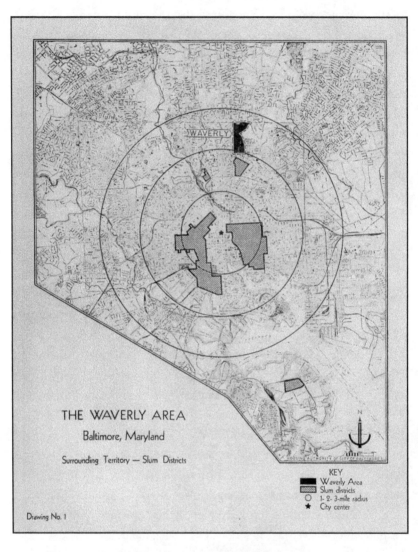

FIGURE 5.2 Map from the Waverly pilot project report showing slum districts in Baltimore.

(Arthur Goodwillie, *Waverly: A Study in Neighborhood Conservation* [Washington, DC: Federal Home Loan Bank Board, 1940, 9]) on the condition that the FHLBB approved the resulting plans as well as provided funds and supplies.[112] In turn, the legal department of the USHA, the parent agency of the HABC, approved all the project decisions.[113]

At the time, the HABC was in the midst of surveying property to demolish for public housing projects. It expressed particular interest in the Waverly plan's field survey component and hoped it could be extended to the entire city. If that was done, it would gain data to help it better negotiate, buy, and option property in designated clearance areas.[114] It was well known that the HABC had made explicitly race-based site selections. Two of the projects, Latrobe and Perkins Homes in East Baltimore, changed sites from mixed-race to all-white. Housing Authority chair James Edmunds said that displacing black people and institutions was intentionally done "to prevent the blight from eating north" and to raise "the value of the white residential neighborhood north of Eager Street, one of the boundaries of the tract."[115] McCulloh Homes eliminated a portion of the eponymous street, two blocks from Eutaw Place. Twenty-five years after Baltimore passed the country's first residential segregation ordinance, it was state and federal money that finally shored up West Baltimore's color line.

CONDUCTING THE WAVERLY PILOT STUDY

Following the initial planning stage, it was time for the Waverly Project's implementation. The project consisted of two parallel operations: neighborhood organization and planning. The advisory committee, chaired by Mowbray, steered both. It consisted of twenty-five members, with representatives from each federal or municipal agency involved with the study. Paisley Lemmon, former Roland Park Company employee, HOLC map consultant, and chief appraiser for the Baltimore insuring office of the FHA, often represented the FHA at committee meetings.[116]

Once project organizers secured funding, they sought local stakeholders. They found lending institutions eager to participate because it would mean both a boom in low-risk government-backed home improvement loans for residents of the project site and general publicity. The president of the regional Provident Savings Bank met with a HOLC representative to stress the bank was "ready, willing, and able to cooperate" because it had a branch on Greenmount Avenue.[117] Provident already ran a loan department, called Friendliloan, that loaned "quick cash" with or without collateral for any "worthy cause," even to customers who did not deposit in the bank.[118] In response to the pilot study, Provident Savings Bank changed Friendliloan's marketing to emphasize FHA-backed home improvement loans. It hoped the project would send property owners from the pilot area through its doors.

Mowbray and the project organizers identified and approved seven local neighborhood associations and reached out to representatives from each to join the advisory committee. Mowbray also contacted a reverend and a member of the board of governors of the Women's Civic League. The Women's Civic League, Mowbray noted, shared the same aims as the pilot study through its "committees on traffic regulations, planning and zoning, and clean city."[119] In addition, Mowbray contacted real estate developer and NAREB member Edward J. Gallagher Jr., who had served on the mayor's blighted area committee in 1937. On the advisory committee, Gallagher represented his company, E. J. Gallagher Realty, one of the largest residential builders in Baltimore. His company developed Ednor Gardens, one of Baltimore City's two A-rated areas not developed by the Roland Park Company. Ednor Gardens bordered the project area. Though acting in a business capacity, he had a personal interest in the pilot study as an Ednor Gardens resident.[120]

With a coalition in place, workers from the Works Progress Administration (WPA) conducted the field survey of both individual properties and the project area as a whole. WPA survey workers went door to door for five months, circulating two questionnaires to property owners. Renters did not participate. One questionnaire gathered "social and economic factors bearing upon physical and functional characteristics of the area." The other asked about physical characteristics of the property.[121] Additional workers collected municipal and court records on anything related to taxes, mortgages, sales information, and permit history. Still others talked to local HOLC workers and real estate firms to ascertain area conditions.

Survey workers sent the data to draftsmen to create maps. They also gave it to tabulators, who created IBM punch cards for mechanized sorting.[122] Once the data was processed, architects and appraisers conducted reviews of each property and made recommendations to property owners for improvements with estimated costs. Officials also considered neighborhood planning. They studied "installed utilities and present street and alley patterns, park facilities, playground provision, land use, block improvement schemes, and zoning ordinances" to determine how to replan the project area. The WPA then supplied the results to the advisory committee, which gave it to personnel from the HABC to disseminate to property owners in the project area.[123]

McNeal and Mowbray initiated an educational campaign to garner support from area residents. Mowbray held meetings where he gave speeches on Waverly's health, stability, and family life. Standing before one of the officially recognized neighborhood groups, the York Road Improvement Association, he opened one such speech by saying, "The thrill of returning home. The pleasure of going again to the old homestead. The home of your father. Place from which you went to Sunday school, then to public school, and from there to life's work." Mowbray crafted a narrative of solidarity based on a shared, imagined domesticity and property ownership. The language of homesteading, though decades removed from westward expansion, echoed the principles of Manifest Destiny and colonialism in which the Roland Park Company had its origins. The ideal environment, he said, "produces our real leaders in national life." By contrast, "the criminal element seldom buys a house." To support this statement, he claimed that "65% of the inmates of prisons come from houses, not homes," an unsupported statistic that played on fears that those who Mowbray called "slum-dwellers" might move into Waverly.[124]

It was these "slum-dwellers" that made the project so urgent. It was necessary, Mowbray asserted, to stop "encroachment from the south." Among possible measures that residents could take, he advised imposing restrictive covenants modeled after those of the Roland Park Company and the Mount

Royal Association, the latter of which covered Eutaw Place.[125] By citing those restrictions, Mowbray linked the future of Waverly to both the Roland Park Company—which had spent years erecting boundaries between it and Guilford—and Mount Royal, the same area the HABC was working to keep white through the siting of McCulloh Homes.

McNeal, meanwhile, focused on the character of residents during the educational campaign. In his address to the Chestnut Hill Association, another officially recognized group, he described Waverly as "a community of substantial citizens" and assured them that as a result, their community's property values were "essentially sound," attributing Waverly's stability to its property owners being good citizens.[126] The project would not fail those good citizens. Its aim, McNeal said, was to "preserve good homes and protect the investments of their owners." He added that these investments represented "a good share of their lifetime savings." Such thrift and diligence, he continued, should not go unnoticed and unrewarded. McNeal acknowledged Waverly residents' hard work and wanted to help them defeat "the encroaching blight that menaced Waverly" before their hard-earned equity disappeared.[127] Project reports confirmed that "the average Waverly resident" resisted the project at first but gradually supported it once they better understood how it would help them.[128]

Though the education campaign proved successful, Mowbray and McNeal faced limits in generating full support from project area residents. Few critiques from residents made it to the press, because the FHLBB tightly controlled publicity.[129] One exception was the comments of Simon Moser, a member of the project's advisory committee and president of one of the officially recognized neighborhood associations. Moser attended meetings in which the board's publicity agent ordered committee members and project area residents not to speak to journalists without Mowbray's approval. Moser nevertheless spoke to the *Baltimore Sun* after his group lodged a complaint with the head of the HABC. Moser's group wanted the area south of Thirty-Third Street included in the pilot project. He reasoned that if the pilot area was extended, then project officials could more closely control conditions there and "Waverly will be doubly protected."[130] Moser and his group bought into the general logic of the study that the area to the south lowered everyone's property values. Moser did not mince words on the subject, calling it a "cancer which [was] breaking down realty value more than anything else."[131] Expanding the pilot boundaries was no moment of inclusionary thinking for Moser's group, who did not express a desire to work with residents south of Thirty-Third Street. Rather, the project could serve multiple functions. While Moser supported the state diverting technical assistance and capital to assist white property owners like himself, he envisioned a different role for the state when it came to the black renters south of the project area: the surveillance and education they would receive as unequal participants would help Moser protect his property value. Moser's proposal went unadopted by project officials.

Instead, the state focused on ensuring access to credit on good terms for the residents of the Waverly project area, including Moser, and them alone. The FHLBB and the FHA reached agreements with lending institutions to increase any current mortgages of Waverly residents to finance the cost of renovations and repairs. The FHA also marked properties in the Waverly project area as eligible for Title I funds for home improvement and Title II mortgage insurance.[132] Though the FHA left individual applications for such funds in the hands of lenders, the aforementioned assurances from local institutions all but guaranteed property owners access to needed federally backed finance.

Renters in the pilot study area lacked the same support and resources that the project directed toward property owners. Renters did not sit on committees, nor did the project include creating any mechanisms to act on tenant grievances about where they lived. Tenants, however, did voice concerns through the WPA study even if they could not fully participate and even though registering complaints could prove harmful for them because of the project's aim to assist property owners. NAREB touted one episode of how the project addressed renters, as a sign of the project's incipient successes. A tenant reported to the advisory committee that the lender who owned his rental house would not make any repairs to the property. The lender told the advisory committee it would make the repairs if it could "get its money back." The tenant's neighbor found out about the situation and purchased the house as an investment property, knowing the lender could repair it. The new property owner then evicted the tenant and found a new one who could pay double the rent, supplying the capital to make the repairs. Here, the project leaders ensured that property owners would profit from improving the building. This included displacing the tenant who initially brought the conditions of the property to the attention of project officials. An article in the NAREB magazine concluded the original tenant "had no business in the neighborhood." It blamed the tenant for "discouraging the necessary repair and reconditioning work" by not making enough money to pay a higher rent.[133]

RESULTS

At the conclusion of the implementation phase of the Waverly test study, the FHLBB published a master plan to "restore and preserve the value" of the project area.[134] Drawing from the 1934 Emmart report and its "ring of blight," the master plan contained extensive recommendations based on stopping blight through neighborhood rehabilitation. The plan went further, however, by calling not just for rehabilitation but for conservation. Whereas the report equated rehabilitation with stabilizing property values, conservation entailed a long-term multipronged approach to protecting and enhancing property value. Drawing on the now well-established ideas about the relationship between property and people, and blight and black people in particular, neighborhood conservation aimed to utilize legal and financial resources to keep Waverly's white population turnover low.

The master plan recommended the adoption of restrictive covenants in the project site. While the final report acknowledged that restrictions could not "be easily established" in already built-up areas such as Waverly, a future nonprofit would make an effort to get property owners to sign on to area-wide restrictions. The benefits of restrictions, according to the report, would be to effectively ward off "undesirable infiltration," "improper land use," and "unattractive street pictures." Overall, they would not only enhance property values but also protect "social values" that would reinforce the neighborhood's long-term economic fortunes. As evidence, the report cited an unnamed section of Baltimore that had been imposing restrictions since it started construction in 1891 and as a result, property values consistently rose.[135] That section was Roland Park.

The plan also called for adjusting the street pattern through the cooperation of city agencies with an incorporated nonprofit group, the Waverly Conservation League. The league and the city would work together to effect strategic street closures, widenings, and changed traffic patterns. They would collaborate to adjust zoning regulations that would remove small industrial plants and "food distribution" stores that predated the city's 1920s zoning laws. For these purposes, the advisory committee voted to furnish the Waverly Conservation League with HOLC data, including surveys and residential security maps, to which the agency tightly controlled access. All told, the master plan would not only "stop future objectionable encroachments from the south" but also "protect the city's investment in Waverly's infrastructure" and bolster the city and state tax base by preventing the depreciation of property. Finally, the master plan would "protect the residential neighborhoods contiguous to [Waverly] on the north, east, and west."[136] In other words, it would protect Roland Park Company developments and Ednor Gardens.

By 1940, the HOLC had changed the name of the pilot study. Its working documents referred to "A Program of Rehabilitation and Protection." The final report, authored by McNeal and HOLC economist Arthur Goodwillie, was titled *Waverly: A Study in Neighborhood Conservation*. NAREB, too, began to characterize the project as conservation rather than rehabilitation. "It is more a matter of conserving latent values," ran a NAREB magazine profile, "than of giving life to a corpse."[137]

Between the beginning of the pilot study and its conclusion in 1940 when the Waverly Conservation League took over, the project met its short-term goals. HOLC foreclosures fell by half. Paid-in-full loans on the HOLC's books had nearly doubled during the year, while the ratio of borrowers in default had dropped from 37 percent to 14 percent. Waverly business substantially improved the overall HOLC figures in the state of Maryland. Conservation depended on continued state investment in Waverly and the continuous ability of the Waverly Conservation League to exert political leverage for municipal resources. Both seemed not just feasible to the authors of the project report, but likely.

American entry into the Second World War in 1942 reduced municipal funding commitments and diverted the priorities of housing authorities. The HOLC wound down lending operations at the beginning of the 1940s, resulting in fewer new potential foreclosures. With the economic upswing from U.S. entry into the war, the HOLC sharply reduced the number of houses left on its books and had an easier time reselling those that remained. As such, it no longer needed to prioritize reconditioning as a matter of financial expediency. Mortgage holders also had an easier time repaying loans during the war, especially as Baltimore became a center for wartime production for the military.[138]

The pilot study remained popular in NAREB, where the board of directors—which included Mowbray—adopted a resolution unanimously approving the project as a way to prevent and mitigate "blight-causing property uses."[139] While its long-term implementation in Waverly largely fell by the wayside, the very principles of blight, rehabilitation, and conservation at the heart of the project became key features in a resurgent debate about national housing policies following the war. It also served as a forerunner for organizations that would be established decades later.[140] The same Realtors, including Mowbray, would once again play central roles. They looked back toward Waverly for lessons in how to craft new legislation. The study's long-term impact can also be measured in another way: the project area remained all white until 1960.[141]

CONCLUSION

Racial capitalism lay at the heart of New Deal housing policies, uniting agencies that on the surface seemed diametrically opposed. Likewise, the shared belief in protecting white investment became the basis for coalitions of Realtors, policymakers, and property owners whose shifting agendas remained otherwise incompatible. The 1930s lay bare some of the most important and wide-ranging examples of how people with power used racial hierarchy to redefine property value and codify it into new structural conditions. Nevertheless, it was a continuation of long-running processes that helped bring them to power in the first place.

NAREB members made themselves indispensable to formulating and implementing New Deal housing policy. Despite having different policy goals, NAREB and local and federal agencies shared personnel and resources across different projects ranging from public housing to neighborhood conservation. They did so because they shared assumptions about the relationship between race, class, and property value that they forged through their working together during the 1930s. These assumptions, outgrowths from suburban developer practices, remained the foundation of widely different responses to reconfiguring the housing market during the Great Depression.

The Waverly study represented one of the earliest applications of that emerging consensus of real estate professionals, local, and federal policymakers, which coalesced first in the discussions around rehabilitation and later as conservation. Both terms centered on protecting and preserving existing neighborhood property values with a long-term investment in retaining white property owners in a bounded area. Because protecting white property investment could take on many forms, Realtors continued to use rehabilitation for the often contradictory aims of advocating both for and against slum clearance, depending on the specific circumstances.

Conservation also helped inculcate the desirability of the single-family home as the focal point of federal lending policies. Mowbray and McNeal reinforced the primacy of the single-family house during the educational campaigns to garner widespread support for the pilot study. They framed the single-family house in two ways: as a federally backed long-term investment that improved the lives of property owners and as a cultural touchstone that showcased the respectability and good character of the project participants by virtue of their position as property owners striving for self-reliance and domestic bliss. Advocates of public housing used the same imagery to promote its benefits to residents of public housing, but the HOLC and the FHA engendered widespread white cross-class support for the New Deal in ways that public housing never achieved, partly because it could not promise the same investment in whiteness and white property ownership. When public housing did get built, however, it was because local Realtors and politicians used site selection to keep adjacent areas white or transform sites into white spaces. The HABC continued its policies, especially as it began to construct temporary housing during the Second World War.[142]

In order to protect white investment, developers played a central role in drawing and redrawing borders to define access to resources. In Baltimore, redefining the borders of Waverly accompanied reclassifying Waverly. It had once been what the since-retired Edward Bouton had called an "eyesore" that needed to be blocked from view along York Road and Greenmount Avenue. Now Waverly's property owners became allies and a necessary bulwark against new undesirable neighbors. As developers redrew neighborhood borders, they set newly divided neighborhoods on diverging paths throughout the country.

Such was the case for the northern and southern halves of Waverly. Many of the players in the pilot study gained more prominent platforms to reshape American cities in an expanded postwar state. Meanwhile, the southern half of Waverly, defined by its redlined borders, would meet the wrecking ball. The person helming that project, a liberal white developer, had deep ties to the Roland Park Company.

6

ADAPTATIONS

Mr. Bouton's boys." That is how Guy T. O. Hollyday described himself and John Mowbray in 1955 when he reached out to a former attendee of the Developers of High-Class Residential Property to borrow the minutes of the meetings held by the group in the 1910s.[1] Hollyday knew the group had included some of the most respected subdividers in the nation, including former Roland Park Company president Edward Bouton, and that they frankly discussed topics such as land planning as well as racial and religious restrictions. In fact, he borrowed the minutes to study restricted suburbs.[2]

Hollyday regarded himself and Mowbray as not just owing their start to Bouton, who had died in 1941; they were Bouton's protégés, who sought to continue the work of early developers. In doing so they formed a continuity with Bouton's generation not just through where they worked and the people they knew, but in their belief that planned suburbs—restricted, homogenous, and with strong boundaries—still held the key to successful development in the postwar era.

Bouton had given "his boys" their start at the Roland Park Company, but both had since gone on to illustrious careers of their own. Having begun as Roland Park Company sales manager, Hollyday branched out into mortgage banking and became head of the Federal Housing Administration (FHA) in 1953. Mowbray succeeded Bouton as president of the Roland Park Company in 1935 and remained in that position, though he, too, branched out into mortgage banking and also assumed prominent positions in the National Association of Real Estate Boards (NAREB). The two continued to cross paths, and in the late 1940s they collaborated on a project that seemed a marked departure from their various business endeavors centered on developing segregated suburbs and lending to white people to live in them: combating poor housing conditions in Baltimore's majority-black neighborhoods. These efforts, called the Baltimore Plan, became a model endorsed by NAREB. The Baltimore Plan called for rehabilitation of existing housing and the enforcement of local housing codes in order to tamp down the growing influence of public housing reformers, who believed a strong centralized federal government could address the problems of inadequate housing and poverty.[3] Ultimately, through professional networks and facilitated by Hollyday's appointment to the FHA, the Baltimore Plan became federal policy.

The Baltimore Plan emerged amid wider debates over public housing, the role of business, and urban development. These debates came to a head in the years following the Second World War when different factions converged on Washington to secure the passage of major legislation. Ultimately, the federal government empowered cities to clear and redevelop large swaths of housing. Ostensibly, the purpose was to allow cities to eliminate slums, provide better housing for their citizens, and enrich municipal tax coffers through the higher property values that accompanied new, modern construction. In reality, federal and local officials, along with developers, who moved between public- and private-sector posts, used federal urban redevelopment programs to "renew and strengthen" racial borders throughout the United States.[4] They did so primarily by creating mechanisms for protecting white property investment at the expense of erasing entire neighborhoods.[5] At its root, the Baltimore Plan was borne from the same exclusionary goals as the urban redevelopment projects to which it stood in contrast. It was, in effect, an attempt at containing black Baltimoreans to particular areas to enhance or preserve property values for white homeowners.

The postwar urban redevelopment of the 1950s marked another generational shift in which a new crop of white developers launched their careers. Urban redevelopment continued to be imbued with exclusionary ideas from earlier decades. Established developers still played their part in its implementation, but the newer generation of developers built their reputations in the context of sustained civil rights activism that moved the dial on acceptable racial discourse after 1945.[6] This combination of continuity and change produced a number of contradictions. No one embodied these contradictions more than James Rouse.

Rouse was a white mortgage banker who got his start enforcing discriminatory guidelines for the FHA during the New Deal. He then gained a reputation in the 1940s among politicians, civic groups, and business associations for his outspoken role in trying to improve conditions in poor black neighborhoods through his involvement, alongside Mowbray and Hollyday, in the Baltimore Plan. He took things a step further than Mowbray and Hollyday, however, by embracing the wholesale demolition of the southern part of Waverly and Cross Keys in some of the country's first federally backed redevelopment projects.

Numerous contradictions point to the limited role that political ideology played in the dawn of postwar housing policy. Rouse enforced and profited from the discriminatory lending practices of the FHA, yet he also tried to create credit opportunities in redlined areas. He founded organizations to promote the benefits of city living, yet he put his vision of urbanism into practice by creating a gated community in Baltimore City that he saw as an extension of suburban Roland Park. He advocated for racial integration, enforced Jewish quotas for the Roland Park Company, and adopted restrictive covenants. Rouse, a self-described liberal, worked with conservatives such as Mowbray and Hollyday to fortify the very socioeconomic and racial borders that earlier suburban developers had created. In doing so, the group of them helped standardize a commercial logic binding real estate's profitability to racial segregation.

REALTORS GO TO WASHINGTON

As the Waverly rehabilitation project wound down in 1940, John Mowbray's star continued to rise at NAREB. In 1941 he joined the association's Housing and Blighted Areas Committee after a stint chairing the powerful Land Developers and Home Builders Division. That year, the committee released a plan for cities to clear and redevelop neighborhoods. It called for the formation of a federal agency to finance land acquisition made by municipal agencies that created master plans for redevelopment. Cities would be able to use federal assistance in conjunction with state-sponsored demolition via eminent domain and other tools to assemble tracts of about twenty to thirty blocks in size, which they would then sell or lease to private developers at below-market value.[7] The committee also proposed that the FHA could insure the loans of these private developers to help guarantee a minimum profit regardless of the project's overall financial success and to incentivize them to redevelop the site in a timely fashion. Cities would be able to plan anything for the site, irrespective of its previous usage.[8]

With the ramping up of the defense industry and America's entry into the Second World War the following year, NAREB retooled its policy proposal from a call for immediate action into a guide for the eventual redevelopment of cities once the war ended. Though the outcome of the war was anything but certain, federal agencies began laying the groundwork for a postwar world in which they could plan and manage everything from natural resources to transportation. State and municipal planning commissions, many of them less than a decade old, also drafted comprehensive plans for what they saw as inevitable postwar growth.[9]

The New Deal had legitimized planning in the 1930s as a necessary economic good that only became more essential as the United States entered the war. Planning efforts received the approval of economists both within and outside government who worried that the end of the war would thrust the economy back into depression. Over the decade, planners and those in adjacent fields such as resource management and architecture came to embrace an ascendant managerial modernism in which they could solve almost any issue by treating cities as blank slates that could be reorganized in rational, functional ways. They believed that these treatments could be applied universally to any city in a top-down manner by experts—their colleagues. Not all planners embraced such thinking, but this approach informed the long-range postwar planning taking place in the early 1940s. It punctuated how the NAREB Housing and Blight Committee justified planned redevelopment as wiping "out the mistakes of the past."[10]

As shown in chapter 5, the Second World War caused NAREB to shift its official stance on the role of federal government in real estate. Even so, the group retained older talking points on matters such as redevelopment for public housing. NAREB's efforts to fight blight were rooted partly in its opposition to public housing, which its leaders had previously called the beginning of real estate nationalization. NAREB continued to view public housing as a dire threat to real estate interests.[11] However, by 1941, little federal public housing was being constructed. Congress instead redirected the moribund program's budget and manpower to construct enough housing for the defense workers it anticipated would migrate to industrial centers should the United States enter the Second World War.

NAREB acknowledged that war necessitated the growth of a federal housing apparatus. It also recognized that opposing federal defense housing might seem unpatriotic. As a solution, it established the Realtors' Washington Committee to lobby for Realtor interests and secure places for Realtors in the expanded state. With its new office in the capitol, NAREB initially continued to propose policy that bore the marks of long-standing concerns of the organization. Much like how the association fought public housing during the 1930s when it was directly financed and constructed by the federal government, NAREB successfully pressured agencies to rescind two orders that would have stopped private companies from building temporary housing for defense workers. As a result, private firms built over three hundred thousand such units in 1943.[12] The Realtors' Washington Committee scored other victories that year. Among them were agreements with eight government agencies, the army, and the navy to use NAREB appraisers for property transactions and to provide the language for boilerplate contracts between the federal government, brokers, appraisers, and real estate managers.[13]

The committee also worked with the newly formed Urban Land Institute (ULI) to identify allies in Congress on postwar redevelopment. Though ostensibly an independent organization, the ULI functioned as an arm of NAREB and was run by the same committee members, but the arrangement allowed NAREB to avoid accusations of self-interest when proposing programs that might affect large populations.[14] The ULI, with its research and education mission, had a sheen of disinterested, objective expertise that neither NAREB nor the Realtors' Washington Committee had.[15]

Like NAREB and the Washington Committee, the ULI also made connections with legislators. In 1943, Washington-based members of the ULI reached out to Florida senator Claude Pepper, who was interested in postwar planning and the elimination of blight. Pepper had already introduced a Senate resolution to establish a joint congressional committee to study the social and economic impacts of the war on areas such as unemployment and trade.[16] He told Realtors he could also add a subcommittee to review urban redevelopment policy. That year, Utah senator Elbert Duncan Thomas also introduced a Senate resolution to establish a postwar redevelopment plan similar to NAREB's, though the resolution did not pass.[17]

Another ally was Senator Robert F. Wagner of New York, who sponsored the Neighborhood Redevelopment Act on behalf of the ULI in 1943.[18] Wagner, who was better known for his support of federally subsidized public housing and organized labor, backed the bill containing every provision that NAREB sought, including "encourag[ing] the development of good neighborhood conditions in towns and cities by private enterprise with the collaboration of public enterprise."[19] The federal government would provide loans and grants for cities to purchase, assemble, and clear land, which cities could lease or sell as they saw fit in accordance with a master metropolitan plan. The bill required contracts between cities and developers to stipulate that redevelopment work begin promptly. Wagner described the measure as "an encouragement-to-enterprise" bill.[20] In language supporting ULI's attempts to distance itself from accusations of Realtor self-interest,

Wagner affirmed to the Senate that the bill was vital to investors and financiers as well.[21]

In spite of its origins in NAREB, the bill divided Realtors.[22] Chief among its opponents was the former chair of the NAREB Housing and Blight Committee, Arthur Binns, who had supported the creation of the original NAREB proposal. Binns objected to the $1 billion appropriated to the new federal body to distribute to cities at its discretion. To Binns, an amount that large would inevitably increase the power and size of the federal government—a process he equated with both socialism and fascism. A growing federal bureaucracy, argued Binns, would prove detrimental to local government, regardless of political party, by engendering "patronage, log rolling and manipulation."[23] Two recent encounters had done much to sway him. The first was a meeting with a public housing advocate who thought the bill called for more government involvement in housing than any public housing group had ever pushed for. The second was an exchange Binns had with mayor of Baltimore and Democrat Howard Jackson. Jackson recounted how in his sixteen years as mayor, federal officials inevitably linked money to patronage through controlling contracts. "Little by little," according to Jackson, "by the process of buying votes through public grants of money, the soul of Baltimore was being sold."[24] Hugh Potter disagreed with Binns. Potter, a suburban developer and former NAREB president during the creation of the FHA, pointed out that corruption and patronage occurred no matter which party was in charge. Nevertheless, he conceded that the bill encouraged "private funds as never before to flow into building projects."[25]

Though Binns and Potter disagreed on the merits of the bill, they agreed that cities required massive redevelopment to protect them against blight. That they held those beliefs in common indicates the degree to which NAREB members reached a consensus on how housing and cities worked despite their different backgrounds and business activities. Potter developed the planned, segregated suburban community of River Oaks in Houston. Binns, meanwhile, bought houses in Philadelphia's black neighborhoods, renovated them, and rented them out. The commonalities outlasted the bill itself, which failed to advance beyond committee in the Senate.

Mowbray had long held that same outlook on blight when he became chairman of the Realtors' Washington Committee in 1945. He assumed the position at the same time a former Home Owners' Loan Corporation (HOLC) official became the committee's secretary.[26] Under Mowbray's stewardship, the Realtors' Washington Committee transitioned from a temporary wartime body to a permanent fixture in postwar politics. During his tenure, Mowbray created a statistical bureau to aid NAREB members in their appearances before Congress.[27] He also received assurances from the federal authorities that NAREB would consult on and participate in "any regulatory procedures" related to real estate.[28]

Mowbray considered these to be important accomplishments, but in his eyes, they paled in comparison to how the committee mobilized thousands of Realtors to defeat commercial rent control legislation on his watch. This victory relied on the help of committee member J. C. Nichols—member of the defunct Developers of High-Class Residential Property and friend to the Roland Park Company—who assembled data, conducted surveys, and organized Realtor efforts.[29] Wagner, the author of the legislation, tabled it himself.

THE BALTIMORE PLAN

The end of the war in 1945 also saw Mowbray move from being involved in forestalling blight with the Waverly project to directly combating it across Baltimore. That year the Baltimore City Planning Commission declared fifty-six census tracts "blighted." They based the number partly on estimates of the tracts that contained the most violations of the municipal Housing and Hygiene Ordinance, which laid out minimum housing standards and health codes. Mayor Theodore McKeldin appointed an advisory committee that recommended a pilot program, dubbed the Baltimore Plan for Housing and Law Enforcement, in which the city marshalled resources allotted under the ordinance to stringently enforce code in a single designated project area.

Though the mayor approved the pilot, the project was the culmination of nearly a decade of effort from civic groups. None had gained the attention of city hall like the Citizens' Housing and Planning Association (CPHA), led by Guilford resident Frances Morton, a social worker who made a name for herself publishing exposés of black poverty in the white press during the 1930s. Drawing on a long tradition of middle-class women housing reformers dating back to the nineteenth century, she believed that improving housing conditions would better the physical and mental well-being of the poor. Inspired by the Waverly rehabilitation directed by Mowbray, the CPHA pursued an approach that combined neighborhood rehabilitation and creating strong health and housing codes to fight the problems of blight. Their efforts, though by no means theirs alone, spurred the passage of the Housing and Hygiene Ordinance during wartime.

To enforce the ordinance, the city established a Housing Division within the Baltimore City Health Department to inspect houses and yards, fine property owners, order properties vacated, and condemn buildings.[30] However, the stresses of wartime migration and manpower shortages diminished the efforts of the Housing Division's capabilities from the outset. After the war, the ordinance received renewed attention from politicians and the real estate industry. They were joined by a mortgage banker who had taken an increasingly active role in the CPHA, James Rouse.

Rouse came to Baltimore in the 1930s to take night classes at the University of Maryland School of Law. He got a job as a clerk at the Baltimore offices of the FHA, which he credited with giving him a formative education in housing and mortgage lending. As part of his job he conducted home visits of applicants for mortgages to determine if they met the agency's criteria.[31] In this way he came to evaluate housing conditions based on FHA criteria, including its underwriting guidelines on race, class, location, and building appearance.

While working for the FHA in 1936, Rouse met Hollyday through mutual family ties on the Eastern Shore of Maryland. Rouse proposed that Hollyday's Title Guarantee and Trust Company open a department specializing in FHA loans. Hollyday hired Rouse to run it.[32] As head of the new department, Rouse became a mortgage correspondent. Correspondents sought insurance companies to buy FHA-backed mortgages. Rouse packaged mortgages issued by Title Guarantee for New York– and New England–based life insurance companies. Title Guarantee, in turn, used the money to issue new mortgages in Maryland.[33] In 1939 Rouse began his own mortgage banking company, which carried on the same activities.

In 1945 the CPHA approached the Housing Division about partnering to implement the Baltimore Plan on a single block in South Baltimore's historically black Sharp Street neighborhood. They dubbed it Block One. The plan established a police squad to search for sanitation violations in the streets and coordinated inspectors from five different agencies—health, housing, building, fire, and zoning—to enter buildings. The inspectors issued violations to tenants or property owners. Each conducted follow-up inspections within thirty days to assess compliance.[34] After two years the CPHA declared the pilot a success. Rouse became a tireless proponent for the project and used his business connections to spread news of it far and wide.

During the pilot, the organizers became increasingly frustrated by the lack of compliance. Landlords, they noted, would rather repeatedly violate code than make any lasting changes. Tenants, meanwhile, either feared eviction or lacked the resources and knowledge to keep buildings in good repair. In 1947 the city and state established the country's first housing court in response to the difficulties identified by the Housing Division. Under the terms of the court, the mayor assigned it all housing cases. The court scheduled all trials at the same time each morning to force defendants to sit through many cases in order to learn different aspects of housing law.[35] The CPHA happily reported that the housing court increased compliance enough to justify widening the scope of the Baltimore Plan from Block One to the surrounding neighborhood.

Code enforcement created unintended consequences for tenants.[36] Baltimore landlords took the opportunity to voluntarily add amenities to justify large rental increases that might cover the cost of other violations. Tenants, anticipating retaliation, refused to report conditions. The enforcement of overcrowding violations became particularly contentious for black tenants who faced higher rents and fewer options for housing than whites with the same income levels.[37] The Baltimore Plan did nothing to remedy the larger mechanisms of housing segregation that created a scarcity of available units where blacks could live. Doubling up families and taking on boarders sometimes became necessary survival strategies.

Residents also remained suspicious of the ability of city inspectors and police officers to protect their interests. Residents either experienced first-hand or were well aware of the history of racialized violence, disinvestment, and neglect. It did not help that one of the CPHA's main rationales for the project was reducing juvenile delinquency among black children.[38] Rouse himself conceived of blight as not only the physical but also the moral decay of city neighborhoods. The belief of white reformers and social scientists that bettering the environment would stop the formation of a pathological black culture was a hallmark of midcentury approaches to tackling issues of poverty.[39]

It is less clear how Mowbray and Hollyday regarded the participants in Block One. Hollyday's priority was to use the Baltimore Plan to fight public housing construction. According to Morton, Hollyday played an instrumental role in circulating the Baltimore Plan to real estate professionals, who then tried to use it to defeat public housing initiatives throughout the country. Morton credited the publicity with bringing the initiative to national prominence but disagreed with the Baltimore Plan being instrumentalized against public housing. After finding themselves thrust into the national spotlight, Morton and other CPHA leaders toured the country explaining that the Baltimore Plan was part of a holistic housing program that required public housing construction to be effective. Public housing and code enforcement would need to be accompanied by bolstering local businesses and vigorously incentivizing new private housing construction open to low-income tenants.[40]

Nevertheless, the Baltimore Plan provided an alternative model for NAREB's fight against the revived interest in public housing in the late 1940s. NAREB employed a three-pronged attack on federal public housing legislation. First, it endorsed the Baltimore Plan as a way to consolidate support for code enforcement. If fighting blight through local housing codes prevented slum formation, then there would be no need for the federal government to support public housing. The Realtors' Washington Committee solicited NAREB member information about local housing codes, health laws, and enforcement.[41] Second, NAREB continued its call for the type of neighborhood rehabilitation statute that provided the impetus for the Waverly pilot study in 1938.[42] Finally, as the Cold War heated up, NAREB mounted a campaign to depict public housing—and the growth of the federal bureaucracy in general—as socialism.[43]

Like Morton, Rouse also objected to the way Realtors wanted to use rehabilitation and housing code enforcement as a substitute for public housing. Realtors, Rouse said, "in their zeal to substitute alternatives grabbed at straws wherever they could find them."[44] However, Rouse lobbied Washington on behalf of the Mortgage Bankers Association to achieve the same goal: to ensure that it was businesses, rather than the federal government, that carried out and managed any urban redevelopment. The issue, according to Rouse, was not federal spending but who received the money. Rouse supported the FHA and postwar veterans mortgage financing as well as federal financing for businesses to carry out municipally planned urban redevelopment. Serving as chair of that association's equivalent of the Realtors' Washington Committee, he crafted a statement opposing public housing.[45]

THE HOUSING ACT OF 1949

Four years of legislative attempts to write a redevelopment policy that also addressed the nationwide postwar housing shortage finally yielded the Housing Act of 1949. Morton, Rouse, and Hollyday all found aspects of the Housing Act to support. Title I of the act contained large sections of the NAREB urban redevelopment plan from earlier in the decade. It adopted parts of the NAREB plan for bringing developers into federal urban redevelopment projects by allotting $100 million per year to cover the difference between the price municipalities paid to assemble tracts through eminent domain and the below-market value at which they sold them to companies to carry out plans. The law required that cities target residential areas for redevelopment and plan projects that kept them primarily residential.[46] Title II increased the amount of money for FHA mortgage insurance. Title III authorized the construction of 810,000 new public housing units but left matters of the racial composition of residents in local hands. However, it also linked Titles I and III by requiring that public housing authorities demolish or renovate one slum dwelling unit for every public housing unit built.[47]

Federal administrators close to deliberations over the act warned that federal housing officials might be accused of using "federal funds and powers to harden into brick and mortar the racially restrictive practices of private real estate and lending operations."[48] An administrator in the federal Race Relations Service named Frank Horne tried to convince housing and redevelopment administrators to build antidiscrimination mechanisms into Title I. Chief among his concerns was that under the local provisions of the act, racial segregation would become the norm. In segregated housing markets all over the country, blacks were disproportionately displaced for urban redevelopment but had little chance of finding the same quality of housing as displaced whites. Horne did not rely on the ethical implications of displacement to move his colleagues; he pointed to the potential legal concern. The legal foundation of racial segregation dated back to the separate but equal doctrine of the Supreme Court's *Plessy v. Ferguson* ruling. But housing displacement, argued Horne, was a special case in which separate but equal provisions could not possibly apply. "No two residential districts are equal," he asserted. The "denial of a right to purchase or occupy property is an injury that is not redressed merely by the opportunity to exercise that right elsewhere."[49] But Horne's warning failed to impress the federal administrators in charge of shaping much of Title I and Title III.

However, a more recent Supreme Court case did move administrators to adopt a narrow set of antidiscriminatory mandates for Title I. In 1948, the sustained pressure of the NAACP brought the case of *Shelley v. Kraemer* to the Court, which subsequently ruled racial restrictive covenants legally unenforceable. This did not render existing racial restrictions illegal, but rather ensured they would not withstand individual legal challenges.[50] As a consequence, Title I of the Housing Act of 1949 conditioned federal financial assistance to local redevelopment agencies on those agencies removing any racial restrictions on the land it acquired. Furthermore, local agencies were forbidden from executing any type of contractual agreement that enabled any subsequent parties from restricting the sale, lease, or occupancy of redeveloped land on the basis of race.[51]

The FHA quickly followed suit by removing explicit racial language from its *Underwriting Manual* in 1949. Nevertheless, appraisers continued to factor race into property valuations. The FHA also began to claim it supported nondiscrimination, blaming the continuation of discrimination on a housing market it could not control.[52] NAREB followed the lead of the FHA in 1950 and revised Article 34 of its code of ethics, which since 1924 had prevented Realtors from "introducing into a neighborhood a character of property or occupancy, members of any race or nationality, or any individual whose presence will clearly be detrimental to property values in that neighborhood."[53] The revision prevented Realtors from "introducing into a neighborhood a character of property or use which will clearly be detrimental to property values in that neighborhood."[54] Gone were the mentions of people, but occupancy counted as a type of use and thus remained as a criterion. Who occupied a property still mattered. The article thus preserved the status quo while Realtors distanced themselves from accusations of discrimination. The association continued to defend racial restrictions and encourage their use in documents not intended for the public eye.[55]

Developers by and large anticipated that their restrictions would go unchallenged in court. More cautious groups of homeowners voted to end restrictive covenants in favor of neighborhood protective associations that had the legal power to screen and select home buyers, allowing them to reject buyers while officially not factoring in race.[56] Crucially, the very idea of restrictions continued to be endorsed by lenders and Realtors.[57] The removal of explicit racial language at the FHA, NAREB, and in restrictive covenants masked rather than stopped active discriminatory practices. Realtors, government officials, and homeowners alike still equated property value with race.

BALTIMORE AS A NATIONAL MODEL

In 1951, at the urging of Rouse, the CPHA and Baltimore City expanded the Baltimore Plan with an East Baltimore pilot study that focused the sanitation police, inspectors, and the plan's growing publicity machine on fourteen square blocks in a predominantly black neighborhood near the Johns Hopkins Hospital.[58] As part of those efforts, Baltimore's mayor elevated the Housing Division into a bureau, giving it more autonomy to coordinate agencies. As part of the reorganization, the city established the Mayor's Advisory Council to make recommendations about future directions of the Baltimore Plan. The mayor selected Rouse and Hollyday to be on the council. Council members grew concerned about the pace at which the plan effected change. Code enforcement worked, in their opinions, but the system needed to be streamlined. The Mayor's Advisory Council calculated that at its current rate, the Baltimore Plan would require three hundred years to fix every blighted block in Baltimore.[59] The council urged the mayor to abolish the housing bureau in favor of a volunteer Commission on Blight. The commission would greatly improve the pace of improvements, the council argued, if the mayor vested in it independent powers like those of a redevelopment or housing authority.[60] The commission's centralization would streamline and coordinate the five agencies involved, reducing the time and manpower required to bring each violation to housing court. The mayor rejected the idea, prompting Rouse, Hollyday, and others to resign from the Mayor's Advisory Council in 1953.

Rouse's frustration with the Baltimore Plan changed his views of urban redevelopment. He came to believe that the most effective way to improve the lives of poor people was to clear blocks and relocate residents to public housing. He maintained that any development should be carried out chiefly by private enterprise. In fact, he saw urban redevelopment in Baltimore as a business opportunity. Rouse soon got his chance to implement some of these ideas as Baltimore conducted one of the first redevelopment projects under the 1949 act.

Like many of the earliest federal redevelopment projects, Baltimore's originated as a municipal- and state-financed initiative prior to the act's passage. In 1947 the Baltimore City Planning Commission approved the site. Even though the Housing Act had not yet passed, the Baltimore City plan contained a provision from the old NAREB blight plan of a multimillion-dollar allocation to fund the difference between the value of land to be redeveloped and the below-market value at which the city would sell the land to developers. The Baltimore City Redevelopment Commission called it "an unprecedented opportunity for private enterprise to participate in a new field of sound investment."[61]

The area selected for the redevelopment was the southern section of Waverly, including the redlined area rebranded South Waverly and omitted from the original 1938 project, in part because of its African American residents.[62] By 1953, when the project got underway, the area's percentage of nonwhite residents remained 51.3 percent. The project area encompassed nine blocks bounded by railroad tracks on the south, Greenmount Avenue on the west, and a zigzagging border of several streets to the north and east.

Plans called for replacing all the structures in the area with a shopping center, new housing, and reconfigured streets in conformity with contemporary planning principles. Varied mixed-use buildings on nine blocks would become two super blocks of identical attached garden apartments set back from the street at angles that maximized light and air circulation. The large blocks created by street closures enabled planners to designate play areas between the buildings at a safe distance from traffic. Selected streets would be widened or extended through the project area on the north to facilitate continuous traffic flow through Waverly to the surrounding areas. All underground utilities such as sewer and water lines would be updated to follow the new street pattern. The design shared much in common with the low-rise public housing begun in the 1930s.[63]

The project required the demolition of 170 residences, along with commercial buildings and scattered small industrial sites. Overall, it would replace 197 units housing 847 people with 291 apartments designed to house 1,024 people. The Housing Authority of Baltimore City (HABC) handled all relocation services on behalf of the Baltimore Redevelopment Commission, the body in charge of coordinating urban redevelopment. The HABC's relocation office dispersed most residents throughout Baltimore in neighborhoods comparable to Waverly, based on what people could afford to buy or rent and the needs of the household. Some gained spots in public housing.

Though 70 percent of Waverly's housing units contained renters, homeowners lived in the area as well. The HABC paid out relocation expenses to both renters and owners, and owners received additional compensation for the property seized by eminent domain. The majority of these property owners were African American. Black homeowners outnumbered white homeowners nineteen to ten. The majority of property owners, black and white, thought their property was worth more than the city paid them.[64] Ten black homeowners and five white homeowners hired attorneys to negotiate higher offers from the city, and all of them secured higher offers.[65]

The HABC assured residents that some of the displaced would be relocated in Waverly.[66] This turned out to be a possibility only for white residents. All 291 new housing units were segregated for whites only. Black residents of Waverly expressed their frustration with being displaced for segregated housing. A city survey found the prime reason displaced black households disliked the redevelopment plan was that "the city" would not let them live in the new units. The Baltimore Redevelopment Commission passed the blame to the private development company, which "select[ed] its own tenants."[67] News of the redevelopment's segregation reached the Urban League, which condemned the project for its racial segregation.[68] The developers of the housing, Harry Bart and Albert Stark, remained unmoved. News also quickly reached federal administrators such as Frank Horne of the federal Race Relations Service. Horne watched as his predictions that redevelopment dollars would fund racial segregation urban were realized. To him, the Waverly pilot study demonstrated "the issue of Federal facilitation of 'Negro clearance' about as sharply as is conceivable."[69] Clarence Mitchell of the NAACP cited Waverly as an example of federal housing policy instituting a "monumental program of segregation" that succeeded in doing what "the courts have forbidden state legislatures and city councils to do and what the Ku Klux Klan has not been able to accomplish by intimidation and violence."[70]

The FHA lent federal dollars to the Title I money funding the segregated redevelopment. Bart and Stark contracted with Rouse's mortgage banking company to arrange financing. They secured a commitment from the FHA to insure a $1,891,500 mortgage on the 291-unit rental project.[71] With that approval, FHA credit finally flowed into the redlined Waverly. However, that credit abetted the same racial segregation that redlining entrenched in the first place. The project also created an additional brick and mortar bulwark against future racial change spreading from East Baltimore into the affluent North Central section of the city near Roland Park Company subdivisions. In 1938 the northern half of Waverly formed this buffer zone, but even then, officials eyed the redlined southern section of the neighborhood as a potential future problem. In 1953 the city, with the aid of developers and federal dollars, finished the job. Because the contract for redevelopment left the property in the hands of the Bart and Stark for decades, continuous vetting of new tenants accomplished what the racially restrictive covenants and zoning changes did in Waverly's northern half.

Rouse created a new company to helm development of the shopping center portion of the Waverly program. To run it, he sought a businessman with more development experience than he possessed. He brought in Baltimore developer Joseph Meyerhoff, whom he knew through mutual connections at the Roland Park Company. Meyerhoff, the son of Jewish immigrants, had built his entire career on selling and renting housing only to white Christians. Meyerhoff survived the Great Depression by buying part of the undeveloped section of Northwood from an overextended Roland Park Company with the agreement that he enforce the company's restrictions on units he built. In fact, if he were given the choice between working with John Mowbray or appeasing angry members of the Baltimore Jewish Council by selling to Jews, Meyerhoff said he would have told "the council to go to Hell."[72]

For the shopping center, Rouse drew on his experience as a mortgage correspondent to secure financing. By 1953 Rouse had established connections with eighteen life insurance companies, to whom he sold FHA-insured mortgages representing over $150 million.[73] He now turned to those same life insurance companies to lend him the capital for the shopping center. The Mutual Benefit Life Insurance Company supplied $650,000.

With the shopping center in Baltimore, life insurance companies joined the array of private businesses that carried out federally backed redevelopment plans under the new policies of the 1949 Housing Act. It was not, however, their first foray into urban redevelopment, nor was it the first time a life insurance company financed a segregated project. In the early 1940s, the New York Metropolitan Life Insurance Company built Stuyvesant Town, an all-white rental complex on twenty demolished blocks of Manhattan's Lower East Side.

Waverly served as a learning experience for Rouse, Baltimore, and federal agencies.[74] The Baltimore Planning Commission wanted to develop mechanisms to allow the "ordinary builder," rather than insurance companies, to take part in future redevelopment projects. Despite this goal, redevelopment projects such as Waverly required a large outlay of capital and the ability to secure large mortgages. FHA financing greatly facilitated the ability of Rouse to arrange a mortgage, a task that builders without contacts in the lending and insurance industry would find difficult to manage. FHA standards for mortgage insurance, including those on size, cost, and building standards, already had the effect of privileging very large suburban developers throughout the country.

The Waverly study had long-term advantages for Rouse's business. He spun off a company from his main firm to manage the Waverly shopping center and collected a portion of rents. It also marked the beginning of Rouse's business relationship with Bart and Stark, who along with Meyerhoff served as chairmen of all Rouse corporate boards for the next two decades.[75] Rouse's sustained involvement in the project through financing the housing and managing the shopping center meant that Rouse likely knew about the racial segregation built into Waverly's relocation policies and tenant selection. At the very least, he willingly worked with and brought into his company people like Stark, Bart, and Meyerhoff, who had long and well-known records of enforcing segregation. On the heels of the Baltimore Plan, Waverly indeed represented a business opportunity for Rouse that demonstrated his ability to compartmentalize the black poverty he built a reputation attacking through code enforcement and the racially segregated housing of the urban redevelopment he profited from.

RENEWAL, REHABILITATION, AND THE 1954 HOUSING ACT

Both the Baltimore Plan and the Waverly pilot study brought Rouse social and political capital. In 1953 President Dwight Eisenhower tapped Rouse to head the urban development subcommittee of the new President's Advisory Committee on Government Housing Policy and Programs. Rouse's committee drafted a report calling for a more expansive version of urban redevelopment, which it termed "urban renewal."[76] Urban renewal incorporated housing rehabilitation with existing provisions on clearance in order to attack "the whole process of urban decay." To use the language of its proponents, it would cover everything from the earliest stages of blight to the full slums that needed to be cleared through public-private partnerships. Public housing construction would be acceptable so long as it primarily served to house those displaced by redevelopment.[77] The committee recommended that urban renewal be spearheaded by local actors on the condition that they present comprehensive master plans for an area's use. The FHA would then finance renewal as well as rehabilitation on terms comparable to the mortgage insurance it already provided. While the emphasis on rehabilitation along the lines of the Baltimore Plan seemed to preclude wholesale demolition of neighborhoods, it was nevertheless predicated on the prevailing association between black residents and lower property values that portended poor conditions. Now, with urban renewal, local actors would gain more the latitude to reshape large swaths of cities.

Rouse also incorporated his experiences working on the Baltimore Plan and in Waverly into testimony defending urban renewal. Renewal, he explained, would save the fabric of the city, and when put under a "vigorous program of law enforcement," all structures would meet minimum local standards. Any structures unfit for such purposes, he argued, "should be demolished; adverse nonconforming uses condemned; congestion relieved; parks and playgrounds provided; public utilities installed; [and] street and traffic patterns planned to protect the neighborhood."[78]

Eisenhower selected Hollyday to help shape his administration's housing policy as head of the FHA. One of Hollyday's first acts was to appoint an advisory committee chaired by Rouse and consisting of large housing developers, fellow mortgage bankers, and leaders of the construction industry. A month later, Hollyday announced the FHA's commitment to expand the ways it facilitated urban redevelopment. Among the new measures was a plan for financing housing rehabilitation along the lines of the Baltimore Plan.

Hollyday and Rouse were instrumental in crafting the Housing Act Eisenhower signed into law in 1954. The act made it easier to construct FHA-backed private housing in redevelopment areas. On the whole, however, urban renewal would not have to target residential streets, nor would new construction have to be residential at all. The act also decoupled the construction of redevelopment housing from the construction of matching numbers of public housing units, which had been required under the 1949 Housing Act. The first funded project completed under the law was the publication of a report explaining the Baltimore Plan for those interested in replicating it elsewhere.[79]

URBAN RENEWAL AND CROSS KEYS

For a time, the area of Baltimore north of Waverly and between the Jones Falls and York Road largely escaped the urban renewal that rendered large swaths of East and West Baltimore unrecognizable to those who had lived there previously. Much of this area, with the exception of Cross Keys, consisted of the Roland Park Company district. Far from the Baltimore Plan inspectors, Cross Keys had gone unnoticed by city and federal administrators. Though the community remained unacknowledged, for

FIGURE 6.1 Falls Road in Cross Keys, before 1956.

(Courtesy of the Maryland Historical Society)

better or worse, by the HOLC, it remained difficult for its black residents to obtain credit, as was the case throughout the country. Former resident Ed Chaney remembered how "even our refrigerator had a coin box on it."[80] Nevertheless, it had grown more prosperous over the 1940s.[81] Detached two-story brick homes joined older ones made of wood as the community of property owners and renters grew. Enough young children lived in Cross Keys that the city added portable classrooms to the local public school in the 1940s.

This began to change in the 1950s, when urban renewal ended the relative peace and prosperity of Cross Keys. Its location in the Jones Falls Valley put it in squarely in the path of a planned expressway. In May 1951, Baltimore City voters approved a $10 million bond for the Jones Falls Expressway.

Construction did not begin until after the passage of the Interstate Highway Act in 1956. The act's generous provisions had the federal government finance 90 percent of a highway project while state and cities agencies covered the other 10 percent. In cities across the country, highways and urban renewal projects went hand in hand. City agencies condemned land on either side of a highway for projects such as public housing or office buildings. Baltimore's proposed highway routes and accompanying urban renewal projects followed this model. They also reflected a national trend in site and project selection in that they reinforced racial boundaries and created others, destroyed black neighborhoods, and, throughout the city, spurred grassroots organizing efforts by people trying to save their homes.[82]

Baltimore and the state of Maryland successfully secured federal financing for the Jones Falls Expressway, which subsequently received the designation Interstate 83. Construction began in 1956. Thirty-two of 104 Cross Keys homes stood in the path of a planned interchange at Cold Spring Lane and Falls Road. There was no community input.[83] To longtime resident Gert West, Falls Road had remained "one big family until word came that the city was going to buy up the houses in Cross Keys and tear them down."[84]

Baltimore followed the national trend of pairing interstate highway construction with urban renewal. In 1960 the Baltimore school board learned that Roland Park's Baltimore Country Club wanted to sell a portion of its golf course.[85] The board requested that the city purchase sixty-three acres for a new educational complex for two of Baltimore's most venerable historically white high schools, Western High School and Baltimore Polytechnic Institute. Advocates reasoned that the new schools would "halt the flight of middle class families to the suburbs."[86] The only site the school board considered consisted of the land between Cold Spring Lane, Falls Road, the Jones Falls, and three acres of the country club. The new school complex would replace the remaining thirty-two properties on the west side of Cross Keys. When combined with the expressway interchange, Cross Keys lost 62 percent of its houses.

The Baltimore Urban Renewal and Housing Agency (BURHA) assumed the responsibility of relocating displaced residents. BURHA had

FIGURE 6.2 Falls Road in Cross Keys, after 1956.

(Courtesy of the Maryland Historical Society)

initially been formed to relocate residents displaced by public housing construction. It later contracted with the Baltimore Redevelopment Commission to relocate all residents displaced by any highway or urban renewal project receiving federal funding. It handled relocation duties of the municipally funded Cross Keys school site because the project was being carried out in tandem with the federally funded expressway. Under BURHA, renters received financial assistance and help from staff members charged with finding them new places to live.

BURHA, like its counterparts across the country, often failed to provide reliable, adequate, or timely assistance, especially when working with black tenants.[87] Cross Keys residents on the school site recalled being treated as afterthoughts. "City Hall just gave us three options," recalled West. "The first offer for your house was one amount of money, the second was for some more, and if you thought your house was worth more, you had to go to court and sue. And who could afford that?"[88] The Baltimore Country

Club could. It successfully sued the city for a higher appraisal that entitled it to be paid more money for its land. By that time, Cross Keys residents had taken whatever money the city offered.[89]

In anticipation of demolishing over half of Cross Keys for a school and highway, the city shuttered the existing public school on the west side of Falls Road. Cross Keys lost its churches, doctor's office, and all but one of its stores. One by one, residents left. A decade later, Cross Keys seemed like a "ghost town" to those who remembered its tight-knit sense of community.[90] They joined ten thousand Baltimore households displaced by urban renewal.[91] Blacks comprised 85 percent of the displaced.[92]

A BURHA spokesperson speaking about Cross Keys displacement commented that every household would now be better off. As evidence, he pointed out that half would be buying new homes. Indeed, some former Cross Keys residents, such as the Hynson family, considered the payout they received good enough that relocation afforded them a chance at upward mobility.[93] Cross Keys residents moved to one of several areas. Some headed up Falls Road to Bare Hills in Baltimore County, a small settlement with historical social and religious ties to Cross Keys. Most, however, joined other African Americans seeking housing in Northwest Baltimore on the other side of the Jones Falls or, like the Hynsons, in Govans on the east side of York Road north of the decades-old black suburb of Wilson Park. Those moving into these areas in the early 1960s faced hostile white landlords who slammed doors in their faces or claimed the homes were already rented.[94]

Speculators capitalized on the mass displacement of urban renewal, the housing shortage for black buyers and renters, and credit discrimination.[95] Those who moved to Govans and Northwest Baltimore faced blockbusting from speculators who bought houses at low prices from whites and either sold them at exorbitant markups to blacks or rented to them at high rates. Because black borrowers continued to be denied federally insured loans, speculators engaged in predatory financial arrangements such as contract selling, in which they would collect a weekly fee toward the purchase of the house but offer none of the legal or financial protections of a mortgage.[96] They were aided by black real estate brokers who contracted with white NAREB members to steer African Americans into particular neighborhoods.[97]

NAREB members could not be accused of violating association ethics about harming property values, and everyone involved profited from commissions and referral fees.

THE VILLAGE OF CROSS KEYS

The Baltimore Country Club soon put the remainder of its property on the west side of Falls Road on the market. Rouse seized the opportunity to purchase it in 1961 and begin his company's first planned community. He named it the Village of Cross Keys. Rouse may have adopted the name Cross Keys, but the community was to be more similar to Roland Park. Whatever the motive, the name changed what Cross Keys would come to mean to all Baltimoreans.[98]

The tract's strong boundaries, which included the Jones Falls, Falls Road, and the new school complex, appealed to Rouse, who envisioned the "island nature" of the land giving rise to an isolated "urban village" complete with an ornamental gatehouse and perimeter fences. When the Roland Park Company created its borders seventy years before, it visually separated Roland Park from Cross Keys with a hedge. In 1961, Rouse proudly declared that the Village of Cross Keys would form a "fine addition to the Roland Park Community."[99]

Rouse knew that the success of the Village of Cross Keys depended on securing the alliance of Roland Park residents. When he needed a zoning variance for the Village of Cross Keys, he held a series of meetings with them. He never consulted with the remaining residents of Cross Keys on the edge of his proposed tract. Roland Park residents agreed to support a zoning variance so long as Rouse signed on to a set of restrictions governing the development, though no race clause was included.[100] Rouse agreed.

The plans for the Village of Cross Keys called for ninety-eight town houses set back and facing away from Falls Road and clustered on an internal network of streets named Bouton, Olmsted, and Palmer Greens. Rouse's company worked hard to convince Baltimoreans that the town houses were not the row houses that dominated Baltimore's housing stock.[101] This distinction served to separate the Village of Cross Keys from Baltimore City, much like the Roland Park Company used the term "suburb" to carve out its own niche in opposition to the city. The focal point of the complex would be a commercial and office complex called the Village Square intended to serve residents. Flanking the clusters of town houses would be garden apartments, mid-rise apartments, and one luxury high-rise named Harper House, after the slaveowner Robert Goodloe Harper who owned the land in the early nineteenth century.

Rouse intended for the Village of Cross Keys to be open to people of all races and religions. His company never advertised that fact, but his past disavowals of housing segregation drew the attention of black organizers. The Congress of Racial Equality (CORE) made it clear to Rouse that they would monitor whether black people indeed bought and rented homes.[102] This made members of Rouse's team uneasy. The project's head of publicity wondered if the consequences of CORE approval would include unwanted attention to "breakthrough" integration. Concerned that prospective white buyers might choose to live elsewhere, company officials resolved to "quietly seek out a qualified Negro" to rent a garden apartment in order to neutralize the publicity of African Americans visiting the Village of Cross Keys and moving in.[103] White Village of Cross Keys residents pressured Rouse by voicing their expectation that racial integration would amount to a small quota of nonwhite residents. One added, "I do think that two colored families are *more* than adequate."[104]

Rouse considered instituting quotas for African Americans. It was not the first time. In 1951, he and a partner had formed a company to manage rentals of a new Roland Park Company apartment building for which they had secured financing. There they instituted a Jewish quota and quelled rumors that they would rent units to black people. Rouse had been offended by pushback from Baltimore's Jewish community, who threatened to fight the quotas in the press. He reasoned that "the simple fact is that a wholly non-Jewish management company has attempted to be effective in opening the doors of a previously closed community, and the fruits of that effort are to be a public statement branding the owners of the apartment building and its managers as anti-Semitic."[105] He ultimately opted not to enforce quotas in the Village of Cross Keys, but Rouse retained a vision of racial integration in which his company allowed a few highly vetted individuals to live in what would unquestionably remain a majority-white community.

CONCLUSION

With its restrictive covenants and orientation toward Roland Park, Rouse's first planned community served as a microcosm of how the very practices begun next door would remain too profitable for the next generation to dispense with. Rouse favored racial integration, but integration meant a small and highly vetted contingent of renters in a firmly majority-white complex of rentals and condominiums. The same thinking made it acceptable to Rouse to adopt the name of a black neighborhood for his first subdivision, purchase land from the party responsible for part of that neighborhood's demolition, name the largest building in the middle of it after a slaveowner, and when he needed to secure zoning changes, consult only with local white residents. Rouse's brand of liberalism allowed him to reconcile his roles in the FHA, the Baltimore Plan, and Waverly as a supporter of both private development and expansive federal power, of both integration and quotas.

This postwar refinement of racial capitalism enabled the most well-known and politically powerful postwar developers to disavow racial inequality but perpetuate it as part of doing business. William Levitt, the developer perhaps most associated with the postwar suburban boom through Levitt and Sons' Levittown subdivisions, told *Time* magazine, "We can solve a housing problem, or we can try to solve a racial problem. But we cannot combine the two."[106] Levittown garnered more national and international attention than any other American suburb of the immediate postwar years. The success of their developments cast Levitt and Sons into the spotlight as industry leaders.

It was the attention on Levittown that prompted the NAACP and other local organizations to pressure the FHA housing director to stop underwriting mortgages to Levittown unless Levitt agreed to a nondiscrimination policy in the wake of *Shelley v. Kraemer.* Though unsuccessful, their efforts prompted Levitt's lawyers to couch the company's position in terms of free enterprise. Attempts to integrate Levittown, they argued, interfered with free enterprise.[107] Taken together, Levitt's comments and the position of company attorneys amounted to a curiously contradictory discourse in which the developer both abdicated responsibility for market conditions while claiming the right to participate in the housing market as he saw fit.

In the context of the Cold War and the building momentum of the 1950s civil rights movement, the shift toward a discourse of free enterprise seemed to mark a shift toward how developers conceived of their role in shaping housing markets. Whereas the developers of the early twentieth century turned to racial segregation as part of a broader experiment with making suburbs profitable, by the 1950s Levitt could plausibly claim, as an NAACP attorney put it, that he "could not take a chance on admitting Negroes and then not being able to sell his houses."[108] Though befitting of the time period, such statements echoed how the previous generation of developers strategically devolved sales decisions to residents. Developers relied on this tactic of popular sovereignty to bolster discriminatory outcomes. In the 1910s and 1920s developers like the Roland Park Company invoked images of hypothetical riots and lynching. In the 1950s the Levitts turned to free enterprise and the common sense of the market.

CONCLUSION

By the 1950s, the Roland Park Company no longer counted as a large developer in the United States. From its heady days in the 1890s, when it transformed the scale of residential building in Baltimore and began experimenting with racial segregation to increase its profit, through the early decades of the twentieth century, when it reshaped the city's political economy via capital and personnel investment and disseminated its practices, the company cultivated a reputation that its officials parlayed into leadership roles in nascent national institutions such as the National Association of Real Estate Boards (NAREB). NAREB provided a venue through which newly branded Realtors crafted an identity as experts through their attempts to standardize practices and ideas about property. The Roland Park Company's daily business operations belied any totalizing top-down schema. Nevertheless, NAREB became a springboard for leading developers to codify practice into policy within the federal government, reshaping cities according to the principles previously articulated by suburban developers decades before.

The Roland Park Company name continued to carry cachet, but it never financially recovered from trying to develop Northwood during the Great

Depression. Under Mowbray's leadership, it spun off a subsidiary that developed a Federal Housing Administration (FHA)–backed 388-unit rental complex called Northwood Apartments near Morgan State University, utilizing a provision of the National Housing Act to insure mortgages to Realtors on limited-dividend rental projects.[1] The Roland Park Company increasingly operated through subsidiaries focused on landscaping, shopping centers, management, and real estate brokerage. By 1952 it had ceased all operations except brokerage. At the end of 1959 it closed its doors completely after sixty-eight years in business.

By the time the Roland Park Company shuttered, the very federal policies that it and developers like it helped codify rendered their firms obsolete. Postwar developers such as Levitt and Sons aimed to achieve economies of scale rather than meticulous design or planning to secure government-backed financing. These newer developers relied on the assembly line–like processes of prefabrication to rapidly produce even bigger new subdivisions near interstate highways on an unprecedented scale. Such a shift was mirrored in the businesses of companies such the Olmsted Brothers, which had shepherded the planned suburb into its most recognizable forms. The Olmsteds' suburban commissions declined after the Second World War along with the Roland Park Company's fortunes, but the former stayed in business thanks to a diversified client base that extended beyond housing developers.[2] Postwar developers may not have needed landscape architects, but they retained echoes of Olmstedian principles found in Roland Park Company developments such as curving streets and pastoral street names intended to distinguish these spaces from cities. The logic that informed the creation of the planned suburb largely formed the foundation for both planned and unplanned postwar suburbs in general. New suburbs continued to be segregated, by and large, through a variety of "technologies of exclusion" including credit discrimination, physical boundaries, threats of violence, and restrictive covenants.[3]

Nor did the postwar decades and the passing of early leaders of NAREB mark the end of the association's growth. On the contrary, it extended its reach globally. Beginning in 1960, just as it was opposing fair housing laws in the United States, NAREB began to cultivate an international network of affiliates, beginning with the Philippine Association of Real Estate Boards.[4] Both domestic and international growth continued over the next three decades. In the 1990s, now called the National Association of Realtors, it joined with the United States Agency for International Development to "encourage the development of international real estate standards, housing policies, private property rights, and real estate financing mechanisms" around the world.[5] By 2017, the National Association of Realtors had partnership agreements with ninety-three associations in seventy-one countries.[6] Its expanded outlook marks what sociologist Kevin Fox Gotham calls a shift on the part of institutions "toward forging international networks and global information channels" to facilitate real estate investment.[7]

The 1960s also marked the return of an influx of transnational capital into American real estate, thanks to the creation of new finance mechanisms both in the United States and around the world.[8] These mechanisms included the expansion of the secondary mortgage market in which institutional lenders such as insurance companies purchased mortgage debt, bundled the mortgages together, and sold them. A major player in the secondary mortgage market was Fannie Mae, which had been created by the federal government during the New Deal to purchase mortgages backed by the FHA and, later, by the Veterans Administration, which adopted FHA underwriting guidelines for its programs. When John Mowbray and James Rouse worked as mortgage correspondents for insurance companies to purchase FHA-backed mortgages, they participated in the secondary mortgage market. Like mortgage correspondents, Fannie Mae then resold the mortgages. In the 1960s Congress changed the scope of Fannie Mae by reorganizing it into a corporation that sold shares to investors and issued securities based on the mortgages it held. In doing so, it authorized Fannie Mae to purchase conventional mortgages in addition to those backed by the FHA and the VA.[9]

As historian David Freund has pointed out, FHA appraisal guidelines reshaped conventional mortgage criteria, essentially changing them to reflect the same rules as those backed by the agency.[10] If the capital circulating on the secondary mortgage market originated with discriminatory mortgages, then the secondary mortgage market also was a form of state-facilitated racial capitalism fueled by both the discriminatory criteria against which people took out loans for homes and discriminatory appraisals that linked a home's value to race. Once these loans were resold, they became seemingly abstracted and distant from the interpersonal and institutional racism that shaped the conditions of the original loan. Even so, mortgage underwriting criteria and appraisals never lost their connection to the race-based developer practices in which they had their origins decades earlier.

Thanks to the secondary mortgage market, transnational capital once again financed the growth of residential real estate as far-flung investors purchased mortgage debt and products backed by those mortgages from places they never saw. These transactions mirrored the business conducted during the late nineteenth century when companies such as the Jarvis-Conklin Mortgage Trust fueled white settlement in the American West by packaging and selling mortgages to British investors. The regulatory context and state involvement differed considerably, but the return of transnational investment based on discriminatory lending brings the story of the exclusionary housing market full circle.

Like in the nineteenth century, when racial capitalism informed investor decisions to finance colonialism and the rise of Jim Crow, firms in the late twentieth century made decisions rooted in racism. These firms packaged not only conventional and government-backed loans but also predatory loans made through a process called "reverse redlining," in which lenders offered mortgages to those denied access to credit, on far worse terms than a conventional mortgage. These debt instruments fueled the subprime housing crisis of 2008, which disproportionately devastated black and brown neighborhoods. The continuities attest to the ways businesses adapted racial capitalism through a century of massive political, social, and economic change.

The secondary mortgage circuit constituted one of two major ways transnational capital flowed back into American residential real estate. Real estate investment trusts (REITs) comprised another. REITs are publicly traded businesses in which shareholders own large parcels of land or a portfolio of mortgages. REITs historically own assets on the peripheries of cities and form a vehicle for international investment in U.S. real estate. It was through a REIT, for example, that a British coal miners pension fund came to own a stake in a California mall.[11] The James W. Rouse Company has operated as a REIT since 1998.[12]

REITs, like the Lands Trust Company, remain beholden to distant investors, receive finance from around the globe, and have far more capital than most local builders. Like developers of the 1890s, REITs tend to opt for homogenous developments on urban peripheries to reduce long-term risk and ensure steady returns for investors year after year.[13] As a result of REITs' resources, scholars have begun to raise questions about how they reconfigure local governance.[14]

REITS also tap deep connections linking American real estate and colonialism, state violence, and dispossession around the world. One of the largest REITs operating in Baltimore in 2018 specialized not only in urban real estate but also in tools of present-day American imperialism: national security and defense property for the U.S. government.[15]

The international financial underpinnings of American real estate continue to be felt most strongly at the local level. This is case with the Roland Park Company's legacy in Baltimore. The company's 2,500 acres remain some of the city's wealthiest and whitest neighborhoods. During its early years, the company used a series of visual strategies to separate Guilford from the mixed-race neighborhoods across York Road and Greenmount Avenue. It created planned limited through streets, disconnected from the existing grid. Single-family homes faced inward toward Guilford or were set back far from the street, separated from the adjacent community by a wall. Company officials explained these tactics as protecting Guilford from "eyesores," but their treatment of borders also signaled that the company could maintain a socioeconomically homogenous space free from those it labeled undesirable neighbors. All of these boundaries remain. In fact, they have multiplied. The few streets that connect to York Road have since been designated one-way, leading out of Guilford. This traffic engineering required city approval.

Restrictive covenants endure just as prevalently as physical borders. Throughout the United States, these agreements remain living documents rather than relics of a different time. They still raise property values because they reduce the risk of long-term change by limiting uses of the property. They still contain rules about property appearance and costs. Each Roland Park Company neighborhood still employs them, with the race restriction removed at an unknown point after 1960, when the company went out of business. Federal fair housing laws passed that decade finally made such racial restrictions illegal, not just unenforceable as in 1948. Despite the removal of racial restrictions and increased legal protections against housing discrimination, racial hierarchy still plays a role in how people purchase housing, where they live, the value of their homes, the credit available to maintain those homes, and how homes are taxed. These are all functions of how developers inscribed their practices into policies, standardizing and coding the logic behind municipal and, later, federal resource distribution. The large racial wealth gap in the United States can be attributed in large part to the continuation of housing inequality.[16]

Roland Park Company neighborhoods also continue to disproportionately receive municipal resources and services. Resource inequality existed long before the developers of the 1890s shifted municipal priorities with their ability to supply city governments with capital and personnel to carry out public works jobs. In the early twentieth century, the Roland Park Company persuaded members of the Baltimore Sewerage Commission to alter its need-based master plan to build sewers in Roland Park and even drain some houses outside its jurisdiction that already had company sewage. Beginning in the late 1960s, Baltimore City paid the Guilford and Homeland neighborhood associations to maintain private parks at their center, while public parks languished in other parts of the city.[17] The arrangement has since ended, but the contours of neighborhood resource disparities appear starkly on maps. A passing glance at a map of Baltimore's trees, for example, quickly reveals the borders of Roland Park Company neighborhoods and York Road.[18] Like sewer pipes, trees are municipal resources purchased, planted, and maintained by city government that impact the overall quality of neighborhood health.[19]

Consequently, affluent residents, regardless of their individual political commitments, still disproportionately shape municipal resource distribution and benefit from how developers helped shaped the mechanisms of governance a century ago. This includes those who benefit from the legacy of neighborhood rehabilitation as housing policy—that is, gentrifiers. Present-day resource disparities would not surprise scholars of metropolitan areas, who have linked both the wealth and race of a neighborhood's residents to the levels of municipal investment that benefit them. They certainly would not surprise Baltimore's poorer and black residents who continue to fight for environmental justice, decent housing, and equal access to city services.[20] However, they might still surprise some residents of Roland Park Company neighborhoods, to whom the structures of inequality seem invisible, abstract, and far removed from their daily lives on their tree-lined streets. The erasure attendant to racial capitalism continues to prove integral for its survival.

And yet, the exclusionary housing market, as invisible and abstract as its mechanisms may seem, found its form through the daily street-level decisions developers made. Chief among developer assumptions was a connection between race and property value that was anything but a given when the Roland Park Company began business in 1891. Block by block, through informal networks and institutions, it helped construct a market wherein the most valuable property, the most resources, and the greatest amount of social, cultural, and political power all accrued to white people in planned suburbs. Together with policymakers, developers helped to build suburban power around an exclusionary housing market—a market that persists to this day. Housing segregation may be persistent, but it is not immutable.[21] By looking at its history, it becomes clear that it was never inevitable, nor is its continuation.

NOTES

INTRODUCTION

1. Over the last twenty years, studies of suburbs have fallen under the rubric of metropolitan history and, a subset of this, the new suburban history. These works focus primarily on federal financing and postwar politics to explain disinvestment and capital movement though they sometimes contain an opening chapter that covers earlier periods. For an early example of the call to reevaluate the framework for studying cities and suburbs, see Greg Hise, *Magnetic Los Angeles: Planning the Twentieth-Century Metropolis* (Baltimore, MD: Johns Hopkins University Press, 1997), 4–5. See also Kevin Kruse and Thomas Sugrue, eds., *The New Suburban History* (Chicago: University of Chicago Press, 2006); Kevin Kruse, *White Flight: Atlanta and the Making of Modern Conservatism* (Princeton, NJ: Princeton University Press, 2007); Matthew Lassiter, *Silent Majority: Suburban Politics in the Sunbelt South* (Princeton, NJ: Princeton University Press, 2007); Robert Self, *American Babylon: Race and the Struggle for Postwar Oakland* (Princeton, NJ: Princeton University Press, 2005); and Andrew Highsmith, *Demolition Means Progress: Flint, Michigan, and the Fate of the American Metropolis* (Chicago: University of Chicago Press, 2016). For a transnational take, see Hillary Jenks, "Seasoned Long Enough in Concentration: Suburbanization and Transnational Citizenship in Southern California's South Bay," *Journal of Urban History* 40, no. 6 (2014): 6–30.

2. Marc Weiss called for a history of the Roland Park Company to be written thirty years ago, but the only scholarly book-length work on the Roland Park Company remains an unpublished master's thesis. Marc Weiss, "Real Estate History: An Overview and Research Agenda," *Business History Review* 63, no. 2 (Summer 1989): 248; Roberta Moudry,

"Gardens, Houses, and People: The Planning of Roland Park" (MA thesis, Cornell University, 1990). For a popular history, see James Waesche, *Crowning the Gravelly Hill: A History of the Roland Park–Guilford–Homeland District* (Baltimore, MD: Maclay and Associates, 1987).

3. Chloe N. Thurston, *At the Boundaries of Homeownership: Credit, Discrimination, and the American State* (Cambridge: Cambridge University Press, 2018), 37. Thurston lists NAREB, the Mortgage Bankers Association of America, the American Bankers Association, and the Life Insurance Association of America as influential.

4. Warren J. Samuels, "Markets and Their Social Construction," *Social Research* 71, no. 2 (2004): 358; Kenneth Lipartito, "Reassembling the Economic: New Departures in Historical Materialism," *American Historical Review* 121, no. 1 (February 2016): 137; Thurston, *At the Boundaries of Homeownership*, 101.

5. Jennifer Schuessler, "In History Departments, It's Up with Capitalism," *New York Times*, April 6, 2013, A1.

6. Like any academic subject of study, the history of capitalism owes its form to institutional networks—conferences, hiring committees, organizers of professional development, and graduate programs. As is the case with the historical actors in this book, not all participants can access these networks, and even when they can, they do not have equal power to shape the history of capitalism or become public faces associated with it.

7. Nan Enstad, "The 'Sonorous Summons' of the New History of Capitalism, or What Are We Talking About When We Talk About Economy?," *Modern American History* 2, no. 1 (March 2019): 83–95. See also Peter Hudson in Sven Beckert, Angus Burgin, Peter Hudson, et. al., "Interchange: The History of Capitalism," *Journal of American History* 101, no. 2 (September 2014): 504–505. Paul Kramer characterized the manner in which some have defined the history of capitalism against cultural history as having a "revanchist edge." Kramer, "Embedding Capital: Political-Economic History, the United States, and the World," *Journal of the Gilded Age and Progressive Era* 15, no. 3 (July 2016): 332.

8. Lani Guinier, "From Racial Liberalism to Racial Literacy: *Brown v. Board of Education* and the Interest-Divergence Dilemma," *Journal of American History* 91, no. 1 (June 2004): 92–118. Special thanks to N. D. B. Connolly, whose Racial Literacy for Historians seminar shaped my thinking on how racism works.

9. Cedric Robinson, *Black Marxism: The Making of the Black Radical Tradition* (Chapel Hill: University of North Carolina Press, 2000), 2–3, 9–28. On Robinson's debt to discussions of apartheid, see Robin D. G. Kelley, "What Did Cedric Robinson Mean by Racial Capitalism?," *Boston Review*, January 12, 2017, http://bostonreview.net/race/robin-d-g-kelley -what-did-cedric-robinson-mean-racial-capitalism.

10. Robinson, *Black Marxism*, 203. Robinson names W. E. B. Du Bois, C. L. R. James, and Richard Wright as the leading figures of the Black Radical Tradition. Subsequent scholarship has criticized Robinson's omission of women and offered fuller pictures of feminism in the Black Radical Tradition. See, for example, Carole Boyce Davies, "A Black Left Feminist View on Cedric Robinson's *Black Marxism*," *Black Perspectives*, November 10, 2016, https://www.aaihs.org/a-black-left-feminist-view-on-cedric-robinsons-black

-marxism. For a critique of the term "Black Radical Tradition," see Paul Gilroy, *The Black Atlantic: Modernity and Double Consciousness* (Cambridge, MA: Harvard University Press, 1993), 122.

11. For Marx, modes of production are inseparable from their historical period. Robinson retains a historically grounded conception of production but rebuts Marx and Engels, who called capitalism a negation of feudalism. Doing so, Robinson argues, permitted them to universalize the experiences of the European proletariat. Robinson, *Black Marxism*, 42–43.

12. See, especially, Barbara Fields, "Ideology and Race in American History," in *Region, Race, and Reconstruction: Essays in Honor of C. Vann Woodward*, ed. Morgan J. Koussar and James McPherson (New York: Oxford University Press, 1982), 143–177; and Barbara Fields, "Slavery, Race and Ideology in the United States of America," *New Left Review* 1, no. 181 (May/June 1990): 95–118.

13. Seth Rockman, "What Makes the History of Capitalism Newsworthy?," *Journal of the Early Republic* 34, no. 3 (Fall 2014): 439–466; Tom Cutterham, "Is the History of Capitalism the History of Everything?," *The Junto*, September 2, 2014, https://earlyamericanists .com/2014/09/02/is-the-history-of-capitalism-the-history-of-everything/.

14. Arnold Hirsch, *Making the Second Ghetto: Race and Housing in Chicago, 1940–1960* (New York: Cambridge University Press, 1983); Thomas Sugrue, *The Origins of the Urban Crisis: Race and Inequality in Postwar Detroit* (Princeton, NJ: Princeton University Press, 1996). The bridging of the history of capitalism and urban history was the subject of Paige Glotzer, "Real Estate and the City: Considering the History of Capitalism and Urban History," *Journal of Urban History* 42, no. 2 (March 2016): 438–445; and N. D. B. Connolly, "Notes on a Desegregated Method: Learning from Michael Katz and Others," *Journal of Urban History* 41, no. 4 (July 2015): 584–591.

15. Guinier, "From Racial Liberalism to Racial Literacy," 100, 114–115. Ruth Wilson Gilmore formulates racial capitalism as antirelational in that it produces and exploits "group-differentiated vulnerabilities to premature death." Gilmore, "Race and Globalization," in *Geographies of Global Change: Remapping the World*, ed. R. J. Johnston, Peter J. Taylor, and Michael Watts (New York: Wiley-Blackwell, 2002), 261. See also Jodi Melamed, "Racial Capitalism," *Critical Ethnic Studies* 1, no. 1 (Spring 2015): 78.

16. Dorothy Adler, *British Investment in American Railways* (Charlottesville: University of Virginia Press, 1970); Charles Blockson, *Black Genealogy* (New York: Prentice-Hall, 1977); Sharon Ann Murphy, "Securing Human Property: Slavery, Life Insurance, and Industrialization in the Upper South," *Journal of the Early Republic* 25, no. 4 (Winter 2005): 615–652.

17. Peter James Hudson, *Bankers and Empire: How Wall Street Colonized the Caribbean* (Chicago: University of Chicago Press, 2017), by contrast, is a transnational book that follows capital and people and briefly connects investors in the Lands Trust Company to Roland Park. However, it largely omits housing development and U.S. cities from discussion of the imperial dimensions of American and British financiers. Another work that briefly mentions Roland Park, but only in a national context, is Carl Nightingale,

Segregation: A Global History (Chicago: University of Chicago Press, 2012), 320–331. This book further differs from Nightingale's primarily comparative approach by employing a transnational lens that follows capital across, as well as within, national boundaries. For a multidirectional approach to suburban development, see Andrew Friedman, *Covert Capital: Landscapes of Denial and the Making of U.S. Empire in the Suburbs of Northern Virginia* (Berkeley: University of California Press, 2013). Friedman calls the suburbs of Northern Virginia the "covert capital" of the United States because of how they supported and shaped a rapidly expanding U.S. intelligence community in the second half of the twentieth century. U.S. activity abroad shaped and was shaped by the agents, strategists, officials and support staff who lived there.

18. Portions of this paragraph are from Paige Glotzer, "The Connections Between Urban Development and Colonialism," *Black Perspectives*, November 27, 2017, https://www.aaihs.org/the-connections-between-urban-development-and-colonialism; and Paige Glotzer, "Who Bankrolled Jim Crow: Global Capital and American Segregation," *Public Seminar*, September 22, 2015, http://www.publicseminar.org/2015/09/who-bankrolled-jim-crow.

19. In contrast to relatively short histories of suburbs that begin after the Second World War, scholars of other topics in American history have used longer histories instead of more common periodizations in their fields to complicate understandings about the interplay between race, class, and politics. Two examples are Walter Stern, *Race and Education in New Orleans: Creating the Segregated City, 1764–1960* (Baton Rouge: Louisiana State University Press, 2018), 3; and Steven Hahn, *A Nation Under Our Feet: Black Political Struggles in the Rural South from Slavery to the Great Migration* (Cambridge, MA: Harvard University Press, 2003), 4–6.

20. Scholars who have written about black suburbanization describe early black suburbs as often originating in relation to labor demands in nearby planned suburbs at the turn of the twentieth century. Cross Keys residents, however, did not consider themselves suburbanites, nor did Cross Keys form the core of Baltimore's black suburban growth. Scholarship on black suburbs does not adequately account for comparable places. Andrew Wiese, *Places of Their Own: African American Suburbanization in the Twentieth Century* (Chicago: University of Chicago Press, 2004); Todd Michney, *Surrogate Suburbs: Black Upward Mobility and Neighborhood Change in Cleveland, 1900–1980* (Chapel Hill: University of North Carolina Press, 2017); Bruce Haynes, *Red Lines, Black Spaces: The Politics of Race and Space in a Black Middle-Class Suburb* (New Haven, CT: Yale University Press, 2006). The closest approximation to Cross Keys is what Thomas Hanchett calls the "rim villages" around Charlotte in the nineteenth century. Thomas Hanchett, *Sorting the New South City: Race, Class, and Urban Development in Charlotte, 1875–1975* (Chapel Hill: University of North Carolina Press, 1998), 43. There are also parallels between Cross Keys and the enclaves in Colin Gordon, *Citizen Brown: Race Democracy, and Inequality in the St. Louis Suburbs* (Chicago: University of Chicago Press, 2019).

21. Recent work on urban finance, predatory tax sales, and the secondary mortgage market, however, foreground the mechanisms of abstracting debt and the ways those processes

both shaped and were shaped by racial capitalism. David M. P. Freund, *Colored Property: State Policy and White Racial Politics in Suburban America* (Chicago: University of Chicago Press, 2007), 136–139; Louis Hyman, *Debtor Nation: The History of America in Red Ink* (Princeton, NJ: Princeton University Press, 2011), 69–88; Destin Jenkins, *Bonded Metropolis: Debt, Redevelopment, and Racial Inequality* (Chicago: University of Chicago Press, forthcoming); Andrew Kahrl, "Investing in Distress: Tax Delinquency and Predatory Tax Buying in Urban America," *Critical Sociology* 43, no. 2 (2017): 199–219.

22. Some exceptions discuss the population, labor conditions, and property arrangements prior to suburban development; all use those discussions to explicitly link how preexisting settler colonialism, slavery, and imperialism informed the suburban development itself. Jeanette A. Estruth, "Subcontracting: Silicon Valley's Riskiest Work," *Washington Post*, November 16, 2017, https://www.washingtonpost.com/news/made-by-history/wp/2017/11/16/subcontracting-silicon-valleys-riskiest-work; Robert M. Fogelson, *The Fragmented Metropolis: Los Angeles, 1850–1930* (Cambridge, MA: Harvard University Press, 1993), 5–23; Friedman, *Covert Capital*, 42–46; Lisa McGirr, *Suburban Warriors: The Origins of the New American Right* (Princeton, NJ: Princeton University Press, 2001), 24–34.

23. In the words of anthropologist Michel-Rolph Trouillot, power "precedes the narrative proper, contributes to its creation, and to its interpretation." Michel-Rolph Trouillot, *Silencing the Past: Power and Production of History* (Boston: Beacon Press, 1995), 28–29. The global turn in urban history has also introduced a range of comparative and transnational approaches that can historicize developer narratives about space. This book situates itself within this turn, which combines discursive and material approaches to suburbanization. Several examples can be found in A. K. Sandoval-Strausz and Nancy Kwak, eds., *Making Cities Global: The Transnational Turn in Urban History* (Philadelphia: University of Pennsylvania Press, 2018).

24. Sam Bass Warner, *Streetcar Suburbs: The Process of Growth in Boston, 1870–1900* (Cambridge, MA: Harvard University Press, 1962); early chapters of Kenneth Jackson, *Crabgrass Frontier: The Suburbanization of the United States* (Oxford: Oxford University Press, 1985); Dolores Hayden, *Building Suburbia: Green Fields and Urban Growth, 1820–1900* (New York: Pantheon, 2003); Robert Fishman, *Bourgeois Utopias: The Rise and Fall of Suburbia* (New York: Basic Books, 1987), 182–208; Paul H. Mattingly, *Suburban Landscapes: Culture and Politics in a New York Metropolitan Community* (Baltimore, MD: Johns Hopkins University Press, 2001); Margaret O'Mara, *Cities of Knowledge: Cold War Science and the Search for the Next Silicon Valley* (Princeton, NJ: Princeton University Press, 2004). Henry Binford created a typology of suburban characteristics that were both descriptive of space and municipal priorities, in *The First Suburbs: Residential Communities on the Boston Periphery* (Chicago: University of Chicago Press, 1985).

25. In the words of Nancy Fraser and Linda Gordon, "We assume that the terms that are used to describe social life are also active forces in shaping it." Nancy Fraser and Linda Gordon, "A Genealogy of Dependency: Tracing a Keyword of the U.S. Welfare State," *Signs* 19, no. 2 (Winter 1994): 310. See also Richard Harris and Charlotte Vorms, *What's in a Name? Talking About Urban Peripheries* (Toronto: University of Toronto Press, 2017),

3–35. Harris and Vorms also cite a shift occurring in late nineteenth-century London in which "suburb" came to stand in opposition to "slum" (15, 18). The relationship between that shift and the concurrent shift in the meaning of "suburb" in the United States is beyond the scope of this book, but given the financial links discussed, it is worthy of more study.

26. In deed restrictions, racial restrictions are written directly into title deeds. In covenants, they are in a separate document referenced by the deed. "Restrictive covenant" has become the generic name that can refer to both. Clement Vose, *Caucasians Only: The Supreme Court, the NAACP, and the Restrictive Covenant Cases* (Berkeley: University of California Press, 1967), 7–8.

27. Noam Maggor calls for a new history of capitalism for the Progressive Era that "would explore the intimate and always power-laden connections between ostensibly disparate spheres (state and market, science and politics, business and ideology), regions (East and West, core and periphery), landscapes (urban and rural), and geographical scales (local, metropolitan, national, continental, and global)." Noam Maggor, "The Great Inequalizer: American Capitalism in the Gilded Age and Progressive Era," *Journal of the Gilded Age and Progressive Era* 15, no. 3 (July 2016): 242.

28. Davarian Baldwin notes that between 1910 and 1935, the "'old' and 'new' markers of distinction" referred to "a rift between an emerging middle class and an older elite" about how to perceive newcomers during the Great Migration. Over time, "terms such as 'old' and 'new' . . . began to signify one's relationship to ideas about industrialized labor and leisure as expressions of respectability." Davarian L. Baldwin, *Chicago's New Negroes: Modernity, the Great Migration, and Black Urban Life* (Chapel Hill: University of North Carolina Press, 2007), 28.

29. Consumption connects buyers directly to the state, bypassing producers. These works combine bottom-up approaches where consumers make choices independently of developers and a more top-down approach where the state shaped consumer markets. In both cases, work on the "politics of consumption" deemphasizes how the history of development was one of uneven power, where consumers did not have the same type of platform as certain suburban developers to construct a housing market. Meg Jacobs, "State of the Field: The Politics of Consumption," *Reviews in American History* 39, no. 3 (September 2011): 567; Lizabeth Cohen, *Making a New Deal: Industrial Workers in Chicago, 1919–1939* (Cambridge: Cambridge University Press, 1990); Lizabeth Cohen, *A Consumer's Republic: The Politics of Mass Consumption in Postwar America* (New York: Alfred A. Knopf, 2003); Meg Jacobs, *Pocketbook Politics: Economic Citizenship in Twentieth-Century America* (Princeton, NJ: Princeton University Press, 2005); Lawrence Glickman, *Buying Power: A History of Consumer Activism in America* (Chicago: University of Chicago Press, 2009). Two notable exceptions both focus on financial instruments: Hyman, *Debtor Nation*, and Thurston, *At the Boundaries of Homeownership*, which links credit, consumption, and the construction of neighborhood boundaries.

30. Scholars of unplanned suburbs have tried to correct what they see as too much focus on planned suburbs, which were relatively more affluent, homogenous, and relatively few in

number. While their work has provided a needed corrective to the depictions of the periphery, focusing on planned suburbs is necessary in order to understand the power of developers in shaping resource distribution, the evolution of property values, the geography of growth, and the connections between city planning practices and developer practices. For evidence of emulation, see Anne E. Krulikowski, "'A Workingman's Paradise': The Evolution of an Unplanned Suburban Landscape," *Winterthur Portfolio* 42, no. 4 (Winter 2008): 259; LeeAnn Lands, *The Culture of Property: Race, Class, and Housing Landscapes in Atlanta, 1880–1950* (Athens: University of Georgia Press, 2009), 71–106; Patricia Burgess Stach, "Real Estate Development and Urban Form: Roadblocks in the Path to Residential Exclusivity," *Business History Review* 62, no. 2 (Summer 1989): 370. Literature on unplanned suburbs includes Mary Corbin Sies, "North American Suburbs, 1880–1950," *Journal of Urban History* 27, no. 3 (March 2001): 318–319; Richard Harris, *Unplanned Suburbs: Toronto's American Tragedy, 1900 to 1950* (Baltimore, MD: Johns Hopkins University Press, 1999); Becky Nicolaides, *My Blue Heaven: Life and Politics in the Working-Class Suburbs of Los Angeles, 1920–1965* (Chicago: University of Chicago Press, 2002); Elaine Lewinnek, *A Workingman's Reward: Chicago's Early Suburbs and the Roots of American Sprawl* (New York: Oxford University Press, 2014).

31. On the connections between zoning and restrictive covenants, see Freund, *Colored Property*, 45–98; Marc Weiss, *The Rise of the Community Builders: The American Real Estate Industry and Urban Land Planning* (New York: Columbia University Press, 1987), 79–106; Garrett Power, "The Advent of Zoning," *Planning Perspectives* 4, no. 1 (1989): 1–13.

32. Janet Pearl Davies, *Real Estate in American History* (Washington, DC: Public Affairs Press, 1958), 101. On NAREB, developers, and professionalization, see Freund, *Colored Property*, 51–98; William S. Worley, *J. C. Nichols and the Shaping of Kansas City* (Columbia: University of Missouri Press, 1990), 89–123; Weiss, *Rise of Community Builders*, 17–78; Jeffrey Hornstein, *A Nation of Realtors: A Cultural History of the Twentieth-Century American Middle Class* (Durham, NC: Duke University Press, 2005), 53–117; Rose Helper, *Racial Policies and Practices of Real Estate Brokers* (Minneapolis: University of Minnesota Press, 1969), 201–217.

33. Freund, *Colored Property*, 92–98; Margaret Garb, *City of American Dreams: A History of Home Ownership and Housing Reform in Chicago, 1871–1919* (Chicago: University of Chicago Press, 2005), 177–202.

34. The religion of real estate professionals needs more attention than is provided in this book. On the formation of institutional culture including performance of race, gender, and religion, see Bethany Moreton, *To Serve God and Wal-Mart: The Making of Christian Free Enterprise* (Cambridge, MA: Harvard University Press, 2009), 67–85; Jessica Ann Levy, "Black Power Inc.: Global American Business and the Post-Apartheid City" (PhD diss., Johns Hopkins University, 2018), 161–167. On race and institutional culture, see Sharon M. Collins, *Black Corporate Executives* (Philadelphia: Temple University Press, 1997), 111–113. On racialized performance at business meetings, see Hudson, *Bankers and Empire*, 135–136. On the role religion played for

black women fighting suburban segregation, see Betty Livingston Adams, *Black Women's Church Activism: Seeking Social Justice in a Northern Suburb* (New York: New York University Press, 2016).

35. At different points in time, as Joe Trotter notes, scholarship on African American migration and international migration have been connected and disconnected from each other. Joe Trotter, "The Great Migration, African Americans, and Immigrants in the Industrial City," in *Not Just Black and White: Historical and Contemporary Perspectives on Immigration, Race, and Ethnicity in the United States*, ed. Nancy Foner and George Frederickson (New York: Russell Sage Foundation, 2005), 82–99.

36. On office tools such as the organization and content of standardized forms, I draw from Margot Canaday, *The Straight State: Sexuality and Citizenship in Twentieth-Century America* (Princeton, NJ: Princeton University Press, 2009) to make a case that daily business decisions helped construct the mechanisms of exclusion.

37. On the constant making and remaking of racial hierarchy, see Madeline Y. Hsu, "Asian American History and the Perils of a Usable Past," *Modern American History* 1, no. 1 (March 2018): 74.

38. Todd Michney and LaDale Winling describe federal agencies as seeking a "social scientific veneer" to property valuations, but this underplays the tensions in NAREB between valuing sources of academic knowledge and the primacy of daily business experience, which went unresolved during the 1930s. This book does seek to deemphasize the focus on social scientific expertise in New Deal housing. At the same time, it argues for how daily business practices and long-standing networks shaped and reshaped many forms of exclusion, including property valuation. In particular, much attention has been paid to Richard Ely and Homer Hoyt. Todd Michney and LaDale Winling, "New Perspectives on New Deal Housing Policy: Explicating and Mapping HOLC Loans to African Americans," *Journal of Urban History*, January 9, 2019 (advanced online publication), 2, https://doi.org/10.1177/0096144218819429.

39. Sugrue, *Origins of the Urban Crisis*, 60–61.

40. Gail Radford, *Modern Housing for America: Policy Struggles in the New Deal Era* (Chicago: University of Chicago Press, 1996), 199.

41. See, for example, Rhonda Williams, *The Politics of Public Housing: Black Women's Struggles Against Urban Inequality* (New York: Oxford University Press, 2005); D. Bradford Hunt, *Blueprint for Disaster: The Unraveling of Chicago's Public Housing* (Chicago: Chicago University Press, 2010).

42. Dara Orenstein and Aaron Carico, "Editors' Introduction: The Fictions of Finance," *Radical History Review* 14, no. 118 (2014): 8.

43. Notable exceptions that serve as useful models for how to retain a focus on racial capitalism and developers in the mid-twentieth century are Self, *American Babylon*, and N. D. B. Connolly, *A World More Concrete: Real Estate and the Remaking of Jim Crow South Florida* (Chicago: University of Chicago Press, 2014). Literature on the Sunbelt and Silicon Valley emphasizes the roles of postwar developers and boosters who attracted capital and created sprawling metropolitan areas where many of those major

political changes occurred. Their analytic foci vary widely. See, for example, Elizabeth Tandy Shermer, *Sunbelt Capitalism: Phoenix and the Transformation of American Politics* (Philadelphia: University of Pennsylvania Press, 2013); and Margaret O'Mara, *The Code: Silicon Valley and the Remaking of America* (New York: Penguin, 2019).

44. Digital Scholarship Lab, "Renewing Inequality: Urban Renewal, Family Displacements, and Race, 1955–1966," in *American Panorama*, ed. Robert K. Nelson and Edward L. Ayers, accessed February 1, 2019, http://dsl.richmond.edu/panorama/renewal, counts 8,600 households. This figure underestimates the total number of displaced households because it is based on what the federal government classified as urban renewal. For a breakdown of additional categories of displacement closely associated with urban renewal projects, such as school construction and selected public housing sites, see Baltimore Urban Renewal and Housing Agency, "Anticipated Displacement of Households in the Six Year Period 1962–1967. Baltimore, MD," R0019, Special Collections, Langsdale Library, University of Baltimore.

1. FLOWS

1. "Lands Trust Company," *Financial Times*, March 24, 1891.

2. Tracing the economic connections through investment adds another layer to the racial capitalism that spawned a "global history of segregation." Carl Nightingale, *Segregation: A Global History* (Chicago: University of Chicago Press, 2012), 1–13, 300–332.

3. On investment and empire, see Peter James Hudson, *Bankers and Empire: How Wall Street Colonized the Caribbean* (Chicago: University of Chicago Press, 2017), 82–83; Sven Beckert, "Emancipation and Empire: Reconstructing the Worldwide Web of Cotton Production in the Age of the American Civil War," *American Historical Review* 109, no. 5 (December 2004): 1405–1438; Anne Laurence, "Women Investors, 'That Nasty South Sea Affair,' and the Rage to Speculate in Early Eighteenth-Century England," *Accounting, Business and Financial History* 16, no. 2 (2006): 245–264. Some historians have drawn intellectual connections between housing segregation and British imperialism while others have examined the links between the ways Americans conceived of imperial relations abroad and racial relations at home. Amy Kaplan, *The Anarchy of Empire in the Making of U.S. Culture* (Cambridge, MA: Harvard University Press, 2005), 18.

4. Josephine Maltby and Janette Rutterford, "Editorial: Women, Accounting, and Investment," *Accounting, Business and Financial History* 16, no. 2 (2006): 136.

5. Josephine Maltby and Janette Rutterford, "She Possessed Her Own Fortune: Women Investors from the Late Nineteenth Century to the Early Twentieth Century," *Business History* 48, no. 2 (2006): 231.

6. Dorceta E. Taylor, *The Rise of the American Conservation Movement: Power, Privilege, and Environmental Protection* (Durham, NC: Duke University Press, 2016), 20–21; Mae Ngai, "Chinese Gold Miners and the 'Chinese Question' in Nineteeth-Century California and Victoria," *Journal of American History* 101, no. 4 (2015): 1085.

7. Hudson, *Bankers and Empire*, 24.

8. The conveyancer was Uria Brown. Wilma Dunaway cites Brown as an example of the "crucial role played by antebellum real estate middlemen" in protecting the interests of large property owners and enabling land speculation. Wilma A. Dunaway, *The First American Frontier: Transition to Capitalism in Southern Appalachia, 1700–1860* (Chapel Hill: University of North Carolina Press, 1996), 64; Deed from Prudence Gough and James Carroll to Solomon Moonier, Liber 147 Folio 151 CE 66-197, Maryland State Archives, Annapolis.

9. Land records index, CE 15-2, 330, Maryland State Archives.

10. Deed from Prudence Gough and James Carroll to Solomon Moonier.

11. Deed from Prudence Gough and James Carroll to Ann Cutler, Liber 147 Folio 169 CE 66-197, Maryland State Archives.

12. Megan Ming Francis and Michael C. Dawson, "Race, Capitalism, and Conflict Then and Now," *Items: Insights from the Social Sciences*, October 3, 2017, https://items.ssrc.org/reading-racial-conflict/race-capitalism-and-conflict-then-and-now.

13. Seth Rockman, *Scraping By: Wage Labor, Slavery, and Survival in Early Baltimore* (Baltimore, MD: Johns Hopkins University Press, 2009), 7.

14. Eric Robert Papenfuse, *The Evils of Necessity: Robert Goodloe Harper and the Moral Dilemma of Slavery* (Philadelphia: American Philosophical Society, 1997), 70–72. In and near Baltimore it was also common to hire out enslaved people of African descent, which led to what Rockman calls a labor force with varying degrees of "unfreedom." Rockman, *Scraping By*, 50, 72.

15. Daina Ramey Berry, *The Price for Their Pound of Flesh: The Value of the Enslaved from Womb to Grave in the Building of a Nation* (Boston: Beacon Press, 2017).

16. James Waesche, *Crowning the Gravelly Hill: A History of the Roland Park–Guilford–Homeland District* (Baltimore, MD: Maclay and Associates, 1987), 21–23.

17. Census, 1870 District 9, Baltimore, Maryland, Roll: M593_570. James Holechek gives a figure of five hundred but does not say when Cross Keys had that population. James Holechek, *Baltimore's Two Cross Keys Villages: One Black, One White* (Lincoln, NE: iUniverse, 2003), 7.

18. Census, 1880 Cross Keys, Baltimore, Maryland, Roll: 496, Page: 136D, Enumeration District: 242.

19. Holechek, *Baltimore's Two Cross Keys Villages*, 45.

20. "The Workingmen's Part in Baltimore County," *Baltimore Sun*, September 11, 1877, 4.

21. *Laborer* was a catchall term used in antebellum Baltimore for people in various states of what Seth Rockman called *freedom* and *unfreedom*, including slaves, indentured servants, and people who had full legal recognition to control their own labor. When using it to count African American men, especially, census takers likely elided a range of skills, employment arrangements, and skills. Rockman, *Scraping By*, 23–27.

22. The majority of black women in Cross Keys are listed on the 1880 census as "kept house." According to Mary Ellen Hayward, census takers listed women this way if men in the household "had a skilled job. But if a man worked as a common 'laborer' or had an un-

skilled occupation, his wife had to make extra money by taking in laundry." Mary Ellen Hayward, *Baltimore's Alley Houses: Homes for Working People Since the 1780s* (Baltimore, MD: Johns Hopkins University Press, 2008), 187. Most employees of Jones Falls Valley mills in the late nineteenth century were rural white migrants from Maryland and Virginia. Bill Harvey, "Hampden-Woodberry: Baltimore's Mill Villages," in *The Baltimore Book: New Views of Local History*, ed. Elizabeth Fee, Linda Shopes, and Linda Zeidman (Philadelphia: Temple University Press, 1991), 46.

23. Natasha Lightfoot, *Troubling Freedom: Antigua and the Aftermath of British Emancipation* (Durham, NC: Duke University Press, 2015), 168–169.

24. For evidence that the process is sped up, see "On the Chemistry of Sugar Manufacture and Sugar Refining," *Barbados Agricultural Reporter*, January 29, 1869; "(Alfred) Fryer's Concretor and Its Products," *Barbados Agricultural Reporter*, June 30, 1868.

25. Muscavado carried lower import duties than refined white sugar. Many of the questions that potential buyers of the Concretor asked Fryer pertained to the expected duties on concrete. "The Concretor," *Saint Christopher Advertiser and Weekly Intelligencer*, April 24, 1866; Susan Lowes, "The Peculiar Class: The Formation, Collapse, and Reformation of the Middle Class of Antigua, West Indies, 1834–1940" (PhD diss., University of Michigan, 1994), 49.

26. "The Concretor."

27. See, for example, W. J. Read, "The Concretor at Work," *Saint Christopher Gazette and Charibbean* [sic] *Courier*, September 7, 1866.

28. Lightfoot, *Troubling Freedom*, 169–173.

29. Natasha Lightfoot, "'Their Coats Were Tied Up Like Men': Women Rebels in Antigua's 1858 Uprising," *Slavery and Abolition* 34, no. 4 (2010): 532, 538–539.

30. Lightfoot, *Troubling Freedom*, 173.

31. Keithlyn B. Smith and Fernando C. Smith, *To Shoot Hard Labour: The Life and Times of Samuel Smith, an Antiguan Workingman, 1877–1982* (Scarborough, ON: Edan's Publishers, 1986), 73; Lightfoot, "'Their Coats,'" 529.

32. Peter James Hudson, "The Racist Dawn of Capitalism," *Boston Review*, March 14, 2016, http://bostonreview.net/books-ideas/peter-james-hudson-slavery-capitalism.

33. The estates and number of enslaved individuals were as follows: Belvidere, 120; Bendals, 221; Bath Lodge, 200; Bodkin's, 188; Green Castle, 306; and George Byam's, 137. Numbers obtained from Centre for the Study of the Legacies of British Slave-Ownership, *Legacies of British Slave-Ownership*, University College London Department of History, accessed July 15, 2019, https://www.ucl.ac.uk/lbs. The database does not hold information on Halliday's Mountain and the leased estate, Rigsby. Names of estates purchased or leased by Fryer's Concrete Company obtained from "Fryer's Concrete Company," BT 39/69/4352, National Archives of the United Kingdom, London; Lowes, "Peculiar Class," 53.

34. Smith and Smith, *To Shoot Hard Labour*, 41–42, 73.

35. "The Concretor."

36. The Concretor was especially popular with planters in Trinidad. "Agricultural Report and Packet Summary," *Barbados Agricultural Reporter*, May 8, 1868.

37. "Claim of Mssrs. Manlove and Alliott, Protest Against the Courts," FO 23/94, "Fryer's Concrete Company," BT 39/69/4352, National Archives of the United Kingdom. In the Dominican Republic and Puerto Rico they sold sugar machinery as well as held mortgage securities and other debts from planters to whom they sold the sugar machinery. Gricel M. Surillo Luna, "Moving Forward: Railways in Puerto Rico" (PhD diss., City University of New York, 2017), 83.

38. Ursula Mellor Bright, ed., *Speeches of Jacob Bright, M.P., 1869–1884* (London: Simpkin, Marshall, and Company, 1885), 352; *The Bankers' Magazine, Journal of the Money Market and Commercial Digest* 44 (July 1884): 922.

39. Jacob Bright, "The Congo Treaty," *Bristol Selected Pamphlets*, 1884, http://greystoke.unl.edu/doc/llg.ber.002.01.html.

40. Portions of this paragraph have been published as Paige Glotzer, "The Connections Between Urban Investment and Colonialism." *Black Perspectives*, November 27, 2017, https://www.aaihs.org/the-connections-between-urban-development-and-colonialism.

41. Eugene Moehring cites Utah territorial leaders' support for a railway as a deliberate act of colonialism that would link Mormon towns together and improve social organization. Eugene Moehring, *Urbanism and Empire in the Far West, 1840–1890* (Reno: University of Nevada Press, 2003), 115. Noam Maggor argues that the "incorporation of the West into the economic orbit of the United States hinged on an uneasy relationship between financial networks that penetrated the deep interiors of North America and emergent state institutions." Noam Maggor, "To Coddle and Caress These Great Capitalists: Eastern Money, Frontier Populism, and the Politics of Market-Making in the American West," *American Historical Review* 122, no. 1 (February 2017): 58–59.

42. Ned Blackhawk, *Violence Over the Land: Indians and Empire in the Early American West* (Cambridge, MA: Harvard University Press, 2008), 263–268.

43. Hudson, *Bankers and Empire*, 29.

44. George Thomas, *The of Institutions Under Irrigation* (New York: Macmillan, 1920), 212–214; Mira Wilkins, *The History of Foreign Investment in the United States to 1914* (Cambridge, MA : Harvard University Press, 1989), 229.

45. Hudson, *Bankers and Empire*, 23.

46. Jonathan Levy, "The Mortgage That Worked Hardest: The Fate of Landed Independence in Nineteenth-Century America," in *Capitalism Takes Command: The Social Transformation of Nineteenth-Century America*, ed. Michael Zakim and Gary Kornblith (Chicago: University of Chicago Press, 2011), 40–41.

47. Larry McFarlane, "British Investment in Midwestern Farm Mortgages and Land, 1875–1900: A Comparison of Iowa and Kansas," *Agricultural History* 48, no.1 (January 1974): 192.

48. Kenneth Snowden, "Covered Farm Mortgage Bonds in the United States During the Late Nineteenth Century," *Journal of Economic History* 70, no. 4 (December 2010): 784. Snowden uses the example of a Jarvis-Conklin competitor, the J. B. Watkins Mortgage Company of Lawrence, Kansas. McFarlane describes the two firms as very similar and also mentions that Jarvis-Conklin issued debentures. McFarlane, "Iowa and Kansas," 193–194.

49. Wilkins, *The History of Foreign Investment*, 229–230; McFarlane, "Iowa and Kansas," 182, 195–197; Larry McFarlane, "British Investment and the Land, Nebraska 1877–1946," *Business History Review* 57, no. 2 (Summer 1983): 266–267.

50. *The London Stock Exchange Yearbook*, 1881–1891, Baker Library, Harvard Business School, Cambridge, Massachusetts.

51. McFarlane, "Iowa and Kansas," 190, 193–194.

52. Alfred Fryer, *The Great Loan Land* (Manchester, UK: Brook and Crystal, 1887), 19–23.

53. For more on different interpretations of Turner, his pivotal role in the formation of the American historical profession, and the survival of the frontier thesis, see Patricia Nelson Limerick, *Something in the Soil: Legacies and Reckonings in the New West* (New York: W. W. Norton, 2000).

54. William Cronon, *Nature's Metropolis: Chicago and the Great West* (New York: W. W. Norton, 1991), 364; Rebecca Tinio McKenna, *American Imperial Pastoral: The Architecture of US Colonialism in the Philippines* (Chicago: University of Chicago Press, 2017), 76–77, 96.

55. See, for example, David Chang, *The Color of Land: Race, Nation, and the Politics of Land Ownership in Oklahoma, 1832–1929* (Chapel Hill: University of North Carolina Press, 2010), 109–148.

56. For more on how "racialized logics inform natural resource struggles," see Sharlene Mollett, "The Power to Plunder: Rethinking Land Grabbing in Latin America," *Antipode* 48, no. 2 (2016): 412–432; Hudson, *Bankers and Empire*, 24.

57. Fryer, *The Great Loan Land*, 43, 45.

58. Fryer, *The Great Loan Land*, 20.

59. The ad appeared in various newspapers, including the *Freeman's Journal*, August 13, 1889, 8; the *Manchester Courier*, August 13, 1889, n.p.; the *Sheffield Daily Telegraph*, August 13, 1889, n.p.; the *Standard*, August 13, 1889, n.p.; the *York Herald*, August 13, 1889, n.p.; and the *Guardian*, August 10, 1889, n.p.

60. Stock Exchange Application for the Lands Trust Company 23B S4, Guildhall Library, London.

61. Stock Exchange Application for the Lands Trust Company 23B S4, Guildhall Library.

62. Tracy Jean Boisseau, *White Queen: May French-Sheldon and the Imperial Origins of American Feminist Identity* (Bloomington: Indiana University Press, 2004), 9.

63. Boisseau, *White Queen*, 2, 10.

64. "List of Persons Holding Shares," Lands Trust Company Limited BT 31/4141/26712, National Archives of the United Kingdom.

65. "List of Persons Holding Shares."

66. Alan Fowler, *Lancashire Cotton Operatives and Work, 1900–1950: A Social History of Lancashire Cotton Operatives in the Twentieth Century* (Aldershot, UK: Ashgate, 2003), 16; "List of Persons Holding Shares."

67. "Some American Land and Mortgage Companies, Experience of the 'Friends,'" *The Statist*, June 24, 1893, 691.

68. Joseph Smith, *Supplement to "A Catalog of Friends Books"* (London: Edward Hicks, 1893), 161.

69. "List of Persons Holding Shares."
70. Literature on the work singles out the South Sea Company and the Royal African Company as two enterprises characterized by the investments of women. Anne Laurence, "Women Investors"; Ann M. Carlos, Karen Maguire, and Larry Neal, "Financial Acumen, Women Speculators, and the Royal African Company During the South Sea Bubble," *Accounting, Business and Financial History* 16, no. 2 (2006): 219–243. In the 1850s, women composed half of the East India Company's Court of Proprietors, the body that elected directors.
71. Accumulating and spending money in certain ways carried gendered connotations. Janice Traflet, "Gendered Dollars: Pin Money, Mad Money, and Changing Notions of a Woman's Proper Place," *Essays in Economic and Business History* 26 (2008): 189–202; Mark Freeman, Robin Pearson, and James Taylor, "'A Doe in the City': Women Shareholders in Eighteenth- and Early Nineteenth-Century Britain," *Accounting, Business and Financial History* 16, no. 2 (2006): 265–291.
72. Lance E. Davis and Robert Huttenback, *Mammon and the Pursuit of Empire: The Political Economy of British Imperialism* (Cambridge: Cambridge University Press, 2009), 199. Table 7.2 was used to calculate the total of women shareholders in the sample and the total shareholders. The authors divide shareholders into domestic, foreign, and empire firms. To find what percentage of women shareholders invested in nondomestic firms, the three categories were totaled and then the percentage of combined foreign and empire found.
73. Quoted in Maltby and Rutterford, "Editorial," 137.
74. Shares refers to common stock.
75. "List of Persons Holding Shares."
76. George Robb, "Ladies of the Ticker: Women, Investment, and Fraud in England and America, 1850–1930," in *Victorian Investments: New Perspectives on Finance and Culture*, ed. Nancy Henry and Cannon Schmitt (Bloomington: Indiana University Press, 2009), 123.
77. "File of Proceedings in the Matter of the Lands Trust Company Limited, 1895," J 13/1119, National Archives of the United Kingdom.
78. For more on the relationship between women, investment, and modes of thinking, see Nancy Henry, *Women, Literature, and Finance in Victorian Britain* (London: Palgrave, 2018). In the American context, the increase in women investment primarily took place a little later, during the Liberty Bond drive during the First World War. This mirrors the difference of several decades between democratization of investment in Great Britain and in the United States. Julia Ott, *When Wall Street Met Main Street: The Quest for an Investors' Democracy* (Cambridge, MA: Harvard University Press, 2011), 75–100. However, like in Britain, investment in the United States tied women directly to the expansion of imperial activity. Hudson, *Bankers and Empire*, 207.
79. Thomas Hanchett uses the term "sorting" to describe how Charlotte, North Carolina, changed from a "salt and pepper" pattern to wedges of a pie. A nearly identical morphology characterized Baltimore. Thomas Hanchett, *Sorting the New South City: Race,*

Class, and Urban Development in Charlotte, 1875–1975 (Chapel Hill: University of North Carolina Press, 1998), 224.

80. "Real Estate Transaction 1," *Baltimore Sun*, July 9, 1891, 4; "Untitled," *Baltimore Sun*, May 9, 1892, 4. Real estate speculators also routinely used the courts to litigate business disputes. This task usually fell to Laura Lee Capron, whose name appeared alone in court records. "Baltimore County," *Baltimore Sun*, October 6, 1890; "A Suit for $30,000," *Baltimore Sun*, September 3, 1891.

81. Mary P. Ryan, *Taking the Land to Make the City: A Bicoastal History of North America* (Austin: University of Texas Press, 2019), 73–75.

82. Builders manipulated ground rent in various ways, including by turning the rights to ground rent into a financial instrument to sell on its own. For more on the ground rent system, see Mary Ellen Hayward and Charles Belfoure, *The Baltimore Rowhouse* (Princeton, NJ: Princeton Architectural Press, 2001), 83–166; Mary Ellen Hayward, "Urban Vernacular Architecture in Nineteenth-Century Baltimore," *Winterarthur Portfolio* 16, no. 1 (Spring 1981): 40; Martha J. Vill, "Building Enterprise in Late Nineteenth-Century Baltimore," *Journal of Historical Geography* 12, no. 2 (1986): 170, 173–174.

83. Hayward, *Baltimore's Alley Houses*, 32–33.

84. Joseph Arnold, "Suburban Growth and Municipal Annexation," *Maryland Historical Magazine* 73, no. 2 (1978): 111–114; "The Belt Annexation: A Boom for City Extension, a Delegation of Sixty," *Baltimore Sun*, March 1, 1888, 1; Sherry Olson, *Baltimore: The Building of an American City* (Baltimore, MD: Johns Hopkins University Press, 1980), 217–219.

85. Capron was invited to Maryland's capitol to lobby the state senate to pass the bill. "Belt Annexation," 1; "For Better Roads: Progress of the Movement at Govanstown, Baltimore County," *Baltimore Sun*, August 1, 1890, 4.

86. Olson, *Baltimore*, 217.

87. Real estate transactions increased so suddenly and voluminously following annexation that Sherry Olson discusses it in terms often reserved for American expansion and European colonialism. She describes annexation as a Baltimore "land boom" and a "scramble." Olson, *Baltimore*, 217.

88. William S. Worley, *J. C. Nichols and the Shaping of Kansas City* (Columbia: University of Missouri Press, 1990), 53.

89. Box 204, Folder 19, Roland Park Company Records, MS 504, Special Collections, Johns Hopkins University (hereafter RPC Records).

90. Worley, *J. C. Nichols*, 52.

91. Thomas was a director of the Maryland Life Insurance Company, the Mercantile Trust and Deposit Company, the Safe Deposit and Trust Company, and the Savings Bank of Baltimore. He also served as president of the Mercantile-Mechanics First National Bank.

92. Bound Meeting Minutes, 1891–1903, Box 178, Folder 1, RPC Records. These tracts were called Oakland, Woodlawn, Hepburn, the Armath tract, the Maynadier tract, and Poplar Hill. Jarvis and Conklin discussed the arrangement in Jarvis and Conklin to Bouton, February 18, 1892, Box 2, Folder 27, RPC Records.

93. Bound Meeting Minutes, 1891–1903.

94. Vill, "Building Enterprise," 169.

2. INFRASTRUCTURE

1. Edward Bouton to Alfred Fryer, quoted in James Waesche, *Crowning the Gravelly Hill: A History of the Roland Park–Guilford–Homeland District* (Baltimore, MD: Maclay and Associates, 1987), 46.

2. Seth Rockman, "What Makes the History of Capitalism Newsworthy?," *Journal of the Early Republic* 34, no. 3 (Fall 2014): 448. Two alternative formulations to infrastructure are the technologies of exclusion and the arsenal of exclusion. Both encompass a wide range of legal, political, and planning strategies that reinforce each other in the service of creating and enforcing housing segregation. For technologies, see Gerald Frug, "The Legal Technology of Exclusion in Metropolitan America," in *The New Suburban History*, ed. Kevin Kruse and Thomas Sugrue (Chicago: University of Chicago Press, 2006), 205–219. For arsenal, see Tobias Armborst, Daniel D'Oca, and Georgeen Theodore, *The Arsenal of Exclusion and Inclusion* (Barcelona: Actar, 2017).

3. Elizabeth Blackmar, "Accountability for Public Health: Regulating the Housing Market in Nineteenth-Century New York City," in *Hives of Sickness: Public Health and Epidemics in New York City*, ed. David Rosner (New York: Museum of the City of New York, 1995), 45; Jon C. Teaford, *Municipal Revolution in America: Origins of Modern Urban Government, 1650–1825* (Chicago: University of Chicago Press, 1975), 102–109.

4. Nayan Shah, *Contagious Divides: Epidemics and Race in San Francisco's Chinatown* (Berkeley: University of California Press, 2001), 51–53; David Freund, *Colored Property: State Policy and White Racial Politics in Suburban America* (Chicago: University of Chicago Press, 2007), 69; Margaret Garb, *City of American Dreams: A History of Home Ownership and Housing in Chicago, 1871–1919* (Chicago: University of Chicago Press, 2005), 32, 62–63. On nuisance as a legal category, see Christine Meisner Rosen, "'Knowing' Industrial Pollution: Nuisance Law and the Power of Tradition in a Time of Rapid Economic Change, 1840–1864," *Environmental History* 8, no. 4 (October 2003): 565–566.

5. Shah, *Contagious Divides*, 51–53; Mary Ryan, *Taking the Land to Make the City: A Bicoastal History of North America* (Austin: University of Texas Press, 2019), 167; Seth Rockman, *Scraping By: Wage Labor, Slavery, and Survival in Early Baltimore* (Baltimore, MD: Johns Hopkins University Press, 2009), 131. N. D. B. Connolly writes about the tensions among different groups in Miami. These differences were papered over by white violence and Jim Crow property relations, both of which reproduced these people as black. N. D. B. Connolly, *A World More Concrete: Real Estate and the Remaking of Jim Crow South Florida* (Chicago: University of Chicago Press, 2014), 54–62; Warwick Anderson, *Colonial Pathologies: American Tropical Medicine, Race, and Hygiene in the Philippines* (Durham, NC: Duke University Press, 2006), 197.

6. Shah, *Contagious Divides*, 73.

7. Michael Jones-Correa, "The Origins and Diffusion of Racial Restrictive Covenants," *Political Science Quarterly* 115, no. 4 (Winter 2000–2001): 541; Marc Weiss, *The Rise of the Community Builders: The American Real Estate Industry and Urban Land Planning* (New York: Columbia, 1987), 80–99; Robert M. Fogelson, *Bourgeois Nightmares: Suburbia, 1870–1930* (New Haven, CT: Yale University Press, 2005), 247–272.

8. Cindy I-Fen Cheng, *Citizens of Asian America: Democracy and Race During the Cold War* (New York: New York University Press, 2013), 25–26; Mary Ting Yi Lui, *The Chinatown Trunk Mystery: Murder, Miscegenation, and Other Dangerous Encounters in Turn-of-the-Century New York City* (Princeton, NJ: Princeton University Press, 2005), 67.

9. Dorceta E. Taylor, *The Rise of the American Conservation Movement: Power, Privilege, and Environmental Protection* (Durham, NC: Duke University Press, 2016), 18.

10. Bound Meeting Minutes, 1891–1903, Box 178, Folder 1, Roland Park Company Records, MS 504, Special Collections, Johns Hopkins University (hereafter RPC Records).

11. William S. Worley, *J. C. Nichols and the Shaping of Kansas City: Innovation in Planned Residential Communities* (Columbia: University of Missouri Press, 1993), 54.

12. Individual lots had remained the focus of deed restrictions dating back to mid-eighteenth-century England, when aristocrats leased parts of their estates for decades at a time and imposed restrictions to ensure the land remained valuable to lease again once the term ended. The short-term emphasis came from the needs of American builders. Fogelson, *Bourgeois Nightmares*, 43, 46.

13. Bouton to Waring, January 2, 1892, Box 155, RPC Records; Harry G. Schlack, "Planning Roland Park, 1891–1910," *Maryland Historical Magazine* 6, no. 4 (Winter 1972): 419.

14. Waring to Bouton, January 6, 1892, Box 2, Folder 15, RPC Records; Waring to Bouton, January 18, 1892, Box 2, Folder 15, RPC Records.

15. Blackmar, "Accountability for Public Health," 45; Sonia Hirt, *Zoned in the USA: The Origins and Implications of American Land-Use Regulation* (Ithaca, NY: Cornell University Press, 2014), 118.

16. Ryan, *Taking the Land*, 131–132.

17. Blackmar, "Accountability for Public Health," 45.

18. William J. Clark quoted in "Will Complete Waring's Report," *Brooklyn Daily Eagle*, October 31, 1898, 3. For more on the links between imperialism and suburban developments including Roland Park at the turn of the century, see Carl Nightingale, *Segregation: A Global History* (Chicago: University of Chicago Press, 2012), 320, 324.

19. George Whitlock and Samuel D. Schmucker to Edward Bouton, October 5, 1893, Box 2, Folder 7, RPC Records; Antero Pietila, *Not in My Neighborhood: How Bigotry Shaped a Great American City* (Chicago: Ivan R. Dee, 2010), 35; Fogelson, *Bourgeois Nightmares*, 62; *Barbier v. Connolly*, 113 U.S. 27 (1885).

20. Hirt, *Zoned in the USA*, 130; Shah, *Contagious Divides*, 65–66. According to Cindy I-Fen Cheng, "restrictions leveled against the Chinese during the late nineteenth century became antecedents to the prohibitions directed against blacks during the first part of the twentieth century." Cheng, *Citizens of Asian America*, 27.

21. William R. Ming Jr., "Racial Restrictions and the Fourteenth Amendment: The Restrictive Covenant Cases," *University of Chicago Law Review* 16, no. 2 (1949): 203n1.

22. *Gandolfo v. Hartman*, 49 F. 181 (1892); Taylor, *The Rise of the American Conservation Movement*, 18; Cheng, *Citizens of Asian America*, 26–27. The court was likely constructing the judicial enforcement of a contract as government action, making it subject to the Fourteenth Amendment. Harold Kahen, "Validity of Anti-Negro Restrictive Covenants: A Reconsideration of the Problem," *University of Chicago Law Review* 12, no. 2 (1945): 199.

23. Fogelson, *Bourgeois Nightmares*, 46; Edward Bouton to George Waring, September 3, 1891, Box 155, RPC Records.

24. Contract of Sale, Box 272, Folder 32, RPC Records.

25. See, for example, Baltimore City Ordinance No. 52 (1858); Maryland Public Local Laws (1860), Article 4; Baltimore City Ordinance No. 72 (1860); Baltimore City Ordinance No. 33 (1860).

26. On the matter of how infrastructure affected value, Margaret Garb cites examples of developers in Chicago in the nineteenth century laying out infrastructure into order to raise the value of their holdings. Garb, *City of American Dreams*, 88.

27. Kessler to Bouton, May 17, 1891, Box 1, Folder 24, RPC Records.

28. "Classified Ad Six," *Baltimore Sun*, June 6, 1892.

29. Bouton to Stuart and Young, November 3, 1898, Box 5, Folder 17, RPC Records.

30. Bouton to Stuart and Young, November 3, 1898.

31. Bouton to Stuart and Young, October 12, 1898, Box 5, Folder 17, RPC Records.

32. *Roland Park Company v. Charles W. Hull et al.*, 92 Md. 301, 48 A. 366 (1901).

33. Schlack, "Planning Roland Park," 422.

34. Bouton to Jarvis and Conklin, September 14, 1893, quoted in Schlack, "Planning Roland Park," 419.

35. *Baltimore Daily News*, June 1892. James Waesche also notes the disappearance of proximity as an emphasized feature. Waesche, *Crowning the Gravelly Hill*, 55.

36. Fryer to Jarvis-Conklin Mortgage Trust Company, June 25, 1892, Box 2, Folder 28, RPC Records.

37. T. Cole, "Science of Health: Its History and Progress," *Sanitary World*, December 27, 1884, 618; Executive Council of the International Health Exhibition, *The Health Exhibition Literature*, vol. 7, *Health Related to Civic Life* (London: William Clowes and Sons, 1884), 428.

38. "Issues, 1891," *Prospectuses of Public Companies and etc. Advertised in the Times* (London: Times, February 7, 1891), 13.

39. See, for example, "Classified Ad 13," *Baltimore Sun*, June 29, 1867, 3.

40. Kenneth Jackson, *Crabgrass Frontier: The Suburbanization of the United States* (Oxford: Oxford University Press, 1985), 85–86; Dolores Hayden, *Building Suburbia: Green Fields and Urban Growth, 1820–1900* (New York: Pantheon, 2003), 26–27; John W. Reps, *The Making of Urban America: A History of City Planning in the United States* (Princeton, NJ: Princeton University Press, 1965), 339–350.

41. Quoted in Christopher G. Boone, "Obstacles to Infrastructure Provision: The Struggle to Build Comprehensive Sewer Works in Baltimore," *Historical Geography* 31 (2003): 151.

42. "Classified Ad 6," *Baltimore Sun*, June 6, 1892, 1.

43. *Baltimore Daily News*, February 18, 1892, quoted in Waesche, *Crowning the Gravelly Hill*, 55.

44. "Display Ad 13," *Baltimore Sun*, July 25, 1895.

45. Edmonds to Bouton, June 12, 1894, Box 1, Folder 13, RPC Records.

46. Edmonds to Bouton, July 27, 1894, Box 1, Folder 13, RPC Records.

47. "Roland Park, an Incomparable Suburb," *Weekly Herald*, July 24, 1892.

48. Bouton to Jarvis, October 13, 1893, Box 290, RPC Records. Quoted in Waesche, *Crowning the Gravelly Hill*, 60.

49. Robert Rydell, *All the World's a Fair: Visions of Empire and American International Exhibitions, 1876–1916* (Chicago: University of Chicago Press, 1984), 107–108.

50. Olmsted Brothers to Bouton, December 20, 1898, Box 5, Folder 20, RPC Records.

51. Roy Rosenzweig and Elizabeth Blackmar, *The Park and the People: A History of Central Park* (Ithaca, NY: Cornell University Press, 1992), 88–91.

52. Olmsted Brothers to Bouton, September 17, 1898, Box 6, Folder 26A, RPC Records.

53. "How Roland Park Was Founded and Developed," *Baltimore Sun*, December 27, 1908, 24; Henry Rodgers to Bouton, August 8, 1891, Box 2, Folder 5, RPC Records.

54. Manuscript Census, 1900; Bouton to O. Parker Baker, March 10, 1898, Box 156, Vol. 2, RPC Records.

55. Bouton to Baker, March 10, 1898.

56. Baker to Bouton, April 30, 1898, Box 5, Folder 11, RPC Records; Baker to Bouton, June 22, 1898, Box 5, Folder 11, RPC Records; Baker to Bouton, July 13, 1898, Box 5, Folder 11, RPC Records.

57. Bouton to Baker, June 24, 1898, Box 156, Vol. 2, RPC Records.

58. Baker to Bouton, May 10, 1898, Box 156, Vol. 2, RPC Records; Bouton to Baker, May 11, 1898, Box 156, Vol. 2, RPC Records; Bouton to Baker, July 14, 1898, Box 156, Vol. 2, RPC Records.

59. Roland Park Company Ledger, 64, Box 190, Folder 1, RPC Records.

60. Baker to Bouton, May 7, 1898, Box 5, Folder 11, RPC Records; Baker to Bouton, July 21, 1898, Box 5, Folder 11, RPC Records.

61. Baker to Bouton, July 17, 1898, Box 6, Folder 1, RPC Records.

62. Bouton to the Olmsted Brothers, January 27, 1898, Box 156, RPC Records.

63. Bouton to Stuart and Young, October 12, 1898, Box 5, Folder 17, RPC Records.

64. Bouton to Baker, October 24, 1899, Box 156, Vol. 4, RPC Records.

65. Bouton to Baker, July 14, 1898, Box 156, Vol. 2, RPC Records.

66. Marchant to Hynson, March 9, 1908, Box 33, Folder 22, RPC Records.

67. "Killed Every Dog in Town," *Baltimore Sun*, February 9, 1908, 20.

68. William F. Holmes, "Whitecapping: Agrarian Violence in Mississippi, 1902–1906," *Journal of Southern History* 35, no. 2 (May 1969): 166.

69. James Holechek, *Baltimore's Two Cross Keys Villages: One Black, One White* (Lincoln, NE: iUniverse, 2004), 30.

70. Holechek, *Baltimore's Two Cross Keys Villages*, 30.

71. "How Roland Park Was Founded and Developed," 24.

72. Bouton to E. R. Eliss, June 25, 1907, Box 27, Folder 12, RPC Records.

73. Marchant to D. W. Egner, September 12, 1908, Box 31, Folder 6, RPC Records.

74. Hirt, *Zoned in the USA*, 121–126.

75. Manuscript Census, 1900; Zimmerman to Bouton, October 2, 1911, Box 59, Folder 23, RPC Records.

76. White workers could be either foreign or native-born, but they came from Ireland, Germany, Great Britain, or, in one case, Switzerland rather than Eastern or Southern Europe. Manuscript Census, 1900.

77. Census 1910, Ward 13, District 218, Sheets 5B and 6A.

78. Tera Hunter, *To 'Joy My Freedom: Southern Black Women's Lives and Labors After the Civil War* (Cambridge, MA: Harvard University Press, 1998), 54.

79. Jackson, *Crabgrass Frontier*, 97–99.

80. Bouton to Stuart and Young, June 28, 1898, Box 5, Folder 17, RPC Records. Bouton and the British investors were uncertain enough about the country club's success that they commissioned a clubhouse that could be converted to a "country hotel" if need be. Bouton to Stuart and Young, June 28, 1898, Box 5, Folder 17, RPC Records.

81. Bouton to Stuart and Young, June 18, 1898, Box 5, Folder 17, RPC Records.

82. Andrew Williamson to Bouton, July 13, 1898, Box 5, Folder 17, RPC Records; Stuart and Young to Bouton, August 1, 1898, Box 5, Folder 17, RPC Records.

83. Purchase by Edward H. Bouton of the Stock of the Roland Park Company Owned by the Lands Trust Company, July 1, 1903, Box 203, Folder 13, RPC Records.

84. Purchase by Edward H. Bouton of the Stock of the Roland Park Company Owned by the Lands Trust Company, July 1, 1903, Box 203, Folder 13, RPC Records. Dividend figure quoted from page 24.

85. Caroline Remington, *Society Visiting List or "Blue Book"* (Baltimore, MD: Lucas Brothers Press, 1906), 376, 424, 428. The Elk Ridge Fox Hunting Club became the Elk Ridge Club. It remained racially segregated until 2005. David Nitkin, "Club Admits Black Member," *Baltimore Sun*, November 11, 2005.

86. Schlack names Garrett and a "group whose social interests centered on the Maryland Club" in the reorganization, but Garrett's involvement did not seem to include becoming a shareholder in 1903. He would later become a Roland Park Company director, along with members of his company, Robert Garrett and Sons. Schlack, "Planning Roland Park," 423.

87. *Baltimore Sun*, April 1, 1905, quoted in Charles Euchner, "The Politics of Sewage Expansion: Baltimore and the Sewerage Question, 1859–1905," *Maryland Historical Magazine* 86 (Fall 1991): 270. The final tally was 37,111 votes in favor to 25,253 against.

88. Robin Einhorn, *Property Rules: Political Economy in Chicago, 1833–1872* (Chicago: University of Chicago Press, 1991), 141; Ryan, *Taking the Land*, 132, 243–244, 254; Matthew

Crenson, *Baltimore: A Political History* (Baltimore, MD: Johns Hopkins University Press, 2017), 333–334.

89. *Annual Report of the Sewerage Commission, 1905* (Baltimore, MD: City Printer, 1906), 10–11, Legislative Reference Library, Baltimore.

90. Many scholars have recognized how Progressive-Era politics was often less about reform than about shoring up class and race status. Among the earliest was Robert Wiebe with *The Search for Order, 1877–1920* (New York: Hill and Wang, 1967).

91. Euchner, "The Politics of Sewage Expansion," 280.

92. *Annual Report of the Sewerage Commission, 1908* (Baltimore, MD: City Printer, 1909), 24, Legislative Reference Library, Baltimore.

93. B. T. Fendall to Mayor Barry Mahool, July 20, 1908, Baltimore Record Group 9-14-103 273 (2), Baltimore City Archives (hereafter BCA).

94. Joseph Shirley to Edward Bouton, October 21, 1911, Box 60, Folder 1, RPC Records.

95. Quick to Marchant, August 14, 1911, Box 59, Folder 2, RPC Records.

96. Meeting minutes of the Sewerage Commission, BCA BRG 9-14-15-4.

97. See, for example, *Annual Report of the Sewerage Commission, 1905*, 32, and *Annual Report of the Sewerage Commission, 1906* (Baltimore, MD: City Printer, 1907), 43, Legislative Reference Library, Baltimore.

98. Boone, "Obstacles to Infrastructure Provision," 164.

99. Edward Bouton to Calvin Hendrick, February 7, 1908, BCA BRG 9-14-5-1. The city's Department of Law established the power of the Sewerage Commission to determine the "location and character" of local sewers leading up to "private households" whether or not the commission actually built them. Private drains did not come under the purview of the commission, but it facilitated the commission adopting them into the larger sewer system. The Roland Park Company did not have to seek out Sewerage Commission specifications, but in the interest of city cooperation it decided to facilitate integration.

100. Meeting minutes, November 4, 1908, BCA BRG 9-14-5-1.

101. Meeting minutes, May 6, 1908, BCA BRG 9-14-5.

102. Meeting minutes, April 8, 1909, BCA BRG 9-14-5.

103. BCA BRG 9-14-5. Also see various letters in the Roland Park Company Records, especially in Boxes 39, 41, 59, and 60.

104. Meeting minutes, November 1, 1910, BCA BRG 9-14-5.

105. Bouton to the Sewerage Commission, November 7, 1910 Box 41, Folder 7, RPC Records; Meeting minutes, December 20, 1910, BCA BRG 9-14-5.

106. *Annual Report of the Sewerage Commission, 1907*, 5, Legislative Reference Library, Baltimore.

107. Palmer to Bouton and Frederick Olmsted Jr., 1910, Box 40, Folder 18, RPC Records.

108. Peter James Hudson, *Bankers and Empire: How Wall Street Colonized the Caribbean* (Chicago: University of Chicago Press, 2017), 31.

109. Michael E. Neagle, *America's Forgotten Colony: Cuba's Isle of Pines* (Cambridge: Cambridge University Press, 2016), 152–155.

3. BOUNDARIES

1. Antero Pietila, *Not in My Neighborhood: How Bigotry Shaped a Great American City* (Chicago: Ivan R. Dee, 2010), 8; Dennis P. Halpin, "'The Struggle for Land and Liberty': Segregation, Violence, and African American Resistance in Baltimore, 1898–1918," *Journal of Urban History* 44, no. 4 (July 2018): 691–693.

2. N. D. B. Connolly, *A World More Concrete: Real Estate and the Remaking of Jim Crow South Florida* (Chicago: University of Chicago Press, 2014), 34, 38, 52–53; David M. P. Freund, *Colored Property: State Policy and White Racial Politics in Suburban America* (Chicago: University of Chicago Press, 2007), 14–15; Elaine Lewinnek, *The Working Man's Reward: Chicago's Early Suburbs and the Roots of American Sprawl* (New York: Oxford University Press, 2014), 153–154; Thomas Sugrue, *The Origins of the Urban Crisis: Race and Inequality in Postwar Detroit* (Princeton, NJ: Princeton University Press, 1996), 24.

3. Historians agree that it was the first comprehensive segregation ordinance in the United States. Christopher Silver, "The Racial Origins of Zoning in American Cities," in *Urban Planning and the African American Community: In the Shadows*, ed. June Manning Thomas and Marsha Ritzdorf (Thousand Oaks, CA: Sage, 1997), 26; Garrett Power, "Apartheid, Baltimore Style: The Residential Segregation Ordinances of 1910–1913," *Maryland Law Review* 42 (1983): 289; Gretchen Boger, "The Meaning of Neighborhood in the Modern City: Baltimore's Residential Segregation Ordinances, 1910–1913," *Journal of Urban History* 35, no. 2 (January 2009): 236.

4. Quoted in Silver, "The Racial Origins of Zoning" 26–27.

5. Carl Nightingale, "The Transnational Contexts of Early Twentieth-Century American Urban Segregation," *Journal of Social History* 39, no. 3 (Spring 2006): 667.

6. "Baltimore Tries Drastic Plan of Race Segregation," *New York Times*, December 25, 1910, SM2; Matthew Crenson, *Baltimore: A Political History* (Baltimore, MD: Johns Hopkins University Press, 2017), 340.

7. Glenda Gilmore, *Gender and Jim Crow: Women and the Politics of White Supremacy in North Carolina, 1896–1920* (Chapel Hill: University of North Carolina Press, 1996), 21. Quoted in Elizabeth A. Herbin-Triant, *Threatening Property: Race, Class, and Campaigns to Legislate Jim Crow Neighborhoods* (New York: Columbia University Press, 2019), 114.

8. Herbin-Triant, *Threatening Property*, 123.

9. Herbin-Triant, *Threatening Property*, 125.

10. Hawkins paid at least $2,000 for a property that had been valued at $2,400 some years earlier. Pietila, *Not in My Neighborhood*, 18. This price was a sign that property values had not yet declined precipitously, or, more likely, that Hawkins had paid an inflated price, as was typical of the first black buyers in a predominantly white block. See, for example, Kevin Boyle, *Arc of Justice: A Saga of Race, Civil Rights, and Murder in the Jazz Age* (New York: Henry Holt and Company, 2004), 146.

11. Pietila, *Not in My Neighborhood*, 35; Power, "Apartheid, Baltimore Style," 304.

12. Helen Monchow conducted an early study of deed restrictions and found that racial restrictions seldom appeared in the oldest developments. Helen Monchow, *The Use of*

Deed Restrictions in Subdivision Development (Chicago: Institute for Research in Land Economics and Public Utilities, 1928), 50. This study should be used with caution. For example, table 1 lists nuisances prohibited in each restrictive covenant sampled, but Guilford's race clause, discussed later in this chapter, is not included. It is listed separately in a section about racial restrictions (28).

13. Herbin-Triant, *Threatening Property*, 128.

14. Connolly, *A World More Concrete*; Quincy T. Mills, *Cutting Along the Color Line: Black Barbers and Barber Shops in America* (Philadelphia: University of Pennsylvania Press, 2013); Tiffany Gill, *Beauty Shop Politics: African American Women's Activism in the Beauty Industry* (Urbana: University of Illinois Press, 2010).

15. Pietila, *Not in My Neighborhood*, 16; Power, "Apartheid, Baltimore Style," 310–311.

16. On international impact, see Carl Nightingale, *Segregation: A Global History* (Chicago: University of Chicago Press, 2012), 306.

17. James Waesche, *Crowning the Gravelly Hill: A History of the Roland Park–Guilford–Homeland District* (Baltimore, MD: Maclay and Associates, 1987), 89.

18. Waesche, *Crowning the Gravelly Hill*, 23. The exact acreage depends on how it is counted; 336 acres were platted but not all of this was developed as Guilford. Waesche puts the figure at 296 (89).

19. "Preliminary Draft of Proposed Restrictions for Guilford," Box 203, Folder 30, Roland Park Company Records, MS 504, Special Collections, Johns Hopkins University (hereafter RPC Records).

20. Deed Agreement and Restrictions for Guilford, Box 265, RPC Records.

21. Crenson, *Baltimore*, 336–339; Joseph Heathcott, "Black Archipelago: Politics and Civic Life in the Jim Crow City," *Journal of Social History* 38, no. 3 (Spring 2005): 714; Thomas Hanchett, *Sorting Out the New South City: Race, Class, and Urban Development in Charlotte, 1875–1975* (Chapel Hill: University of North Carolina Press, 1998), 81–87, 210; Michelle Alexander, *The New Jim Crow: Mass Incarceration in the Age of Colorblindness* (New York: New Press, 2010), 33–35.

22. "Preliminary Draft of Proposed Restrictions for Guilford."

23. Baltimore City Liber S. C. L. 2829 Folio 1; Baltimore County Liber W. P. C. 412, Folio 177, June 26, 1913, Maryland State Archives.

24. Edward Bouton to William H. Grafflin, February 20, 1911, Box 162, Folder 7, RPC Records.

25. "Preliminary Draft of Proposed Restrictions for Guilford."

26. Garrett Power, "The Unwisdom of Allowing City Growth to Work Out on Its Own," *Maryland Law Review* 47, no. 3 (1988): 651; Bouton to Robert Garrett, February 20, 1913, Box 165, Folder 6, RPC Records.

27. Roland Park Company, *Guilford: Information for Buyers, Owners, and Architects* (Baltimore, MD: Roland Park Company, 1914), 20, https://archive.org/details/cu31924014929719 /page/n5.

28. Clearwater Deed Restriction, Box 18, John Nolen Pamphlet Collection #6333, Rare and Manuscript Division, Cornell University; Bouton to Nolen, July 9, 1915, Box 291, RPC

Records; Fred Todd to Edward Bouton, March 31, 1913, Box 207, Folder 32, RPC Records; Todd to Bouton, August 6, 1913, Box 207, Folder 32, RPC Records.

29. William Worley, *J. C. Nichols and the Shaping of Kansas City: Innovation in Planned Residential Communities* (Columbia: University of Missouri Press, 1990), 141–143.

30. Bouton to George B. Ford, August 11, 1911, Box 61, Folder 10, RPC Records.

31. "Subdivisions and the Best Manner of Handling Them: Text of Great Paper by J. Nichols of Kansas City at the National Convention," *National Real Estate Journal* 5, no. 6 (1912): 460.

32. C. L. Strobel to Bouton, May 22, 1911, Box 45, RPC Records.

33. David Freund calls early planning courses "a benchmark of planning's new orientation and prominence." Freund, *Colored Property*, 50.

34. George B. Ford to Bouton, July 21, 1911, Box 61, Folder 10, RPC Records; Bouton to Ford, August 11, 1911, Box 61, Folder 10, RPC Records; George B. Ford, "Lecture Course on City Planning," 1911–1912, John Nolen Pamphlet Collection #6337, Box 2, Folder 2-1, Rare and Manuscript Division, Cornell University.

35. Monchow, *The Use of Deed Restrictions*, 27.

36. Monchow, *The Use of Deed Restrictions*, 27, 49. For more on the terms of employment for the Olmsted Brothers, see Paige Glotzer, "The Roland Park Company: The Critical Planning Role of the Olmsted Brothers," *The Olmstedian* 21, no. 1 (2015): 1–2. On Los Angeles–area restrictions against Mexicans, see Steven Bender, *Tierra y Liberdad: Land, Liberty, and Latino Housing* (New York: New York University Press, 2010), 100.

37. David Armenti, "'Is He White or Colored?' Chinese in Baltimore City Public Schools," Maryland Historical Society, August 15, 2013, http://www.mdhs.org/underbelly/2013/08/15/is-he-white-or-colored-chinese-in-baltimore-city-public-schools.

38. "Is He White or Colored?," *Baltimore Sun*, February 19, 1897. For more on Jim Crow segregation and Asian Americans, see Leslie Bow, *Partly Colored: Asian Americans and the Racial Anomaly in the Segregated South* (New York: New York University Press, 2010).

39. Scott Kurashige, *The Shifting Grounds of Race: Black and Japanese Americans in the Making of Multiethnic Los Angeles* (Princeton, NJ: Princeton University Press, 2008), 18.

40. Samuel Kelton Roberts Jr., *Infectious Fear: Politics, Disease, and the Health Effects of Segregation* (Chapel Hill: University of North Carolina Press, 2009), 76–77, 82.

41. Edward Bouton to Robert Garrett and Sons, May 5, 1915, Box 167, Folder 7, RPC Records; Roland Park Company, *Guilford*, 10.

42. Ledger showing Heathbrook rentals, portions of Tuxedo Park and Evergreen had been connected since at least 1904, Box 274, Vol. 7, RPC Records; Richard Marchant Jr. to the law firm of Steele, Semmes, and Cary, June 20, 1904, Box 14, Folders 8–9, RPC Records.

43. "Cross Keys in the Line of Progress," *Roland Park Review*, May 1915, 2.

44. According to Tera Hunter, black women were "the pivots upon which so much of the anxiety about race relations turned in the eyes of black (and white) middle class reformers." Tera Hunter, "Writing of Labor and Love: Gender and African American History's Challenge to Present Day Assumptions and Misinterpretations," *Souls* 18, no. 1 (January–March 2016): 150.

45. Edward Bouton to George Waring, September 23, 1891, Box 155, Vol. 1, RPC Records.

46. DeCoursey Thom to Barry Mahool, August 1, 1908, Box 31, Folder 26, RPC Records.

47. Thom to Mahool, August 1, 1908.

48. Elizabeth Dowling Taylor, *The Original Black Elite: Daniel Murray and the Story of a Forgotten Era* (New York: HarperCollins, 2017), 325.

49. "Display Ad 1," *Baltimore Afro-American*, December 25, 1909, 2.

50. "Display Ad 1"; "The Struggle for Land and Liberty," *Baltimore Afro-American*, November 22, 1913. For genealogy of black property ownership and claims to citizenship, see Connolly, *A World More Concrete*, 11.

51. "Banker Dead," *Baltimore Afro-American*, February 25, 1939, 5. Wilson Park should not be confused with property held by D. S. Wilson since at least the 1870s. The Roland Park Company referred to the latter when they discussed "the Wilson Tract." See, for example, Edward Bouton to John W. Marshall, April 6, 1915, Box 249, Folder 7, RPC Records. Today, the Wilson Tract constitutes the neighborhood of Kernewood.

52. Charles Belfoure, "Pride Flows Forth from Historic Past," *Baltimore Sun*, August 26, 2001; Connolly, *A World More Concrete*, 8–11.

53. "Display Ad 6," *Baltimore Afro-American*, September 22, 1917, 8.

54. "Display Ad 6."

55. "Display Ad 12," *Baltimore Afro-American*, January 31, 1919.

56. "Display Ad 6"; Sara Gantz, "A Push to Recognize Founder of Baltimore's Historic Wilson Park," *Baltimore Sun*, July 11, 2017.

57. National Register of Historic Places, Lauraville Historic District, Baltimore City, Maryland B-4301, Section 8, 7.

58. Eric L. Holcomb, *The City as Suburb: A History of Northeast Baltimore Since 1660* (Santa Fe, NM: Center for American Places, 2005), 215–217; Power, "Apartheid, Baltimore Style," 308.

59. *Diggs v. Morgan College*, 133 Md. 264, 1918.

60. Holcomb, *The City as Suburb*, 218.

61. Joseph Arnold, "Suburban Growth and Municipal Annexation," *Maryland Historical Magazine* 73, no. 2 (1978): 120.

62. Arnold, "Suburban Growth and Municipal Annexation," 121.

63. Harry Benzinger to Bouton, December 14, 1915, Box 211, Folder 4, RPC Records.

64. Francis K. Carey to Bouton, February 4, 1916, Box 70, Folder 5, RPC Records.

65. Elmer Haile to Bouton, August 24, 1914, Box 211, Annexation Folder 4, RPC Records.

66. Arnold argues that Baltimore County never experienced the public services crisis that might be expected of an area with rapidly increasing population and relatively weak county governance, due to the clout of neighborhood organizations that enabled them to lobby for resources. They also could generally rely on "private" infrastructure such as Roland Park's sewers. While this makes sense in the case of residents in a place like Roland Park, it would not seem to hold true for everyone. Arnold, "Suburban Growth and Municipal Annexation," 117.

67. Pamphlet, Box 211, Folder 3, RPC Records.

68. Names were taken from S. S. Field, "For a Greater Baltimore" and matched against Caroline Remington, *Society Visiting List or "Blue Book"* (Baltimore, MD: Lucas Brothers Press, 1906). The clubs were the Baltimore Country Club, the Elk Ridge Club, and the Maryland Club. S. S. Field, "For a Greater Baltimore," Box 211, Folder 2, RPC Records.

69. Field, "For a Greater Baltimore," 37–38, 41–42.

70. "All Ready for Final Drive," *Baltimore Afro-American*, October 27, 1917, 3.

71. "Mid-Year Conf. Closes," *Baltimore Afro-American*, October 20, 1917, 1.

72. "Saturday, September 8, 1917," *Baltimore Afro-American*, September 8, 1917, 4. Despite the *Afro*'s skepticism that the white annexationists would effect positive change for black Baltimoreans, its editorial board supported annexation. See, for example, "City Upheld in Annexation Fight by the Court of Appeals," *Baltimore Afro-American*, August 2, 1918, 4.

73. See, for example, Elizabeth Tandy Shermer, *Sunbelt Capitalism: Phoenix and the Transformation of American Politics* (Philadelphia: University of Pennsylvania Press, 2013), 192–193.

74. Power, "Apartheid, Baltimore Style," 315.

75. The office of Hawkins and McMechen was located at 21 E. Saratoga Street. Black attorneys displaced from the nearby 222 Courtland Street office for Preston Gardens moved into 21 E. Saratoga Street.

76. George C. Wright, "The NAACP and Residential Segregation in Louisville, Kentucky, 1914–1917," *The Register of the Kentucky Historical Society*, 78 no. 1 (Winter 1980): 39–40.

77. "Will File Brief for Segregation," *Baltimore Sun*, March 6, 1917, 16; "Segregation Suit Up Today," *Baltimore Sun*, April 27, 1917, 5.

78. "Confer on Segregation," *Baltimore Sun*, March 22, 1918, 6.

79. Dennis P. Halpin, *A Brotherhood of Liberty: Black Reconstruction and Its Legacies in Baltimore* (Philadelphia: University of Pennsylvania Press, 2019), 175.

80. "Annexation in a Nutshell," *Baltimore Sun*, March 22, 1918, 16.

81. "New Segregation Plan," *Baltimore Sun*, July 2, 1918, 14. Commissioner John Blake referred blacks employed by whites and as live-in laborers in white homes. A previous assistant health commissioner, Dr. Hampton Jones, enumerated the types of employment Blake likely had in mind in a list of occupations of black tuberculosis victims: drivers, laundresses, seamstresses, and servants. Quoted in Roberts, *Infectious Fear*, 171.

82. Freund, *Colored Property*, 46; Silver, "The Racial Origins of Zoning," 23; Power, "The Unwisdom of Allowing City Growth," 669–670.

83. Jon Peterson, "The Birth of Organized City Planning in the United States, 1909–1910," *Journal of the American Planning Association* 75, no. 2 (Spring 2009): 123–131; Freund, *Colored Property*, 51–54.

84. *Buchanan v. Warley*, 245 U.S. 60 (1917), 10.

85. The Supreme Court ruled that states can use police power to regulate land use in *Hadacheck v. Sebastian*. It was not until the 1926 ruling in *Village of Euclid v. Ambler Realty Corporation* that land-use zoning became unambiguously legal.

86. "Some Legislation, Akin to New York's 'Zone Law,' Is Needed to Protect Valuable Property from Invasions That Are Ruinous to Property Values," *Baltimore Municipal Journal*, October 27, 1916, 4; Freund, *Colored Property*, 61.
87. Power, "The Unwisdom of Allowing City Growth," 653, 660, 663.

4. STANDARDS

1. Guy T. O. Hollyday, "Making Use of the Broker in Subdivision Selling," *National Real Estate Journal* 30, no. 18 (September 2, 1929): 28.
2. Guy T. O. Hollyday, Draft Notes for Making Use of the Broker in Subdivision Selling, Box 245, Roland Park Company Records, MS 504, Special Collections, Johns Hopkins University (hereafter RPC Records).
3. Andrew Abbott, *The System of Professions: An Essay on the Division of Expert Labor* (Chicago: University of Chicago Press, 1988).
4. Marc Weiss, *The Rise of the Community Builders: The American Real Estate Industry and Urban Land Planning* (New York: Columbia University Press, 1987), 17–78; David Freund, *Colored Property: State Policy and White Racial Politics in Suburban America* (Chicago: University of Chicago Press, 2007), 51–98; Jeffrey Hornstein, *A Nation of Realtors: A Cultural History of the Twentieth-Century American Middle Class* (Durham, NC: Duke University Press, 2005), 53–117; Janet Pearl Davies, *Real Estate in American History* (Washington, DC: Public Affairs Press, 1958), 53–127; Rose Helper, *Racial Policies and Practices of Real Estate Brokers* (Minneapolis: University of Minnesota Press, 1969), 201–215.
5. In the 1920s, membership in NAREB depended on admission to a local real estate board. Decisions to admit women varied in the 1920s from board to board, but by and large they excluded women. Even though the decision was a local one, at national meetings men debated the inclusion of women. Hornstein, *A Nation of Realtors*, 163–165.
6. Scott Kurashige, *The Shifting Grounds of Race: Black and Japanese Americans in the Making of Multiethnic Los Angeles* (Princeton, NJ: Princeton University Press, 2008), 14.
7. Freund, *Colored Property*, 74–75.
8. One is undated.
9. Nayan Shah, *Contagious Divides: Epidemics and Race in San Francisco's Chinatown* (Berkeley: University of California Press, 2001), 45–76. Shah notes that the manner of regulation of bodies and space was inherently gendered.
10. Natalia Molina, *Fit to Be Citizens? Public Health and Race in Los Angeles, 1879–1939* (Berkeley: University of California Press, 2006), 49.
11. Exceptions include David Freund, who looks at both Detroit and the national association, as well as Marc Weiss, who has chapters on the national association and the Los Angeles real estate board but treats them as parallel rather than interrelated stories prior to the Great Depression.
12. Hornstein, *A Nation of Realtors*, 13–16; Davies, *Real Estate in American History*, 26, 36–37, 55–56; Weiss, *The Rise of the Community Builders*, 5, 21; Elaine Lewinnek, *The Working*

Man's Reward: Chicago's Early Suburbs and the Roots of American Sprawl (New York: Oxford University Press, 2014), 20.

13. NAREB by-laws article 2, *United Realty* 1, no. 1 (1908), National Association of REALTORS® Library and Archives, Chicago (hereafter NAR Archives).

14. Weiss, *The Rise of the Community Builders*, 24.

15. Davies, *Real Estate in American History*, 63.

16. W. W. Hannan, "The National Association of Real Estate Exchanges," *National Real Estate Journal* 1, no. 1 (March 15, 1910): 1. On NAREB, developers, and professionalization, see Freund, *Colored Property*, 51–98; William S. Worley, *J. C. Nichols and the Shaping of Kansas City* (Columbia: University of Missouri Press, 1990), 89–123; Weiss, *The Rise of the Community Builders*, 17–78; Hornstein, *A Nation of Realtors*, 53–117; Helper, *Racial Policies and Practices*, 201–215; and Davies, *Real Estate in American History*, 201–215.

17. Weiss, *The Rise of the Community Builders*, 13.

18. E. St. Elmo Lewis, "Business Building Power of Advertising in Your Home Town," in *Annals of Real Estate Practice* (Chicago: National Association of Real Estate Boards, 1926), 212.

19. "Come On In, Fellows! The Water's Fine!," *United Realty* 1, no. 1 (June 26, 1908): 1, NAR Archives.

20. "Ethics of the Real Estate Profession," NAR Archives.

21. Jeanne F. Backof and Charles L. Martin, "Historical Perspectives: Development of the Codes of Ethics in the Legal, Medical and Accounting Professions," *Journal of Business Ethics* 10 (1991): 99–110.

22. "Ethics of the Real Estate Profession."

23. Tom Ingersoll, "'Movie' Flashes for Journal Readers," *National Real Estate Journal* 15, no. 5 (May 1917): 94.

24. Worley, *J. C. Nichols and the Shaping of Kansas City*, 91, 128.

25. Freund, *Colored Property*, 51; Jon A. Peterson, "The Birth of Organized City Planning in the United States, 1909–1910," *Journal of the American Planning Association* 75, no. 2 (Spring 2009): 123–133.

26. Freund, *Colored Property*, 52; Weiss, *The Rise of the Community Builders*, 55–58; Worley, *J. C. Nichols and the Shaping of Kansas City*, 91–92.

27. Proceedings of the First Annual Conference of Developers of High-Class Residential Property, 1917, 9–10, Jemison Companies Miscellany, Collection #2838 Rare and Manuscript Division, Cornell University, Ithaca, New York.

28. Proceedings of the Third Annual Conference of Developers of High-Class Residential Property, 1919, 547, Jemison Companies Miscellany, Collection #2838 Rare and Manuscript Division, Cornell University, Ithaca, New York.

29. John Mowbray to Edward Bouton, Box 104, Folder 8, RPC Records.

30. Kenneth Jackson called it "conventional wisdom" among affluent households that it was more difficult to find servants after the First World War. Kenneth Jackson, *Crabgrass Frontier: The Suburbanization of the United States* (New York: Oxford University Press, 1985), 185. He does not differentiate by race or geography.

31. Proceedings of the Third Annual Conference, 553–563.

32. Proceedings of the Third Annual Conference, 553–563.

33. Wiese describes land near or between railroad tracks "or other nuisance-prone land" as common sites for small black communities on the edges of cities at the time. Andrew Wiese, *Places of Their Own: African American Suburbanization in the Twentieth Century* (Chicago: University of Chicago Press, 2005), 17.

34. Proceedings of the Third Annual Conference, 553–563.

35. James Loewen, *Sundown Towns: A Hidden Dimension of American Racism* (New York: New Press, 2005), 113.

36. Proceedings of the Third Annual Conference, 553–563.

37. Proceedings of the Third Annual Conference, 553–563.

38. "Organizations of New Divisions," *National Real Estate Journal* 24, no. 3 (January 29, 1923): 18.

39. "The Fifteenth Annual at San Francisco," *National Real Estate Journal* 23, no. 13 (June 19, 1922): 21; Freund, *Colored Property*, 54–61.

40. Meyer Eiseman, "Small Farm Subdivisions," *National Real Estate Journal* 24, no. 15 (July 16, 1923): 31.

41. For more on Jewish members of NAREB, see Hornstein, *A Nation of Realtors*, 112–113. On Eiseman's religion and family background, see Henry E. Chambers, *A History of Louisiana*, vol. 2 (Chicago: American Historical Society, 1925), 7–8.

42. "Michigan Real Estate Association Holds Conference at Saginaw," *National Real Estate Journal* 23, no. 1 (January 2, 1922): 33–34; "Idaho Realtors Meet," *National Real Estate Journal* 23, no. 6 (March 13, 1922): 30; "Minnesota Associations Takes Lead in Big State Booster Program," *National Real Estate Journal* 24, no. 8 (April 9, 1923): 36; "South Dakota to Form Realty Association," *National Real Estate Journal* 24, no. 23 (November 5, 1923): 21.

43. "Organizations of New Divisions," *National Real Estate Journal* 24, no. 3 (January 29, 1923): 18.

44. Frank D. Chase, "Basic Considerations in Locating Industries," convention speech reprinted in *National Real Estate Journal* 24, no. 15 (July 16, 1923): 28.

45. Mae Ngai, *Impossible Subjects: Illegal Aliens and the Making of Modern America* (Princeton, NJ: Princeton University Press, 2004), 3.

46. Ngai, *Impossible Subjects*, 25; Charlotte Brooks, *Alien Neighbors, Foreign Friends: Asian Americans, Housing, and the Transformation of Urban California* (Chicago: University of Chicago Press, 2009), 58.

47. Proceedings of the Third Annual Conference, 576.

48. Proceedings of the Third Annual Conference, 574–576.

49. Proceedings of the Third Annual Conference, 575–576; Clement Vose, *Caucasians Only: The Supreme Court, the NAACP, and the Restrictive Covenant Cases* (Berkeley: University of California Press, 1959), 25–28.

50. Proceedings of the Third Annual Conference, 577.

51. This theory of succession predated the Chicago School of Sociology's concentric zone theory of urban succession and growth, which Robert Park and Ernest Burgess first published in 1925.

52. Proceedings of the Third Annual Conference, 566.

53. Proceedings of the Third Annual Conference, 579.

54. Proceedings of the Third Annual Conference, 578.

55. Proceedings of the Third Annual Conference, 580; Worley, *J. C. Nichols and the Shaping of Kansas City*, 148–155.

56. Proceedings of the Third Annual Conference, 571.

57. Richard Marchant to Union Credit Company, October 15, 1908, Box 34, Folder 23, RPC Records.

58. Richard Marchant Jr. to Union Credit Company, October 15, 1908, Box 31, Folder 15, RPC Records.

59. Edward Bouton to Joseph Ames, November 7, 1913, Box 166, Folder 5, RPC Records; Bouton to Lilian Welsh, November 7, 1913, Box 166, Folder 5, RPC Records; Bouton to Ames, November 10, 1913, Box 166, Folder 5, RPC Records.

60. Proceedings of the Second Annual Conference of Developers of High-Class Residential Property, 1918, 122–123, Jemison Companies Miscellany, Collection #2838 Rare and Manuscript Division, Cornell University.

61. Exclusion File of Frank Carozza, Box 252, Folder 12, RPC Records.

62. Exclusion File of Frank Carozza.

63. Thomas Guglielmo, *White on Arrival: Italians, Race, Color, and Power in Chicago, 1890–1945* (New York: Oxford University Press, 2003), 7.

64. N. D. B. Connolly, *A World More Concrete: Real Estate and the Making of Jim Crow South Florida* (Chicago: University of Chicago Press, 2014), 58–63; Ngai, *Impossible Subjects*, 38–42. On the category "nonwhite," see Cindy I-Fen Cheng, *Citizens of Asian America: Democracy and Race During the Cold War* (New York: New York University Press, 2013), 21–56.

65. Exclusion File of Mrs. Mildred Wonneman, also known as Mrs. Bracket, Box 252, Folder 12, RPC Records.

66. "Professor Boas of Hopkins Dies at 88," *Baltimore Sun*, March 18, 1980, C1.

67. Hollyday to Joseph S. Ames, November 1926, Box 252, Folder 12, RPC Records.

68. Hollyday to Ames, November 1926.

69. Ames to Hollyday, November 29, 1926, Box 252, Folder 12, RPC Records.

70. Hollyday, note added to November 29 letter from Ames to Hollyday, December 3, 1926, Box 252, Folder 12, RPC Records.

71. Exclusion File of Mr. and Mrs. Charles F. Diehl, Box 252, Folder 12, RPC Records.

72. Note on Melville Felsenheld, Box 252, Folder 12, RPC Records.

73. Exclusion Files of J. Cacome, Vincent DiPaula, and Felice Iula, Box 252, Folder 12, RPC Records; John Mowbray to Edward Bouton, July 27, 1925, Box 104, Folder 8, RPC Records.

74. Exclusion File of M. T. Cavacos, Box 252, Folder 12, RPC Records.

75. Edward Bouton to Joseph Ames, November 7, 1913, Box 166, Folder 5, RPC Records; Bouton to Lilian Welsh, November 7, 1913, Box 166, Folder 5, RPC Records; Bouton to Ames, November 10, 1913, Box 166, Folder 5, RPC Records.

76. For biographical information on Edith McHenry, see "Green Spring Valley Society," *Baltimore Sun*, July 16, 1907; "Miss Dorothy Winants Will Be Honored Guest," *Baltimore Sun*, September 30, 1934; "News of Society," *Baltimore Sun*, November 8, 1913; "Social Calendar," *Baltimore Sun*, April 19, 1914; "Fair Baltimoreans Who Can Drive Their Own Automobiles," *Baltimore Sun*, May 31, 1914; "Society—Fashionable World Take to the Out-of-Doors: Gibson Island to Be Scene of Big Event Formal Opening of New Rendezvous for Society Will Take Place with Elaborate Celebration on Memorial Day," *Baltimore Sun*, May 25, 1924; "Baltimoreans Settling for Winter," *Baltimore Sun*, November 17, 1929; "Edith McHenry," *Baltimore Sun*, December 26, 1973. For Confederate links, see biographical note in the Cary-McHenry Family Papers Collection, MS3085, Maryland Historical Society, Baltimore, which includes information on her brother James Howard McHenry, born in 1892. For link between Edith McHenry and James Howard McHenry, see "Society," *Baltimore Sun*, September 28, 1927. On joining the Roland Park Company, see "Additions to Staff," *Roland Park Company's Magazine* 1, no. 12 (December 1926): 8.

77. Personnel management was a response to Taylorism theorized by women. However, the investigations she conducted had more in common with two lines of work that expanded during the Progressive Era: social work and eugenics fieldwork. Both were largely dominated by educated middle-class and affluent women whose jobs centered on the domestic life and health conditions of their objects of interest. Social workers and eugenics fieldworkers also were often motivated by a Progressive-Era sociomedical view of how race affected behavior. Hornstein, *A Nation of Realtors*, 227n26; Angel Kwolek-Folland, *Engendering Business: Men and Women in the Corporate Office* (Baltimore, MD: Johns Hopkins University Press, 1998), 75; Sharon H. Strom, *Beyond the Typewriter: Gender, Class, and the Origins of Modern American Office Work* (Urbana: University of Illinois Press, 1992), 68–70, 110–112, 120; Alice Wexler, *The Woman Who Walked Into the Sea: Huntington's and the Making of a Genetic Disease* (New Haven, CT: Yale University Press, 2008), 132–150; Amy Sue Bix, "Experiences and Voices of Eugenics Field-Workers: 'Women's Work' in Biology," *Social Studies of Science* 27, no. 4 (1997): 625–668.

78. Exclusion File of William Laukaitis, Box 252, Folder 12, RPC Records.

79. A. G. Morse, "Educate Foreigners to American Citizenship Standards," *National Real Estate Journal* 23, no. 14 (July 3, 1922): 43.

80. The Laukaitis family eventually did live in a Roland Park Company neighborhood. William Laukaitis's obituary mentioned a Homeland house, Homeland being the company's third development, which they opened in 1924. "William Laukaitis, Postmaster, Magistrate," *Baltimore Sun*, October 14, 1990, 6E.

81. Charlotte Brooks details the different outcomes of attempts to discriminate against blacks in San Francisco and Los Angeles. Brooks, *Alien Neighbors*, 30. Of Monchow's limited national sample, two of the three covenants that excluded "Asiatics" or "Mongolians" were in California.

82. As when Edith McHenry called the Laukaitises "foreign," designating the Chows as "Chinese" did not indicate where they were born or how they thought of themselves; it was simply the identity a company employee had assigned to them.

83. On Roland Park Company interactions, see Exclusion File of Dr. and Mrs. Bacon F. Chow, Box 252, Folder 12, RPC Records. For biographical information, see "Dr. Chow, Hopkins Professor, Dies," *Baltimore Sun*, September 28, 1973, A15. On self-described Chinese identity, see Helen Henry, "Maryland Couple Adopts Chinese Twins," *Baltimore Sun*, August 10, 1969, M18. On purchasing a house in Lauraville, see "Real Estate, Business News," *Baltimore Sun*, March 20, 1949, 87.

84. J. C. Nichols, "Responsibilities and Opportunities of a Real Estate Board," in *Proceedings of the General Sessions of the National Association of Real Estate Boards at the Seventeenth Annual Convention* (Chicago: National Association of Real Estate Boards, 1924), 21, quoted in Hornstein, *A Nation of Realtors*, 110; Freund, *Colored Property*, 76.

85. *National Real Estate Journal* 25, no. 8 (April 21, 1924): 167, NAR Archives.

86. Davies, *Real Estate in American History*, 121–124.

87. Hornstein, *A Nation of Realtors*, 84–86; Paul Stark, "Real Estate Education," *Annals of Real Estate Practice* (Chicago: National Association of Real Estate Boards, 1926), 30, NAR Archives; Lewis, "Business Building Power of Advertising."

88. Freund, *Colored Property*, 75–76, 104–120; Hornstein, *A Nation of Realtors*, 84–117; Jennifer Light, *The Nature of Cities: Ecological Visions and the American Urban Professions, 1920–1960* (Baltimore, MD: Johns Hopkins University Press, 2009), 12, 25–60.

89. In a reprint of convention speeches, editor Leo Bozell wrote, "Thus this volume becomes a text book on real estate subdivisions." It is based on "the results they have obtained by application of their theories." Leo Bozell, ed., *Proceedings of the First Annual Convention Conferences of the Homebuilders and Subdividers Division of the National Association of Real Estate Boards* (Chicago: National Association of Real Estate Boards, 1923), 8.

90. L. S. Knight, "Restrictions for the Sub-Division," in Bozell, *Proceedings of the First Annual Convention*, 51.

91. Historians have treated legal rulings as relatively uniform and their adoption by Realtors as a settled question by the 1920s. See, for example, Thomas J. Sugrue, "Jim Crow's Last Stand: The Struggle to Integrate Levittown," in *Second Suburb: Levittown, Pennsylvania*, ed. Dianne Harris (Pittsburgh: University of Pittsburgh Press, 2010), 177.

92. For a condensed version of the bidirectional flow of ideas in the National Association of Real Estate Boards, see Paige Glotzer, "Exclusion in Arcadia: How Developers Circulated Ideas About Discrimination, 1890–1950," *Journal of Urban History* 41, no. 3 (May 2015): 479–494.

93. Report from Irenaeus Shuler to the President and Board of Directors of the National Association of Real Estate Boards, January 1924, NAR Archives.

94. A. John Berge, "How to Build and Use a Prospect File," in *New Selling Ideas for Real Estate Brokers* (Chicago: National Association of Real Estate Boards, 1929), 19.

95. The printer is listed only as "M. & R. Co," with no location. More work on the location and businesses that printed and distributed business forms might yield new information on the formation of professional networks or how business standards developed across professions.

96. See, for example, the illustrated samples in Berge, "How to Build and Use a Prospect File," 21.

97. "Code of Ethics," 1924, 4, NAR Archives. See also Cheng, *Citizens of Asian America*, 29; Freund, *Colored Property*, 15; Hornstein, *A Nation of Realtors*, 107; Thomas Sugrue, *The Origins of the Urban Crisis: Race and Inequality in Postwar Detroit* (Princeton, NJ: Princeton University Press, 1996), 46; Kevin Fox Gotham, *Race, Real Estate, and Uneven Development: The Kansas City Experience, 1900–2000* (Albany: State University of New York Press, 2002), 34–35.

98. Davies, *Real Estate in American History*, 63.

99. "The Seventh Annual Convention," 1914, NAR Archives.

100. Meetings—June 1928, NAR Archives.

101. "The Fifteenth Annual at San Francisco," *National Real Estate Journal* 23, no. 13 (June 19, 1922): 20.

102. "24th Annual Convention, National Asso. of Real Estate Boards Baltimore May 27-28-29-30-1931," Meetings—1931 May (Baltimore, MD), NAR Archives.

103. "24th Annual Convention."

104. "Program of the 24th Annual Convention," pp. 15–16, Meetings—1931 May (Baltimore, MD), NAR Archives.

105. I. Norwood Griscom, "The Job of Selling Real Estate," *Idea Services*, 1929, 2, NAR Archives. The speech bears some resemblance to those given to salesmen in the life insurance industry. See, for example, Kwollek-Folland, *Engendering Business*, 86.

106. Freund, *Colored Property*, 58–59, 93.

5. POLICIES

1. Jennifer Light, *The Nature of Cities: Ecological Visions and the American Urban Professions, 1920–1960* (Baltimore, MD: Johns Hopkins University Press, 2009), 54. Daniel Carpenter calls this ability "reputational uniqueness." If politicians think a group is the only one that can provide policy solutions, then the group has leverage to develop those solutions themselves. This is not to say that NAREB was the only source of real estate knowledge, but that it successfully created that image. Carpenter calls "network-based reputations" the "very essence of state legitimacy." Daniel Carpenter, *The Forging of Bureaucratic Autonomy: Reputations, Networks, and Policy Innovation in Executive Agencies, 1862–1928* (Princeton, NJ: Princeton University Press, 2001), 5.

2. Light, *The Nature of Cities*, 46–47.

3. Wendell E. Pritchett, "The Public Menace of Blight," *Yale Law and Policy Review* 21, no. 1 (2003): 6.

4. Gerald R. Frug, "The Legal Technology of Exclusion in Metropolitan America," in *The New Suburban History*, ed. Kevin Kruse and Thomas Sugrue (Chicago: University of Chicago Press, 2006), 205–219. David Freund describes the Federal Housing Administration as allocating resources on racial terms. David Freund, *Colored Property: State*

Policy and White Racial Politics in Suburban America (Chicago: University of Chicago Press, 2007), 156.

5. Marc Weiss, "Richard T. Ely and the Contribution of Economic Research to National Housing Policy, 1920–1940," *Urban Studies* 26 (1989): 115–126; Benjamin Looker, *A Nation of Neighborhoods: Imagining Cities, Communities, and Democracy in Postwar America* (Chicago: University of Chicago Press, 2015), 76–82.

6. Gail Radford, *Modern Housing for America: Policy Struggles in the New Deal Era* (Chicago: University of Chicago Press, 1996), 199.

7. For a range of different approaches, see Arnold Hirsch, *Making the Second Ghetto: Race and Housing in Chicago, 1940–1960* (New York: Cambridge University Press, 1983); Michael B. Katz, *In the Shadow of the Poorhouse: A Social History of Welfare in America* (New York: Basic Books, 1986), 259–334; Rhonda Williams, *The Politics of Public Housing: Black Women's Struggles Against Urban Inequality* (New York: Oxford University Press, 2005), 37; George Lipsitz, *How Racism Takes Place* (Philadelphia: Temple University Press, 2011); Michael B. Katz, ed., *The "Underclass" Debate: View from History* (Princeton, NJ: Princeton University Press, 1993); Annelise Orleck, *Storming Caesar's Palace: How Black Mothers Fought Their War on Poverty* (Boston: Beacon Press, 2006).

8. Jason Scott Smith, *Building New Deal Liberalism: The Political Economy of Public Works, 1933–1956* (Cambridge: Cambridge University Press, 2006), 1.

9. Louis Lee Woods II, "The Federal Home Loan Bank Board, Redlining, and the National Proliferation of Racial Lending Discrimination, 1921–1950," *Journal of Urban History* 38, no. 6 (November 2012): 1038–1039; Freund, *Colored Property*, 431n29. Todd Michney and LaDale Winling do not try to absolve the HOLC themselves, but they attribute others' attempts to a "perceived disjuncture between HOLC guiding theories and actual practice." I go further than Michney and Winling to argue that not only was there no "disjuncture," but white supremacy was foundational to HOLC operations based on its rhetoric, the ways it structured its policies, and the ongoing conversations among its administrators. Todd Michney and LaDale Winling, "New Perspectives on New Deal Housing Policy: Explicating and Mapping HOLC Loans to African Americans," *Journal of Urban History*, January 9, 2019 (advanced online publication), 2, https://doi.org/10.1177/0096144218819429.

10. Kevin Fox Gotham, "Urban Space, Restrictive Covenants and the Origins of Racial Residential Segregation in a US City, 1900–1950," *International Journal of Urban and Regional Research* 24, no. 3 (2000): 616–633; Michael Jones-Correa, "The Origins and Diffusion of Racial Restrictive Covenants," *Political Science Quarterly* 115, no. 4 (2000–2001): 541–568. See also Jeffrey Gonda, *Unjust Deeds: The Restrictive Covenant Cases and the Making of the Civil Rights Movement* (Chapel Hill: University of North Carolina Press, 2015). For an example of restrictive covenants in the 1920s adopting color-blind language to exclude based on race and religion, see Virginia Dawson, "Protection from Undesirable Neighbors: The Use of Deed Restrictions in Shaker Heights, Ohio," *Journal of Planning History* 18, no. 2 (2019): 117–121.

11. On New Deal policies as protection of white property investment, see Freund, *Colored Property*, 155, and N. D. B. Connolly, *A World More Concrete: Real Estate and the Remaking of Jim Crow South Florida* (Chicago: University of Chicago Press, 2014), 93–95.

12. Hornstein, *A Nation of Realtors*, 147

13. Hornstein, *A Nation of Realtors*, 134–135; Dan Immergluck, *Foreclosed: High-Risk Lending, Deregulation, and the Undermining of America's Mortgage Market* (Ithaca, NY: Cornell University Press, 2009), 37; Freund, *Colored Property*, 108–109.

14. Board of Directors Meeting, National Association of Real Estate Boards, November 18, 1932, National Association of Realtors Library and Archives, Chicago (hereafter NAR Archives).

15. Board of Directors Meeting, November 18, 1932. The RFC did not limit its focus to cities. It approved two loans: one for Knickerbocker Village in New York City and the other for homes in rural Kansas.

16. Board of Directors Meeting, November 18, 1932.

17. "Association Backs Hull Resolution to Eliminate Tax Exemption of Securities," News Service, March 4, 1933, NAR Archives.

18. Janet Pearl Davies, *Real Estate in American History* (Washington, DC: Public Affairs Press, 1958), 117.

19. Freund, *Colored Property*, 112; Louis Hyman, *Debtor Nation: The History of American in Red Ink* (Princeton, NJ: Princeton University Press, 2011), 48.

20. Woods, "The Federal Home Loan Bank Board," 1038.

21. Woods, "The Federal Home Loan Bank Board," 1038.

22. Paige Glotzer, "Exclusion in Arcadia: How Suburban Developers Circulated Ideas About Discrimination, 1890–1950," *Journal of Urban History* 41, no. 3 (May 2015): 490.

23. Secretaries' Weekly Report, February 9, 1932, NAR Archives.

24. Secretaries' Weekly Report, February 9, 1932.

25. Freund, *Colored Property*, 115.

26. Secretaries' Weekly Report no. 19, June 18, 1934, NAR Archives.

27. The HOLC also issued bonds with government-insured interest during its first year of operation. Freund, *Colored Property*, 112.

28. "Minutes, General Sessions, Mid-Winter Business Meeting, National Association of Realtors, Coral Gables Florida," 1934, 7, NAR Archives; "Effects on Home Values of Appraisals by the Home Owners' Loan Corporation," *Federal Home Loan Bank Review* 1, no. 4 (January 1935): 120.

29. "Effects on Home Values of Appraisals," 123.

30. "Effects on Home Values of Appraisals," 123.

31. Kenneth Jackson, *Crabgrass Frontier: The Suburbanization of the United States* (New York: Oxford University Press, 1985), 198.

32. Proceedings of the Third Annual Conference of Developers of High-Class Residential Property, 1919, 575–576, Jemison Companies Miscellany, Collection #2838 Rare and Manuscript Division, Cornell University. See chapter 4 for an extended discussion of the Conference of Developers of High-Class Residential Property.

33. Woods, "The Federal Home Loan Bank Board," 1037.
34. NS Form 8, "Area Description," RG195 Box 106, Baltimore, Maryland, Master File Rev. Security Area Map and Descriptions, National Archives and Records Administration, College Park, Maryland.
35. "Ask Direct Loans for Builders," *National Real Estate Journal* 34, no. 11 (October 1933): 12. NAREB's reversal on the PWA contrasts with accounts that report general disdain from the business community. See, for example, Hyman, *Debtor Nation*, 50–52.
36. Radford, *Modern Housing for America*, 93.
37. "Slum" and the closely related "ghetto" have a fraught history extending far beyond the temporal and geographic scope of this book. "Ghetto," in particular, was frequently used in mid- to late twentieth-century housing scholarship. For an overview of this scholarship, see Roger Biles, "Black Milwaukee and the Ghetto Synthesis," *Journal of Urban History* 33, no. 4 (May 2007): 539–543.
38. Meeting of Board of Directors and the Advisory Board of the National Association of Real Estate Boards, October 26–27, 1934. NAR Archives.
39. Meeting of Board of Directors and the Advisory Board, October 26–27, 1934.
40. Secretaries' Letter no. 19, June 18, 1934, 1, NAR Archives. NAREB was invited by a senator to use his office to craft the Home Owners' Loan Act the previous year. Freund, *Colored Property*, 111.
41. Secretaries' Letter no. 17, June 2, 1934, 2, NAR Archives.
42. Secretaries' Letter no. 18, June 16, 1934, 1, NAR Archives.
43. Gotham, "Urban Space, Restrictive Covenants," 57.
44. Secretaries' Letter no. 19.
45. Secretaries' Letter no. 19.
46. Secretaries' Letter no. 16, May 26, 1934, NAR Archives.
47. Secretaries' Letter no. 16.
48. Woods, "The Federal Home Loan Bank Board," 1056n21.
49. Hornstein, *A Nation of Realtors*, 150.
50. "Racial Content of FHA Underwriting Practices, 1934–1962," pp. 3–4, American Civil Liberties Union of Maryland Records, Box S3A-B2, Folder 20, Langsdale Libraries Special Collections, University of Baltimore; Freund, *Colored Property*, 157–158.
51. Andrew Wiese, *Places of Their Own: African American Suburbanization in the Twentieth Century* (Chicago: University of Chicago Press, 2005), 19, 69, 85; Todd M. Michney, *Surrogate Suburbs: Black Upward Mobility and Neighborhood Change in Cleveland, 1900–1980* (Chapel Hill: University of North Carolina Press, 2017), 22.
52. John Mowbray to Robert Jemison Jr., July 22, 1935, Box 132, Folder 14, Roland Park Company Records, MS 504, Special Collections, Johns Hopkins University (hereafter RPC Records).
53. "Bibliographic Note," in Robert K. Nelson et al., "Mapping Inequality: Redlining in New Deal America," in *American Panorama*, ed. Robert K. Nelson and Edward L. Ayers, accessed March 10, 2017, https://dsl.richmond.edu/panorama/redlining; N. D. B. Connolly, "How Did African Americans Discover They Were Being 'Redlined?,'" *Talking*

Points Memo, August 9, 2015, http://talkingpointsmemo.com/primary-source/redlining
-holc-fha-wilkins-weaver.

54. "NAREB Tackles Problem of Replanning Blighted Areas," *National Real Estate Journal* 36, no. 4 (April 1935): 44.

55. "Memorandum on Protection and Development of Residential Areas and Rehabilitation and Reconstruction of Blighted Areas in Cities," Box 214, Folder 23, RPC Records.

56. "Neighborhood Protective and Improvement Districts: A Suggested State Statute Authorizing the Creation of Such Districts by Property Owners in Cities, Towns, and Villages," 3, Box 214, Folder 22, RPC Records.

57. "Neighborhood Protective and Improvement Districts," 3.

58. John Mowbray to Herbert U. Nelson, June 15, 1935, Box 214, Folder 23, RPC Records.

59. Mowbray to Nelson, June 15, 1935.

60. Herbert U. Nelson to John Mowbray, April 15, 1935, Box 214, Folder 23, RPC Records.

61. Nelson to Mowbray, April 15, 1935.

62. Connolly, *A World More Concrete*, 99.

63. "Neighborhood Protective and Improvement Districts," 3.

64. Herbert U. Nelson to John Mowbray, June 7, 1935, Box 214, Folder 23, RPC Records.

65. "Address to Be Delivered at Real Estate Convention," Box 214, Folder 23, RPC Records.

66. "Address to Be Delivered."

67. Mary Ellen Hayward, *Baltimore's Alley Houses: Homes for Working People Since the 1780s* (Baltimore, MD: Johns Hopkins University Press, 2008), 240–241.

68. Peter H. Henderson, "Local Deals and the New Deal State: Implementing Federal Public Housing in Baltimore, 1933–1968" (PhD diss., Johns Hopkins University, 1994), 99.

69. P. Stewart Macaulay, "A Basis for a Baltimore City Plan," *Baltimore Sun*, January 6, 1935, MS1; Hayward, *Baltimore's Alley Houses*, 242; Williams, *The Politics of Public Housing*, 31–32; "2 Exhibits at Library," *Baltimore Sun*, June 30, 1935, 62.

70. Quoted in Williams, *The Politics of Public Housing*, 31. Hirsch writes that "the report and recommendations equated black areas of residence with 'blight' and used the terms almost interchangeably." Arnold Hirsch, "Public Policy and Residential Segregation in Baltimore, 1900–1968," Case MJG 95-309 no. 3 (2003), 17, R0002 ACLU S03A B01 F003, Special Collections, Langsdale Library, University of Baltimore.

71. P. Stewart Macaulay, "Prospects for Baltimore's City Plan," *Baltimore Sun*, February 3, 1935, MS1; "Slum Clearance Held Biggest Task," *Baltimore Sun*, December 20, 1935, 4.

72. "City Planner Visualizes New Era Here," *Baltimore Sun*, December 12, 1934, 24.

73. Hirsch, "Public Policy and Residential Segregation," 18.

74. Henderson, "Local Deals and the New Deal State," 104.

75. Hayward Farrar, *The Baltimore* Afro-American, *1892–1950* (Westport, CT: Greenwood Press, 1998), 105; Henderson "Local Deals and the New Deal State," 116–118.

76. Real Estate Board of Baltimore to Mayor Howard Jackson, Mortgage Rehabilitation Division, Home Owners' Loan Corporation, September 1935, RG 195 Box 107, National Archives and Records Administration.

77. Williams, *The Politics of Public Housing*, 33; Farrar, *The Baltimore* Afro-American, 105.

78. Emory Niles to W. Don Morrow, August 30, 1935, Mortgage Rehabilitation Division, Home Owners' Loan Corporation, September 1935, RG 195 Box 107, National Archives and Records Administration.

79. Williams, *The Politics of Public Housing*, 33.

80. "To Map Policy on Blighted Areas," *Baltimore Sun*, May 10, 1937, 18; Henderson, "Local Deals and the New Deal State," 128.

81. "Mayor's Committee Backs Housing Authority Plan," *Baltimore Sun*, November 11, 1937, 2.

82. Hirsch, "Public Policy and Residential Segregation," 4.

83. Williams, *The Politics of Public Housing*, 34.

84. Proceedings Creating and Establishing the Housing Authority of Baltimore City, November 2, 1937, BCA 48-1, Microfilm Reel BCA1316.

85. Oliver C. Winston III to Julius P. Robinson, December 9, 1939, BCA 48-39-35.

86. Total number of security maps comes from Arthur Goodwillie, *Waverly: A Study in Neighborhood Conservation* (Washington, DC: Federal Home Loan Bank Board, 1940), 7.

87. "Baltimore, MD Report #1," RG195 Box 106, Baltimore, Maryland Master File Rev. Security Area Map and Descriptions, National Archives and Records Administration.

88. "Baltimore City Map," RG 195 Box 107, Baltimore-Maryland #1, National Archives and Records Administration; "Baltimore, MD Report #1"; Proceedings Creating and Establishing the Housing Authority of Baltimore City.

89. Area Descriptions, RG195 Box 106, Baltimore, Maryland Master File Rev. Security Area Map and Descriptions, National Archives and Records Administration. One of these two areas was Towson, the Baltimore County seat. The Towson area description was from a slightly earlier version of the Baltimore map that used the ratings "Best, Still Desirable, Definitely Declining, and Hazardous." The colors associated with each (green, blue, yellow, and red respectively) remained the same. The one "concentration of negroes" referred to East Towson, an enclave that, like Cross Keys, had been settled by emancipated African Americans from nearby plantations in the nineteenth century.

90. Area Descriptions.

91. African American property owners in these highly rated areas still likely faced credit discrimination for a multitude of reasons, including disadvantages faced by black financial institutions and the fact that lending applications usually involved face-to-face transactions. In other words, their absence from HOLC maps did not shield them from the effects more often associated with redlining.

92. This, too, was inaccurate, because Merrymount Lane in Roland Park's northernmost plat was the last part to be built in the 1910s, after Guilford opened.

93. Proceedings Creating and Establishing the Housing Authority of Baltimore City.

94. Williams, *The Politics of Public Housing*, 31.

95. Proceedings Creating and Establishing the Housing Authority of Baltimore City; Hayward, *Baltimore's Alley Houses*, 245.

96. Land Summary, Project Number MD 2-2 Area B, United States Housing Authority Land Review Division, BCA 48-39-45; Cleveland Bealmar to Thomas E. Barrett Jr., May 9, 1940, BCA 48-39-45.

97. Bealmar to Barrett, May 9, 1940; Report of Optionist John E. Buccino, November 30, 1939, BCA 48-39-45. Bealmar was a signatory in the Baltimore Real Estate Board's 1935 letter to Jackson.

98. C. Lowell Harriss, *History and Policies of the Home Owners' Loan Corporation* (New York: National Bureau of Economic Research, 1951), 101, 105, 114; Goodwillie, *Waverly*, 6; Richard Harris, *Building a Market: The Rise of the Home Improvement Industry, 1914–1960* (Chicago: University of Chicago Press, 2012), 192; Richard Harris, "A New Form of Credit: The State Promotes Home Improvement," *Journal of Policy History* 21, no. 4 (October 2009): 401.

99. "Home Reconditioning Under the Home Owners' Loan Corporation," *Federal Home Loan Bank Review* 1, no. 3 (December 1934): 85; "A Technic for Handling Reconditioning Loans," *Federal Home Loan Bank Review* 1, no. 5 (February 1935): 155,

100. Goodwillie, *Waverly*, 8.

101. Donald McNeal to Herbert U. Nelson, July 7, 1938, Box 215, Folder 16, RPC Records.

102. John Mowbray to Herbert U. Nelson, December 6, 1938, Box 215, Folder 16, RPC Records.

103. John Mowbray to E. L. Ostendorf, December 6, 1938, Box 216, Folder 16, RPC Records.

104. "A Program of Neighborhood Rehabilitation and Protection," March 15, 1939, Box 222, Folder 6, RPC Records.

105. Goodwillie, *Waverly*, 22; Harriss, *History and Policies*, 108.

106. "Program of Neighborhood Rehabilitation and Protection"; Goodwillie, *Waverly*, 8, 55.

107. Area description of D6, RG 195 Box 107, National Archives and Records Administration.

108. Area description of D6.

109. Goodwillie, *Waverly*, 55.

110. Goodwillie, *Waverly*, 55.

111. News Release for September 28, 1938, News Service, FHLBB, Box 222, Folder 5, RPC Records.

112. "Chairman's Report—Advisory Committee Meeting 12/1/39 Waverly Conservation Program," 2, Box 222, Folder 4, RPC Records.

113. "Chairman's Report—Advisory Committee Meeting 12/1/39," 2.

114. Mowbray correspondence, Box 215, RPC Records.

115. Williams, *The Politics of Public Housing*, 35–36; Proceedings Creating and Establishing the Housing Authority of Baltimore City.

116. "Minutes of the Advisory Committee Meeting, Waverly Conservation Program," December 1, 1939, Box 255, Folder 4, RPC Records.

117. "Chairman's Report—Advisory Committee Meeting 12/1/39," 3.

118. "Display Ad 25," *Baltimore Sun*, November 6, 1939, 9; "Display Ad 32," *Baltimore Sun*, February 5, 1940, 11; "Display Ad 36," *Baltimore Sun*, June 26, 1940, 13.

119. "Chairman's Report—Advisory Committee Meeting 12/1/39," 2.

120. "Edward J. Gallagher," 1940 Census Baltimore, Baltimore City, Maryland; Roll: T627_1515; Page: 3A; Enumeration District: 4-194.

121. "Program of Neighborhood Rehabilitation and Protection."

122. "Program of Neighborhood Rehabilitation and Protection."

123. Goodwillie, *Waverly*, 10; "Chairman's Report—Advisory Committee Meeting, 12/1/39," pp. 2–3.

124. John Mowbray, "York Road Improvement Association—11/14/39," card 3, Box 222, Folder 5, RPC Records; Goodwillie, *Waverly*, 11.

125. Mowbray, "York Road Improvement Association—11/14/39," cards 5–6.

126. "A Message to Waverly Home Owners," attached to a letter from McNeal to Mowbray, December 8, 1938, Box 222, Folder 5, RPC Records.

127. "Message to Waverly Home Owners."

128. Goodwillie, *Waverly*, 58.

129. "Discussion by Mr. Howard Acton, Department of Public Relations, FHLBB (from the Minutes of the Advisory Committee Meeting, Waverly Neighborhood Conservation Program, Baltimore, Md., December 1, 1939)," 2, Box 222, Folder 4, RPC Records.

130. "Minutes of the Advisory Committee Meeting, Waverly Conservation Program," December 1, 1939; "Discussion by Mr. Howard Acton."

131. "Broadening of Slum Survey in Waverly Area Suggested," *Baltimore Sun*, October 5, 1938, 9.

132. Goodwillie, *Waverly*, 84–85.

133. Richard E. Saunders, "Saving a Neighborhood," *Freehold*, February 1, 1940, 94.

134. "Waverly: A Demonstration of Neighborhood Conservation," *Federal Home Loan Bank Review* 6, no. 11 (August 1940): 373.

135. "Waverly: A Demonstration," 373–374; Goodwillie, *Waverly*, 65.

136. Amy Hillier, "Redlining and the Home Owners' Loan Corporation," *Journal of Urban History* 29, no. 4 (May 2003): 399–400.

137. Saunders, "Saving a Neighborhood," 93.

138. Light, *The Nature of Cities*, 95.

139. "Forum," *Freehold*, December 1, 1938, 400.

140. One of those organizations was Neighborhood Housing Services in the 1970s. Marc Weiss and John T. Metzger, "The American Real Estate Industry and the Origins of Neighborhood Conservation," in *Proceedings of the Fifth Annual Conference on American Planning History*, ed. Society for American City and Regional Planning History (Hilliard, OH: Society for American City and Regional Planning History, 1993): 761.

141. Weiss and Metzger, "The American Real Estate Industry," 763.

142. Light notes that Arthur Goodwillie of the HOLC used his experiences in the Waverly project to help the Washington Housing Authority segregate housing during the Second World War by framing racial selection of wartime housing tenants as "conserving" community wealth to bolster the war effort. Light, *The Nature of Cities*, 82–83.

6. ADAPTATIONS

1. Guy T. O. Hollyday to Robert Jemison, November 23, 1955, Robert Jemison Miscellany, #2838 Box 1, Cornell University Rare and Manuscript Collections.

2. Hollyday to Jemison, November 23, 1955.

3. Gail Radford, *Modern Housing for America: Public Struggles in the New Deal Era* (Chicago: University of Chicago Press, 1996), 188–189; D. Bradford Hunt, *Blueprint for Disaster: The Unraveling of Chicago Public Housing* (Chicago: University of Chicago Press, 2009), 129.

4. Arnold Hirsch, *Making the Second Ghetto: Race and Housing in Chicago, 1940–1960* (Chicago: University of Chicago Press, 1983), 9, 259–275; Robert O. Self, *American Babylon: Race and the Struggle for Postwar Oakland* (Princeton, NJ: Princeton University Press, 2005), 139–144; Arnold Hirsch, "'Containment' on the Home Front: Race and Federal Housing Policy from the New Deal to the Cold War," *Journal of Urban History* 26, no. 2 (January 2000): 158–189; Kevin Fox Gotham, *Race, Real Estate, and Uneven Development: The Kansas City Experience, 1900–2000* (Albany: State University of New York Press, 2002), 82, 89; Preston H. Smith II, *Racial Democracy and the Black Metropolis: Housing Policy in Postwar Chicago* (Minneapolis: University of Minnesota Press, 2012), 141–149; Beryl Satter, *Family Properties: How the Struggle Over Race and Real Estate Transformed Chicago and Urban America* (New York: Metropolitan Books, 2009), 49–50; Thomas J. Sugrue, *The Origins of the Urban Crisis: Race and Inequality in Postwar Detroit* (Princeton, NJ: Princeton University Press, 1995), 57–88.

5. N. D. B. Connolly, *A World More Concrete: Real Estate and the Remaking of Jim Crow South Florida* (Chicago: University of Chicago Press, 2014), 8; Gotham, *Race, Real Estate, and Uneven Development*, 72–73; Sugrue, *The Origins of the Urban Crisis*, 47; Self, *American Babylon*, 138, 152.

6. David M. P. Freund, *Colored Property: State Policy and White Racial Politics in Suburban America* (Chicago: University of Chicago Press, 2007), 8.

7. Arthur Binns, "Housing and Blighted Areas," *National Real Estate Journal* 42, no. 11 (November 1941): 15; Alexander von Hoffman, "A Study in Contradictions: The Origins and Legacy of the Housing Act of 1949," *Housing Policy Debate* 11, no. 2 (2000): 304. The purchase of land at its assessed value and the sale at a lower value was called a "write-down." For more on write-downs, see Hirsch, *Making the Second Ghetto*, 269–271.

8. *Headlines* 10, no. 49 (December 6, 1943), National Association of Realtors Library and Archives, Chicago (hereafter NAR Archives).

9. Wendell E. Pritchett, "The 'Public Menace' of Blight," *Yale Law and Policy Review* 21, no. 1 (2003): 26–27.

10. Binns, "Housing and Blighted Areas," 15.

11. Gotham, *Race, Real Estate, and Uneven Development*, 75.

12. *Headlines* 10, no. 15 (April 10, 1943), NAR Archives.

13. *Headlines* 10, no. 15 (April 10, 1943).

14. "Is the Wagner Bill for Rebuilding Our Cities Desirable?," *National Real Estate Journal* 44 (October 1943): 17.

15. The NAREB secretary defended the Realtors' Washington Committee from unattributed criticisms by NAREB by asking, "In what other way could the average citizen make his needs known to Congress and the administration except through organized groups?" *Headlines* 10, no. 23 (June 5, 1943). For an example of criticism of NAREB lobbying activities, see Trist Coffin, "The Slickest Lobby," *The Nation*, March 23, 1946, 340–342.

16. *Headlines* 10, no. 8 (February 20, 1943), NAR Archives.

17. *Headlines* 10, no. 15 (April 10, 1943); 78 Bill Profile S. 953 (1943–1944).

18. 1943 Congressional Senate Record, 5357.

19. 78 Bill Profile S. 1163 (1943).

20. *Headlines* 10, no. 24 (June 12, 1943), NAR Archives; "Wagner Offers Bill to Stimulate Urban Housing," *New York Herald Tribune*, June 7, 1943, 26A; 1943 Congressional Senate Record, 5357.

21. 1943 Congressional Senate Record, 5357.

22. Gotham, *Race, Real Estate, and Uneven Development*, 87.

23. "Is the Wagner Bill," 16.

24. "Is the Wagner Bill," 18.

25. "Is the Wagner Bill," 17.

26. Report of the Executive Vice President on Association Affairs, Board of Directors Meeting, May 20, 1945, 14, NAR Archives.

27. Realtors' Washington Committee Report, Board of Directors Meeting, May 25, 1945, 5, NAR Archives; Establishment of Statistical Bureau by RWC, Board of Directors Meeting, May 26, 1945, 19, NAR Archives.

28. Control of Real Estate Prices, Board of Directors Meeting, August 15, 1945, 6, NAR Archives.

29. Report by the Realtors' Washington Committee, Board of Directors Meeting, November 29, 1945, 13, NAR Archives.

30. Morton Hoffman, "The Role of Government in Influencing Changes in Housing in Baltimore: 1940 to 1950," *Land Economics* 30, no. 2 (1954): 17, 20.

31. Joshua Olson, *Better Places, Better Lives: A Biography of James Rouse* (Washington, DC: Urban Land Institute, 2003), 15.

32. Paul Marx, *Jim Rouse: Capitalist/Idealist* (Lanham, MD: University Press of America, 2008), 43.

33. Marx, *Jim Rouse*, 43–44.

34. Letter to the editor, *Baltimore Sun*, April 8, 1953.

35. Elmore McKee, *The People Act: Stories of How Americans Are Coming Together to Deal with Their Community Problems* (New York: Harper and Brothers, 1955), 129–132.

36. Satter, *Family Properties*, 151–152.

37. Alexander von Hoffman, "Enter the Housing Industry Stage Right: A Working Paper on the History of Housing Policy" (working paper, Joint Center for Housing Studies, Harvard University, 2008), 23–24.

38. Khalil Gibran Muhammed, *The Condemnation of Blackness: Race, Crime, and the Making of Modern Urban America* (Cambridge, MA: Harvard University Press, 2010), 226–268. Alice O'Connor argues that of all their applications, urban ecology models most impact understandings of juvenile delinquency beginning in the 1920s. Alice O'Connor, *Poverty Knowledge: Social Science, Social Policy, and the Poor in Twentieth-Century U.S. History* (Princeton, NJ: Princeton University Press, 2001), 51. The CPHA was engaged in what Muhammed characterizes as the "sociological and statistical crime gaze" of white reformers, which most often targeted African Americans in cities (146).

39. O'Connor, *Poverty Knowledge*, 77.

40. Oral History of Frances Morton Froelicher, January 5, 1976, OH8109, Maryland Historical Society.

41. Minutes of the Executive Council, Realtors' Washington Committee, National Association of Real Estate Boards, April 24–25, 1947, 3, Box 218, Folder 20, Roland Park Company Records, MS 504, Special Collections, Johns Hopkins University.

42. *Headlines*, November 15, 1948.

43. Jeffrey M. Hornstein, *A Nation of Realtors: A Cultural History of the Twentieth-Century American Middle Class* (Durham, NC: Duke University Press, 2005), 157, 185–189.

44. Nicholas Dagen Bloom, *Merchants of Illusion: James Rouse, America's Salesman of the Businessman's Utopia* (Columbus: Ohio State University Press, 2004), 71.

45. Marx, *Jim Rouse*, 51.

46. Jon Teaford, "Urban Renewal and Its Aftermath," *Housing Policy Debate* 11, no. 2 (2010): 444.

47. Arnold Hirsch, "Searching for a 'Sound Negro Policy': A Racial Agenda for the Housing Acts of 1949 and 1954," *Housing Policy Debate* 11, no. 2 (2010): 401, 410; Andrew Wiese, *Places of Their Own: African American Suburbanization in the Twentieth Century* (Chicago: University of Chicago Press, 2004), 138–140; Stephen Grant Meyer, *As Long as They Don't Move in Next Door: Segregation and Racial Conflict in American Neighborhoods* (Boston: Rowman and Littlefield, 2000), 85–87.

48. Frank Horne quoted in Hirsch, "Searching for a 'Sound Negro Policy,'" 399.

49. Hirsch, "Searching for a 'Sound Negro Policy,'" 399.

50. Both Thomas Sugrue and Beryl Satter point out that by 1948, property owners often ignored or failed to enforce racial restrictions anyway when it became profitable to sell or rent to blacks. That restrictions failed to serve as strong barriers to entry in these neighborhoods likely influenced the Supreme Court decision to rule them unenforceable. David Freund also claims covenants were unnecessary by the time of the Supreme Court ruling because zoning accomplished the same goals. Sugrue, *The Origins of the Urban Crisis*, 45; Satter, *Family Properties*, 391n18; Freund, *Colored Property*, 98.

51. "A Guide to Slum Clearance and Urban Redevelopment Under Title I of the Housing Act of 1949," Office of the Administrator, Housing and Home Finance Agency, February 1950, 24–25, Box 2, Folder 3, #3669 Historical Planning Publications, Rare and Manuscript Collections, Cornell University.

52. Freund, *Colored Property*, 187.

53. "Code of Ethics, National Association of Real Estate Boards," 1924, 7, NAR Archives.

54. "Code of Ethics, National Association of Real Estate Boards," 1950, n.p., NAR Archives.

55. Lowell Baker to Ruth Dillon, August 3, 1949, Housing—Racial Aspects Folder, NAR Archives; Paige Glotzer, "Exclusion in Arcadia," *Journal of Urban History* 41, no. 3 (May 2015): 490; Sugrue, *The Origins of the Urban Crisis*, 46.

56. Self, *American Babylon*, 105.

57. Rose Helper, *Racial Policies and Practices of Real Estate Brokers* (Minneapolis: University of Minnesota Press, 1969), 55, 117.

58. Jessica I. Elfenbein, "'Church People Work on the Integration Problem': The Brethren's Interracial Work in Baltimore, 1949–1972," in *Baltimore '68: Riots and Rebirth in an American City*, ed. Jessica Elfenbein, Thomas L. Hollowak, and Elizabeth M. Nix (Philadelphia: Temple University Press, 2011), 104.

59. James Rouse, Letter to the editor, *Baltimore Sun*, April 8, 1953, R46 Correspondence, 1953–1955, University of Baltimore Special Collections.

60. Von Hoffman, "Enter the Housing Industry Stage Right," 25.

61. Baltimore Redevelopment Commission, "The Legal Basis for Redevelopment in Maryland," September 30, 1949, Box 65, Folder 16, #3669 Historical Planning Publications, Cornell University Rare and Manuscript Collections.

62. Baltimore City Planning Commissioners such as Clark S. Hobbs still occasionally referred to it as South Waverly in the 1950s, but by and large people reverted to called it Waverly. Clark S. Hobbs to Mayor Thomas D'Alesandro Jr., May 22, 1950, in Baltimore Redevelopment Commission, "Redevelopment Project 1-A," May 1950, Box 66, Folder 17, #3669 Historical Planning Publications, Cornell University Rare and Manuscript Collections.

63. Compare the proposed layout of the sites in Radford, *Modern Housing for America*, 62, 164. The lineage of garden apartments can be traced back to the Garden City movement of Ebenezer Howard in Great Britain. Early examples in the United States include Sunnyside Gardens in Queens, New York. Early low-rise public housing combined garden apartments with different strands of modernist apartment housing that concentrated on using scientific principles to maximize hygienic aspects of housing such as light, air, and ventilation, usually in a deliberate break from an existing street plan.

64. Baltimore Redevelopment Commission, "Attitudes of Waverly Occupants Toward the Redevelopment Plan," September 18, 1950, Box 19 R0032-10F CPHA Records, University of Baltimore Special Collections.

65. Baltimore Redevelopment Commission reports minimized the role of the attorneys in securing higher offers, writing that making multiple offers was standard negotiating practice. The city also speculated that lawyers quoted their clients lower first offers than the city actually proposed, to make the final settlement seem like it was only obtained because of successful negotiation, justifying higher attorney fees. Baltimore Redevelopment Commission, "Attitudes of Waverly Occupants Toward the Redevelopment Plan."

66. Baltimore Redevelopment Commission, "Where Do You Go from Here?," 10, Box 66, Folder 17, #3669 Historical Planning Publications, Cornell University Rare and Manuscript Collections.

67. Baltimore Redevelopment Commission, "Where Do You Go from Here?," 12.

68. Baltimore Urban League to Mayor Thomas D'Alesandro, July 14, 1950, BCA BRG9-23-3, Box 263.

69. Horne quoted in Hirsch, "Searching for a 'Sound Negro Policy,'" 412.

70. Hirsch, "'Containment' on the Home Front," 167.

71. Albert Stark to the Baltimore Redevelopment Commission, May 19, 1950, in Baltimore Redevelopment Commission, "Redevelopment Project 1-A." Olsen also cites the Moss-Rouse Company role as financiers of the housing.

72. Quoted in Antero Pietilla, *Not in My Neighborhood: How Bigotry Shaped a Great American City* (Chicago: Ivan R. Dee, 2010), 137.

73. Marx, *Jim Rouse*, 78.

74. CPHA Planning Committee Meeting Minutes, January 13, 1953, CPHA II-D Box 1, Special Collections, Langsdale Library, University of Baltimore.

75. Marx, *Jim Rouse*, 64, 78.

76. Howard Gillette Jr., "Assessing James Rouse's Role in American City Planning," *Journal of the American Planning Association* 65, no. 2 (Spring 1999): 156–157.

77. Gillette, "Assessing James Rouse's Role," 156–157.

78. Rouse quoted in Howard Gillette Jr., *Civitas By Design: Building Better Communities from the Garden City to the New Urbanism* (Philadelphia: University of Pennsylvania Press, 2010), 103.

79. "A Report on Urban Renewal Demonstrations Authorized by Section 314 of the Housing Act of 1954," Housing Home and Finance Agency, Urban Renewal Administration, #2646 Jacob Leslie Crane Papers, Box 3, Folder 8, Cornell University Rare and Manuscript Collections.

80. Ed Chaney quoted in James Holechek, *Baltimore's Two Cross Keys: One Black, One White* (Lincoln, NE: iUniverse, 2003), 33.

81. Holechek, *Baltimore's Two Cross Keys*, 30–33.

82. Self, *American Babylon*, 149–155; Emily Lieb, "'White Man's Lane': Hollowing Out the Highway Ghetto in Baltimore," in Elfenbein, Hollowak, and Nix, *Baltimore '68*, 51–69.

83. Holechek, *Baltimore's Two Cross Keys*, 32.

84. Gert West quoted in Holechek, *Baltimore's Two Cross Keys*, 32.

85. Stephen E. Nordlinger, "Plan Group Backs Two School Sites," *Baltimore Sun*, July 14, 1960, 36.

86. Great Baltimore Committee Report, 1960, 17, University of Baltimore Special Collections.

87. Sugrue, *The Origins of the Urban Crisis*, 48–49; Smith, *Racial Democracy and the Black Metropolis*, 105–110.

88. Gert West quoted in Holechek, *Baltimore's Two Cross Keys*, 32–33.

89. George Hiltner, "Sites for Poly, Western High Valued by Jury at $578,000," *Baltimore Sun*, September 27, 1962, 54. Similar incidents were typical of urban renewal throughout the country, though one of the strongest parallels to Cross Keys is the demolition of the Mill Creek Valley area of St. Louis. Both areas were located in what had initially been relatively isolated valley areas and surrounded by water and railroads. Both were demolished for similar reasons, including a highway running through a centrally located corridor. Colin Gordon, *Mapping Decline: St. Louis and the Fate of the American City* (Philadelphia: University of Pennsylvania Press, 2009), 163–168.

90. Michael Douglass quoted in Holechek, *Baltimore's Two Cross Keys*, 34.

91. "Displacement and Relocation, Past and Future," Staff Monograph 5.4, Baltimore Urban Renewal and Housing Agency, March 1965, R19 BURHA Series 10, Box 4, University of Baltimore Special Collections.

92. James Rubenstein, "The Impact of Relocation Activities," Local History Research Collection R58, Box 5, University of Baltimore Special Collections.

93. Holechek, *Baltimore's Two Cross Keys*, 31.

94. Kathy E. Boone, "My Family's Migration to Three Neighborhoods in Baltimore City," April 1984, Local History Research Collection R58, Box 5, University of Baltimore Special Collections.

95. Edward Orser, *Blockbusting in Baltimore: The Edmondson Village Story* (Lexington: University Press of Kentucky, 1994), 93.

96. Satter, *Family Properties*, 3–7.

97. Orser, *Blockbusting in Baltimore*, 86.

98. When Rouse named the development the Village of Cross Keys, it was an act of what Michel-Rolph Trouillot calls "silencing." Trouillot gives an example of Haitian revolutionary Henri Christophe, who killed his enemy Jean-Baptiste Sans Souci and then constructed a palace on the site of his death and named it Sans-Souci. According to Trouillot, this act "erased Sans Souci from Christophe's own past, and it erased him from the future. . . . We know the silencing was effective, that Sans Souci [the man]'s life and death have been endowed with only marginal retrospective significance." Michel-Rolph Trouillot, *Silencing the Past: Power and Production of History* (Boston: Beacon Press, 1995), 60.

99. Orser, *Blockbusting in Baltimore*, 128; Marx, *Jim Rouse*, 109–110.

100. The Village of Cross Keys Restrictions, S10F-B15, R0032. CPHA Citizens Planning and Housing Association, Special Collections, Langsdale Library, University of Baltimore.

101. Orser, *Blockbusting in Baltimore*, 130.

102. For more on CORE's fight for housing integration, see Wiese, *Places of Their Own*, 220–222.

103. Marx, *Jim Rouse*, 113.

104. Quoted in Orser, *Blockbusting in Baltimore*, 129. Abigail Perkiss documents the types of qualifications that appeased white homeowners who faced pressure to integrate neighborhoods. Abigail Perkiss, *Making Good Neighbors: Civil Rights, Liberalism, and Integration in Postwar Philadelphia* (Ithaca, NY: Cornell University Press), 60–62.

105. Quoted in Pietilla, *Not in My Neighborhood*, 141.

106. Craig Thompson, "Growing Pains of a Brand-New City," *Saturday Evening Post*, August 7, 1954, 72.

107. Thomas J. Sugrue, "Jim Crow's Last Stand: The Struggle to Integrate Levittown," in *Second Suburb: Levittown, Pennsylvania*, ed. Dianne Harris (Pittsburgh: University of Pittsburgh Press, 2010), 178.

108. Sugrue, "Jim Crow's Last Stand," 179.

CONCLUSION

1. Today this complex is Marble Hall Gardens. "Roland Park Apartments Demonstrates Realtors' Rental Housing Opportunity," *National Real Estate Journal* 39, no. 12 (November 1938): 26–31, 77.

2. Figures compiled using Lucy Lawliss, Caroline Loughlin, and Lauren Meier, eds., *The Master List of Design Projects of the Olmsted Firm 1857–1979* (Washington, DC: National Association of Olmsted Parks, 2008); Paige Glotzer, "Roland Park Company: The Critical Planning Role of the Olmsted Brothers," *The Olmstedian* 21, no. 1 (Spring 2015): 1–6.

3. Gerald R. Frug, "The Legal Technology of Exclusion in Metropolitan America," in *The New Suburban History*, ed. Kevin Kruse and Thomas Sugrue (Chicago: University of Chicago Press, 2006), 205–220; Kevin Fox Gotham, *Race, Real Estate, and Uneven Development: The Kansas City Experience, 1900–2000* (Albany: State University of New York Press, 2002); Louis Hyman, *Debtor Nation: The History of America in Red Ink* (Princeton, NJ: Princeton University Press, 2012), 173–219. See also Keeanga-Yamatta Taylor, *Race for Profit: How Banks and the Real Estate Industry Undermined Black Homeownership* (Chapel Hill: University of North Carolina Press, 2019).

4. "Affiliation of Philippine Group with NAREB Wins Approval," *Headlines*, December 5, 1960; Charlee Gibson, "What Does the 'R' Mean Overseas?," *Global View Blog*, September 27, 2017, http://theglobalview.blogs.realtor.org/2017/09/27/what-does-the-r-mean -overseas; Rose Helper, *Racial Policies and Practices of Real Estate Brokers* (Minneapolis: University of Minnesota Press, 1969), 277–301.

5. Kevin Fox Gotham, "The Secondary Circuit of Capital Reconsidered: Globalization and the U.S. Real Estate Sector," *American Journal of Sociology* 112, no. 1 (July 2006): 253.

6. Gibson, "What Does the 'R' Mean Overseas?"

7. Gotham, "Secondary Circuit," 253.

8. Gotham, "Secondary Circuit," 241–245.

9. Elizabeth Blackmar, "Of REITs and Rights: Absentee Ownership in the Periphery," in *City, Country, Empire: Landscapes in Environmental History*, ed. Jeffry M. Diefendorf and Kurk Dorsey, 85–86 (Pittsburgh: University of Pittsburgh Press, 2005); David Freund, *Colored Property: State Policy and White Racial Politics in Suburban America* (Chicago: University of Chicago Press, 2007), 190–193.

10. Freund, *Colored Property*, 190–193.

11. Blackmar, "Of REITs and Rights," 94; Thomas Shay Hill, "The Securitization of Security: Reorganization of Land, Military, and State in the Pentagon's Backyard," *Journal of Urban History* 41, no. 1 (January 2015): 88; Blackmar, "Of REITs and Rights," 89.

12. The James W. Rouse Company was acquired by a larger REIT, General Growth Properties, in 2004, spun off as Rouse Properties in 2011, and acquired by Brookfield Asset Management in 2016. For more on institutional investments such as pension funds and mutual funds, see Janice Traflet, "'Never Bought, Always Sold': Salesmanship, the Small Investor, and the Early Postwar Surge in Mutual Fund Participation," *Essays in Economic and Business History* 27 (2009): 5–14.

13. A key difference between REITs and nineteenth-century firms is the legal obligation of the former to pay out over 90 percent of its profits to shareholders. Lands Trust Company managers could exercise more discretion.

14. Hill, "Securitization of Security," 75; Blackmar, "Of REITs and Rights," 95.

15. Hill, "Securitization of Security," 82; Paige Glotzer, "The Connections Between Urban Investment and Colonialism," *Black Perspectives*, November 27, 2017, https://www.aaihs.org/the-connections-between-urban-development-and-colonialism.

16. For more on the racial wealth gap, see Mehrsa Baradaran, *The Color of Money: Black Banks and the Racial Wealth Gap* (Cambridge, MA: Harvard University Press, 2017).

17. Christopher G. Boone et al., "Parks and People: An Environmental Justice Inquiry in Baltimore, Maryland," *Annals of the Association of American Geographers* 99, no. 4 (2009): 767–787.

18. See, for example, the 2007 Baltimore Tree Canopy Map produced by TreeBaltimore, accessed January 2, 2017, http://www.treebaltimore.org/maps.

19. Kirsten Schwarz et al., "Trees Grow on Money: Urban Tree Canopy Cover and Environmental Justice," *PLOS One* 10, no. 4 (2015): 1–17.

20. J. Morgan Grove et al., "The Legacy Effect: Understanding How Segregation and Environmental Injustice Unfold Over Time in Baltimore," *Annals of the American Association of Geographers* 108, no. 2 (2018): 524–537. For examples of grassroots environmental justice activism, see Darryl Fears, "This Baltimore 20-Year-Old Just Won a Huge International Award for Taking Out a Giant Trash Incinerator," *Washington Post*, April 18, 2016; Arlene Karidis, "The Toxic Truth," *Baltimore Magazine*, December 2008.

21. Persistence does not mean a narrative of failure. Michael B. Katz, "The Existential Problem of Urban Studies," *Dissent* 57, no. 4 (Fall 2010): 65–68.

SELECTED BIBLIOGRAPHY

PRIMARY SOURCES

Collections

Baker Library, Harvard Business School
  London Stock Exchange Yearbooks, 1881–1891
Baltimore City Archives
  Department of Housing and Community Development
  Manuscript Volumes of Ordinances and Resolutions
  Mayor's Office Records
Baltimore City Legislative Reference Library
  Annual Reports of the Baltimore Sewerage Commission
Cornell University Rare and Manuscript Division
  Historical Planning Publications
  Jemison Companies Miscellany
  The John Nolen Pamphlet Collection
Guildhall Library, London
  Applications to the London Stock Exchange
Maryland Historical Society
  Cary-McHenry Family Papers Collection
  Oral History Collection
Maryland State Archives
  Baltimore City Land Records
  Baltimore County Land Records

National Archives and Records Administration
    Records of the Federal Home Loan Bank Board
National Archives of the United Kingdom
    Board of Trade Records
    Companies Winding Up Proceedings, High Court of Justice Companies Court
    Foreign Office, Political and Other Departments
National Association of Realtors Library and Archives
Special Collections, Johns Hopkins University Sheridan Libraries
    Roland Park Company Records
Special Collections, University of Baltimore
    American Civil Liberties Union of Maryland Records
    Baltimore Urban Renewal and Housing Authority Records
    Citizens Housing and Planning Association Records
    Greater Baltimore Committee Records
    Local History Research Collection

SECONDARY SOURCES

Digital Collections and Projects

Centre for the Study of the Legacies of British Slave-Ownership. *Legacies of British Slave-Ownership*. University College London Department of History, 2019. https://www.ucl.ac.uk/lbs.

Digital Scholarship Lab. "Renewing Inequality: Urban Renewal, Family Displacements, and Race, 1955–1966." In *American Panorama*, ed. Robert K. Nelson and Edward L. Ayers, 2019. http://dsl.richmond.edu/panorama/renewal.

Glotzer, Paige. "Building Suburban Power: The Business of Exclusionary Housing Markets, 1890–1960." In *Visualizing Historical Networks*. Harvard University Joint Center for History and Economics, 2019. https://histecon.fas.harvard.edu/visualizing/buildingsuburbanpower/index.html.

Nelson, Robert K., LaDale Winling, Richard Marciano, Nathan Connolly, et al. "Mapping Inequality: Redlining in New Deal America." In *American Panorama*, ed. Robert K. Nelson and Edward L. Ayers, 2019. https://dsl.richmond.edu/panorama/redlining.

Publications

Abbott, Andrew. *The System of Professions: An Essay on the Division of Expert Labor*. Chicago: University of Chicago Press, 1988.

Adler, Dorothy. *British Investment in American Railways*. Charlottesville: University of Virginia Press, 1970.

Alexander, Michelle. *The New Jim Crow: Mass Incarceration in the Age of Colorblindness*. New York: New Press, 2010.

Anderson, Warwick. *Colonial Pathologies: American Tropical Medicine, Race, and Hygiene in the Philippines*. Durham, NC: Duke University Press, 2006.

Armborst, Tobias, Daniel D'Oca, and Georgeen Theodore. *The Arsenal of Exclusion and Inclusion*. Barcelona: Actar, 2017.

Armenti, David. "'Is He White or Colored?' Chinese in Baltimore City Public Schools." Maryland Historical Society, August 15, 2013. http://www.mdhs.org/underbelly/2013/08/15/is-he-white-or-colored-chinese-in-baltimore-city-public-schools.

Arnold, Joseph. "Suburban Growth and Municipal Annexation." *Maryland Historical Magazine* 73, no. 2 (1978): 109–128.

Backof, Jeanne F., and Charles L. Martin. "Historical Perspectives: Development of the Codes of Ethics in the Legal, Medical and Accounting Professions." *Journal of Business Ethics* 10 (1991): 99–110.

Baldwin, Davarian. *Chicago's New Negroes: Modernity, the Great Migration, and Black Urban Life*. Chapel Hill: University of North Carolina Press, 2007.

Baradaran, Mehrsa. *The Color of Money: Black Banks and the Racial Wealth Gap*. Cambridge, MA: Harvard University Press, 2017.

Beckert, Sven. "Emancipation and Empire: Reconstructing the Worldwide Web of Cotton Production in the Age of the American Civil War." *American Historical Review* 109, no. 5 (December 2004): 1405–1438.

Beckert, Sven, Angus Burgin, Peter Hudson, et al. "Interchange: The History of Capitalism." *Journal of American History* 101, no. 2 (September 2014): 503–536.

Bender, Steven. *Tierra y Liberdad: Land, Liberty, and Latino Housing*. New York: New York University Press, 2010.

Berry, Daina Ramey. *The Price for Their Pound of Flesh: The Value of the Enslaved from Womb to Grave in the Building of a Nation*. Boston: Beacon Press, 2017.

Biles, Roger. "Black Milwaukee and the Ghetto Synthesis." *Journal of Urban History* 33, no. 4 (May 2007): 539–543.

Binford, Henry C. *The First Suburbs: Residential Communities on the Boston Periphery*. Chicago: University of Chicago Press, 1985.

Bix, Amy Sue. "Experiences and Voices of Eugenics Field-Workers: 'Women's Work' in Biology." *Social Studies of Science* 27, no. 4 (1997): 625–668.

Blackhawk, Ned. *Violence Over the Land: Indians and Empire in the Early American West*. Cambridge, MA: Harvard University Press, 2008.

Blackmar, Elizabeth. "Accountability for Public Health: Regulating the Housing Market in Nineteenth-Century New York City." In *Hives of Sickness: Public Health and Epidemics in New York City*, ed. David Rosner, 42–64. New York: Museum of the City of New York, 1995.

——. "Of REITs and Rights: Absentee Ownership in the Periphery." In *City, Country, Empire: Landscapes in Environmental History*, ed. Jeffry M. Diefendorf and Kurk Dorsey, 81–98. Pittsburgh: University of Pittsburgh Press, 2005.

Blockson, Charles. *Black Genealogy*. New York: Prentice-Hall, 1977.

Bloom, Nicholas. *Merchants of Illusion: James Rouse, America's Salesman of the Businessman's Utopia*. Columbus: Ohio State University Press, 2004.

Boger, Gretchen. "The Meaning of Neighborhood in the Modern City: Baltimore's Residential Segregation Ordinances, 1910–1913." *Journal of Urban History* 35, no. 2 (January 2009): 236–258.

Boisseau, Tracy Jean. *White Queen: May French-Sheldon and the Imperial Origins of American Feminist Identity*. Bloomington: Indiana University Press, 2004.

Boone, Christopher G. "Obstacles to Infrastructure Provision: The Struggle to Build Comprehensive Sewer Works in Baltimore." *Historical Geography* 31 (2003): 151–168.

Boone, Christopher G., Geoffrey L. Buckley, J. Morgan Grove, and Chona Sister. "Parks and People: An Environmental Justice Inquiry in Baltimore, Maryland." *Annals of the Association of American Geographers* 99, no. 4 (2009): 767–787.

Bow, Leslie. *Partly Colored: Asian Americans and the Racial Anomaly in the Segregated South*. New York: New York University Press, 2010.

Boyce Davies, Carole. "A Black Left Feminist View on Cedric Robinson's *Black Marxism*." *Black Perspectives*, November 10, 2016. https://www.aaihs.org/a-black-left-feminist-view -on-cedric-robinsons-black-marxism.

Boyle, Kevin. *Arc of Justice: A Saga of Race, Civil Rights, and Murder in the Jazz Age*. New York: Henry Holt and Company, 2004.

Bozell, Leo, ed. *Proceedings of the First Annual Convention Conferences of the Homebuilders and Subdividers Division of the National Association of Real Estate Boards*. Chicago: National Association of Real Estate Boards, 1923.

Brooks, Charlotte. *Alien Neighbors, Foreign Friends: Asian Americans, Housing, and the Transformation of Urban California*. Chicago: University of Chicago Press, 2009.

Canaday, Margot. *The Straight State: Sexuality and Citizenship in Twentieth-Century America*. Princeton, NJ: Princeton University Press, 2009.

Carlos, Ann M., Karen Maguire, and Larry Neal. "Financial Acumen, Women Speculators, and the Royal African Company During the South Sea Bubble." *Accounting, Business and Financial History* 16, no. 2 (2006): 219–243.

Carpenter, Daniel. *The Forging of Bureaucratic Autonomy: Reputations, Networks, and Policy Innovation in Executive Agencies, 1862–1928*. Princeton, NJ: Princeton University Press, 2001.

Chambers, Henry E. *A History of Louisiana*, vol. 2. Chicago: American Historical Society, 1925.

Chang, David. *The Color of Land: Race, Nation, and the Politics of Land Ownership in Oklahoma, 1832–1929*. Chapel Hill: University of North Carolina Press, 2010.

Cheng, Cindy I-Fen. *Citizens of Asian America: Democracy and Race During the Cold War*. New York: New York University Press, 2013.

Cohen, Lizabeth. *A Consumer's Republic: The Politics of Mass Consumption in Postwar America*. New York: Alfred A. Knopf, 2003.

——. *Making a New Deal: Industrial Workers in Chicago, 1919–1939*. Cambridge: Cambridge University Press, 1990.

Collins, Sharon M. *Black Corporate Executives*. Philadelphia: Temple University Press, 1997.

Connolly, N. D. B. "How Did African Americans Discover They Were Being 'Redlined?'"
Talking Points Memo, August 9, 2015. http://talkingpointsmemo.com/primary-source
/redlining-holc-fha-wilkins-weaver.

———. "Notes on a Desegregated Method: Learning from Michael Katz and Others." *Journal
of Urban History* 41, no. 4 (July 2015): 584–591.

———. *A World More Concrete: Real Estate and the Remaking of Jim Crow South Florida.*
Chicago: University of Chicago Press, 2014.

Crenson, Matthew. *Baltimore: A Political History.* Baltimore, MD: Johns Hopkins University
Press, 2017.

Cronon, William. *Nature's Metropolis: Chicago and the Great West.* New York: W. W. Norton,
1991.

Cutterham, Tom. "Is the History of Capitalism the History of Everything?" *The Junto,*
September 2, 2014. https://earlyamericanists.com/2014/09/02/is-the-history-of-capitalism
-the-history-of-everything.

Davies, Janet Pearl. *Real Estate in American History.* Washington, DC: Public Affairs Press,
1958.

Davis, Lance, and Robert Huttenback. *Mammon and the Pursuit of Empire: The Political
Economy of British Imperialism.* Cambridge: Cambridge University Press, 2009.

Dawson, Virginia. "Protection from Undesirable Neighbors: The Use of Deed Restrictions in
Shaker Heights, Ohio." *Journal of Planning History* 18, no. 2 (2019): 116–136.

Dowling Taylor, Elizabeth. *The Original Black Elite: Daniel Murray and the Story of a
Forgotten Era.* New York: HarperCollins, 2017.

Dunaway, Wilma A. *The First American Frontier: Transition to Capitalism in Southern
Appalachia, 1700–1860.* Chapel Hill: University of North Carolina Press, 1996.

Einhorn, Robin. *Property Rules: Political Economy in Chicago, 1833–1872.* Chicago: University
of Chicago Press, 1991.

Elfenbein, Jessica I. "'Church People Work on the Integration Problem': The Brethren's
Interracial Work in Baltimore, 1949–1972." In *Baltimore '68: Riots and Rebirth in an
American City,* ed. Jessica Elfenbein, Thomas L. Hollowak, and Elizabeth M. Nix,
103–121. Philadelphia: Temple University Press, 2011.

Elfenbein, Jessica, Thomas L. Hollowak, and Elizabeth M. Nix, eds. *Baltimore '68: Riots and
Rebirth in an American City.* Philadelphia: Temple University Press, 2011.

Enstad, Nan. "The 'Sonorous Summons' of the New History of Capitalism, or What Are We
Talking About When We Talk About Economy?" *Modern American History* 2, no. 1
(March 2019): 83–95.

Euchner, Charles. "The Politics of Sewage Expansion: Baltimore and the Sewerage
Question, 1859–1905." *Maryland Historical Magazine* 86 (Fall 1991): 270–291.

Farrar, Hayward. *The Baltimore Afro-American, 1892–1950.* Westport, CT: Greenwood
Press, 1998.

Fee, Elizabeth, Linda Shopes, and Linda Zeidman, eds. *The Baltimore Book: New Views of
Local History.* Philadelphia: Temple University Press, 1991.

Fields, Barbara. "Ideology and Race in American History." In *Region, Race, and Reconstruction: Essays in Honor of C. Vann Woodward*, ed. Morgan J. Koussar and James McPherson, 143–177. New York: Oxford University Press, 1982.

——. "Slavery, Race, and Ideology in the United States of America." *New Left Review* 1, no. 181 (May/June 1990): 95–118.

Fishman, Robert. *Bourgeois Utopias: The Rise and Fall of Suburbia*. New York: Basic Books, 1987.

Fogelson, Robert M. *Bourgeois Nightmares: Suburbia, 1870–1930*. New Haven, CT: Yale University Press, 2005.

——. *The Fragmented Metropolis: Los Angeles, 1850–1930*. Cambridge, MA: Harvard University Press, 1993.

Fowler, Alan. *Lancashire Cotton Operatives and Work, 1900–1950: A Social History of Lancashire Cotton Operatives in the Twentieth Century*. Aldershot, UK: Ashgate, 2003.

Francis, Megan Ming, and Michael C. Dawson. "Race, Capitalism, and Conflict Then and Now." *Items: Insights from the Social Sciences*, October 3, 2017. https://items.ssrc.org/reading-racial-conflict/race-capitalism-and-conflict-then-and-now.

Fraser, Nancy, and Linda Gordon. "A Genealogy of Dependency: Tracing a Keyword of the U.S. Welfare State." *Signs* 19, no. 2 (Winter 1994): 309–336.

Freeman, Mark, Robin Pearson, and James Taylor. "'A Doe in the City': Women Shareholders in Eighteenth- and Early Nineteenth-Century Britain." *Accounting, Business and Financial History* 16, no. 2 (2006): 265–291.

Freund, David M. P. *Colored Property: State Policy and White Racial Politics in Suburban America*. Chicago: University of Chicago Press, 2007.

Friedman, Andrew. *Covert Capital: Landscapes of Denial and the Making of U.S. Empire in the Suburbs of Northern Virginia*. Berkeley: University of California Press, 2013.

Frug, Gerald. "The Legal Technology of Exclusion in Metropolitan America." In *The New Suburban History*, ed. Kevin Kruse and Thomas Sugrue, 205–219. Chicago: University of Chicago Press, 2006.

Garb, Margaret. *City of American Dreams: A History of Home Ownership and Housing Reform in Chicago, 1871–1919*. Chicago: University of Chicago Press, 2005.

Gibson, Charlee. "What Does the 'R' Mean Overseas?" *Global View Blog*, September 27, 2017, http://theglobalview.blogs.realtor.org/2017/09/27/what-does-the-r-mean-overseas.

Gill, Tiffany. *Beauty Shop Politics: African American Women's Activism in the Beauty Industry*. Urbana: University of Illinois Press, 2010.

Gillette, Howard, Jr. "Assessing James Rouse's Role in American City Planning." *Journal of the American Planning Association* 65, no. 2 (Spring 1999): 151–167.

——. *Civitas by Design: Building Better Communities from the Garden City to the New Urbanism*. Philadelphia: University of Pennsylvania Press, 2010.

Gilmore, Glenda. *Gender and Jim Crow: Women and the Politics of White Supremacy in North Carolina, 1896–1920*. Chapel Hill: University of North Carolina Press, 1996.

Gilmore, Ruth. "Race and Globalization." In *Geographies of Global Change: Remapping the World*, 2nd ed., ed. R. J. Johnston, Peter J. Taylor, and Michael Watts, 261–274. New York: Wiley-Blackwell, 2002.

Gilroy, Paul. *The Black Atlantic: Modernity and Double Consciousness.* Cambridge, MA: Harvard University Press, 1993.

Glickman, Lawrence. *Buying Power: A History of Consumer Activism in America.* Chicago: University of Chicago Press, 2009.

Glotzer, Paige. "The Connections Between Urban Development and Colonialism." *Black Perspectives,* November 27, 2017. https://www.aaihs.org/the-connections-between-urban -development-and-colonialism.

——. "Exclusion in Arcadia: How Developers Circulated Ideas About Discrimination, 1890–1950." *Journal of Urban History* 41, no. 3 (May 2015): 479–494.

——. "Real Estate and the City: Considering the History of Capitalism and Urban History." *Journal of Urban History* 42, no. 2 (March 2016): 438–445.

——. "Roland Park Company: The Critical Planning Role of the Olmsted Brothers." *The Olmstedian* 21, no. 1 (Spring 2015): 1–6.

——. "Who Bankrolled Jim Crow: Global Capital and American Segregation." *Public Seminar,* September 22, 2015. http://www.publicseminar.org/2015/09/who-bankrolled-jim -crow.

Goodwillie, Arthur. *Waverly: A Study in Neighborhood Conservation.* Washington, DC: Federal Home Loan Bank Board, 1940.

Gonda, Jeffrey. *Unjust Deeds: The Restrictive Covenant Cases and the Making of the Civil Rights Movement.* Chapel Hill: University of North Carolina Press, 2015.

Gordon, Colin. *Citizen Brown: Race Democracy, and Inequality in the St. Louis Suburbs.* Chicago: University of Chicago Press, 2019.

——. *Mapping Decline: St. Louis and the Fate of the American City.* Philadelphia: University of Pennsylvania Press, 2009.

Gotham, Kevin Fox. *Race, Real Estate, and Uneven Development: The Kansas City Experience, 1900–2000.* Albany: State University of New York Press, 2002.

——. "The Secondary Circuit of Capital Reconsidered: Globalization and the U.S. Real Estate Sector." *American Journal of Sociology* 112, no. 1 (July 2006): 355–371.

——. "Urban Space, Restrictive Covenants and the Origins of Racial Residential Segrega- tion in a US City, 1900–1950." *International Journal of Urban and Regional Research* 24, no. 3 (2000): 616–633.

Grove, Morgan J., Laura Ogden, Steward Pickett, et al. "The Legacy Effect: Understanding How Segregation and Environmental Injustice Unfold Over Time in Baltimore." *Annals of the American Association of Geographers* 108, no. 2 (2018): 524–537.

Guglielmo, Thomas. *White on Arrival: Italians, Race, Color, and Power in Chicago, 1890–1945.* New York: Oxford University Press, 2003.

Guinier, Lani. "From Racial Liberalism to Racial Literacy: *Brown v. Board of Education* and the Interest-Divergence Dilemma." *Journal of American History* 91, no. 1 (June 2004): 92–118.

Hahn, Steven. *A Nation Under Our Feet: Black Political Struggles in the Rural South from Slavery to the Great Migration.* Cambridge, MA: Harvard University Press, 2003.

Halpin, Dennis P. *A Brotherhood of Liberty: Black Reconstruction and Its Legacies in Baltimore.* Philadelphia: University of Pennsylvania Press, 2019.

———. "'The Struggle for Land and Liberty': Segregation, Violence, and African American Resistance in Baltimore, 1898–1918." *Journal of Urban History* 44, no. 4 (July 2018): 691–712.

Hanchett, Thomas. *Sorting the New South City: Race, Class, and Urban Development in Charlotte, 1875–1975.* Chapel Hill: University of North Carolina Press, 1998.

Harris, Richard. *Building a Market: The Rise of the Home Improvement Industry, 1914–1960.* Chicago: University of Chicago Press, 2012.

———. "A New Form of Credit: The State Promotes Home Improvement." *Journal of Policy History* 21, no. 4 (October 2009): 392–423.

———. *Unplanned Suburbs: Toronto's American Tragedy, 1900 to 1950.* Baltimore, MD: Johns Hopkins University Press, 1999.

Harris, Richard, and Charlotte Vorms. *What's in a Name? Talking About Urban Peripheries.* Toronto: University of Toronto Press, 2017.

Harriss, C. Lowell. *History and Policies of the Home Owners' Loan Corporation.* New York: National Bureau of Economic Research, 1951.

Harvey, Bill. "Hampden-Woodberry: Baltimore's Mill Villages." In *The Baltimore Book: New Views of Local History,* ed. Elizabeth Fee, Linda Shopes, and Linda Zeidman, 39–56. Philadelphia: Temple University Press, 1991.

Hayden, Dolores. *Building Suburbia: Green Fields and Urban Growth, 1820–1900.* New York: Pantheon, 2003.

Haynes, Bruce. *Red Lines, Black Spaces: The Politics of Race and Space in a Black Middle-Class Suburb.* New Haven, CT: Yale University Press, 2006.

Hayward, Mary Ellen. *Baltimore's Alley Houses: Homes for Working People Since the 1780s.* Baltimore, MD: Johns Hopkins University Press, 2008.

———. "Urban Vernacular Architecture in Nineteenth-Century Baltimore." *Winterarthur Portfolio* 16, no. 1 (Spring 1981): 33–63.

Hayward, Mary Ellen, and Charles Belfoure. *The Baltimore Rowhouse.* Princeton, NJ: Princeton Architectural Press, 2001.

Heathcott, Joseph. "Black Archipelago: Politics and Civic Life in the Jim Crow City." *Journal of Social History* 38, no. 3 (Spring 2005): 705–736.

Helper, Rose. *Racial Policies and Practices of Real Estate Brokers.* Minneapolis: University of Minnesota Press, 1969.

Henderson, Peter H. "Local Deals and the New Deal State: Implementing Federal Public Housing in Baltimore, 1933–1968." PhD diss., Johns Hopkins University, 1994.

Henry, Nancy. *Women, Literature, and Finance in Victorian Britain.* London: Palgrave, 2018.

Herbin-Triant, Elizabeth A. *Threatening Property: Race, Class, and Campaigns to Legislate Jim Crow Neighborhoods.* New York: Columbia University Press, 2019.

Highsmith, Andrew. *Demolition Means Progress: Flint, Michigan and the Fate of the American Metropolis.* Chicago: University of Chicago Press, 2016.

Hill, Thomas Shay. "The Securitization of Security: Reorganization of Land, Military, and State in the Pentagon's Backyard." *Journal of Urban History* 41, no. 1 (January 2015): 75–92.

Hillier, Amy. "Redlining and the Home Owners' Loan Corporation." *Journal of Urban History* 29, no. 4 (May 2003): 399–400.

Hirsch, Arnold. "'Containment' on the Home Front: Race and Federal Housing Policy from the New Deal to the Cold War." *Journal of Urban History* 26, no. 2 (January 2000): 158–189.

———. *Making the Second Ghetto: Race and Housing in Chicago, 1940–1960.* New York: Cambridge University Press, 1983.

———. "Searching for a 'Sound Negro Policy': A Racial Agenda for the Housing Acts of 1949 and 1954." *Housing Policy Debate* 11, no. 2 (2010): 393–441.

Hirt, Sonia. *Zoned in the USA: The Origins and Implications of American Land-Use Regulation.* Ithaca, NY: Cornell University Press, 2014.

Hise, Greg. *Magnetic Los Angeles: Planning the Twentieth-Century Metropolis.* Baltimore, MD: Johns Hopkins University Press, 1997.

Hoffman, Morton. "The Role of Government in Influencing Changes in Housing in Baltimore: 1940 to 1950." *Land Economics* 30, no. 2 (1954): 125–140.

Holcomb, Eric L. *The City as Suburb: A History of Northeast Baltimore Since 1660.* Santa Fe, NM: Center for American Places, 2005.

Holechek, James. *Baltimore's Two Cross Keys Villages: One Black, One White.* Lincoln, NE: iUniverse, 2003.

Holmes, William F. "Whitecapping: Agrarian Violence in Mississippi, 1902–1906." *Journal of Southern History* 35, no. 2 (May 1969): 166–184.

Hornstein, Jeffrey. *A Nation of Realtors: A Cultural History of the Twentieth-Century American Middle Class.* Durham, NC: Duke University Press, 2005.

Hsu, Madeline Y. "Asian American History and the Perils of a Usable Past." *Modern American History* 1, no. 1 (March 2018): 71–75.

Hudson, Peter James. *Bankers and Empire: How Wall Street Colonized the Caribbean.* Chicago: University of Chicago Press, 2017.

———. "The Racist Dawn of Capitalism." *Boston Review*, March 14, 2016. http://bostonreview .net/books-ideas/peter-james-hudson-slavery-capitalism.

Hunt, D. Bradford. *Blueprint for Disaster: The Unraveling of Chicago's Public Housing.* Chicago: University of Chicago Press, 2010.

Hunter, Tera. *To 'Joy My Freedom: Southern Black Women's Lives and Labors After the Civil War.* Cambridge, MA: Harvard University Press, 1998.

———. "Writing of Labor and Love: Gender and African American History's Challenge to Present Day Assumptions and Misinterpretations." *Souls* 18, no. 1 (January–March 2016): 150–154.

Hyman, Louis. *Debtor Nation: The History of America in Red Ink.* Princeton, NJ: Princeton University Press, 2011.

Immergluck, Dan. *Foreclosed: High-Risk Lending, Deregulation, and the Undermining of America's Mortgage Market.* Ithaca, NY: Cornell University Press, 2009.

Jackson, Kenneth. *Crabgrass Frontier: The Suburbanization of the United States.* Oxford: Oxford University Press, 1985.

Jacobs, Meg. *Pocketbook Politics: Economic Citizenship in Twentieth-Century America.* Princeton, NJ: Princeton University Press, 2005.

——. "State of the Field: The Politics of Consumption." *Reviews in American History* 39, no. 3 (September 2011): 561–573.

Jenkins, Destin. *Bonded Metropolis: Debt, Redevelopment, and Racial Inequality*. Chicago: University of Chicago Press, forthcoming.

Jenks, Hillary. "Seasoned Long Enough in Concentration: Suburbanization and Transnational Citizenship in Southern California's South Bay." *Journal of Urban History* 40, no. 6 (2014): 6–30.

Jones-Correa, Michael. "The Origins and Diffusion of Racial Restrictive Covenants." *Political Science Quarterly* 115, no. 4 (Winter 2000–2001): 541–568.

Kahen, Harold. "Validity of Anti-Negro Restrictive Covenants: A Reconsideration of the Problem." *University of Chicago Law Review* 12, no. 2 (1945): 198–213.

Kahrl, Andrew. "Investing in Distress: Tax Delinquency and Predatory Tax Buying in Urban America." *Critical Sociology* 43, no. 2 (2017): 199–219.

Kaplan, Amy. *The Anarchy of Empire in the Making of U.S. Culture*. Cambridge, MA: Harvard University Press, 2005.

Katz, Michael B. "The Existential Problem of Urban Studies." *Dissent* 57, no. 4 (Fall 2010): 65–68.

——. *In the Shadow of the Poorhouse: A Social History of Welfare in America*. New York: Basic Books, 1986.

——, ed. *The "Underclass" Debate: View from History*. Princeton, NJ: Princeton University Press, 1993.

Kelley, Robin D. G. "What Did Cedric Robinson Mean by Racial Capitalism?" *Boston Review*, January 12, 2017. http://bostonreview.net/race/robin-d-g-kelley-what-did-cedric -robinson-mean-racial-capitalism.

Kramer, Paul. "Embedding Capital: Political-Economic History, the United States, and the World." *Journal of the Gilded Age and Progressive Era* 15, no. 3 (July 2016): 331–362.

Krulikowski, Anne E. "'A Workingman's Paradise': The Evolution of an Unplanned Suburban Landscape." *Winterthur Portfolio* 42, no. 4 (Winter 2008): 243–285.

Kruse, Kevin. *White Flight: Atlanta and the Making of Modern Conservatism*. Princeton, NJ: Princeton University Press, 2007.

Kruse, Kevin, and Thomas Sugrue, eds. *The New Suburban History*. Chicago: University of Chicago Press, 2006.

Kurashige, Scott. *The Shifting Grounds of Race: Black and Japanese Americans in the Making of Multiethnic Los Angeles*. Princeton, NJ: Princeton University Press, 2008.

Kwolek-Folland, Angel. *Engendering Business: Men and Women in the Corporate Office*. Baltimore, MD: Johns Hopkins University Press, 1998.

Lands, LeeAnn. *The Culture of Property: Race, Class, and Housing Landscapes in Atlanta, 1880–1950*. Athens: University of Georgia Press, 2009.

Lassiter, Matthew. *The Silent Majority: Suburban Politics in the Sunbelt South*. Princeton, NJ: Princeton University Press, 2007.

Laurence, Anne. "Women Investors, 'That Nasty South Sea Affair,' and the Rage to Speculate in Early Eighteenth-Century England." *Accounting, Business and Financial History* 16, no. 2 (2006): 245–264.

Lawliss, Lucy, Caroline Loughlin, and Lauren Meier, eds. *The Master List of Design Projects of the Olmsted Firm, 1857–1979*. Washington, DC: National Association of Olmsted Parks, 2008.

Levy, Jessica Ann. "Black Power Inc.: Global American Business and the Post-Apartheid City." PhD diss., Johns Hopkins University, 2018.

Levy, Jonathan. "The Mortgage That Worked Hardest: The Fate of Landed Independence in Nineteenth-Century America." In *Capitalism Takes Command: The Social Transformation of Nineteenth-Century America*, ed. Michael Zakim and Gary Kornblith, 39–68. Chicago: University of Chicago Press, 2011.

Lewinnek, Elaine. *The Workingman's Reward: Chicago's Early Suburbs and the Roots of American Sprawl*. New York: Oxford University Press, 2014.

Lieb, Emily. "'White Man's Lane': Hollowing Out the Highway Ghetto in Baltimore." In *Baltimore '68: Riots and Rebirth in an American City*, ed. Jessica Elfenbein, Thomas L. Hollowak, and Elizabeth M. Nix, 51–69. Philadelphia: Temple University Press, 2011.

Light, Jennifer. *The Nature of Cities: Ecological Visions and the American Urban Professions, 1920–1960*. Baltimore, MD: Johns Hopkins University Press, 2009.

Lightfoot, Natasha. "'Their Coats Were Tied Up Like Men': Women Rebels in Antigua's 1858 Uprising." *Slavery and Abolition* 34, no. 4 (2010): 527–545.

——. *Troubling Freedom: Antigua and the Aftermath of British Emancipation*. Durham, NC: Duke University Press, 2015.

Limerick, Patricia Nelson. *Something in the Soil: Legacies and Reckonings in the New West*. New York: W. W. Norton, 2000.

Lipartito, Kenneth. "Reassembling the Economic: New Departures in Historical Materialism." *American Historical Review* 121, no. 1 (February 2016): 101–139.

Lipsitz, George. *How Racism Takes Place*. Philadelphia: Temple University Press, 2011.

Livingston Adams, Betty. *Black Women's Christian Activism: Seeking Social Justice in a Northern Suburb*. New York: New York University Press, 2016.

Loewen, James. *Sundown Towns: A Hidden Dimension of American Racism*. New York: New Press, 2005.

Looker, Benjamin. *A Nation of Neighborhoods: Imagining Cities, Communities, and Democracy in Postwar America*. Chicago: University of Chicago Press, 2015.

Lowes, Susan. "The Peculiar Class: The Formation, Collapse, and Reformation of the Middle Class of Antigua, West Indies, 1834–1940." PhD diss., University of Michigan, 1994.

Lui, Mary. *The Chinatown Trunk Mystery: Murder, Miscegenation, and Other Dangerous Encounters in Turn-of-the-Century New York City*. Princeton, NJ: Princeton University Press, 2005.

Maggor, Noam. "The Great Inequalizer: American Capitalism in the Gilded Age and Progressive Era." *Journal of the Gilded Age and Progressive Era* 15, no. 3 (July 2016): 241–245.

——. "To Coddle and Caress These Great Capitalists: Eastern Money, Frontier Populism, and the Politics of Market-Making in the American West." *American Historical Review* 122, no. 1 (February 2017): 55–84.

Maltby, Josephine, and Janette Rutterford. "Editorial: Women, Accounting, and Investment." *Accounting, Business and Financial History* 16, no. 2 (2006): 133–142.

——. "She Possessed Her Own Fortune: Women Investors from the Late Nineteenth Century to the Early Twentieth Century." *Business History* 48, no. 2 (2006): 220–253.

Marx, Paul. *Jim Rouse: Capitalist/Idealist*. Lanham, MD: University Press of America, 2008.

Mattingly, Paul H. *Suburban Landscapes: Culture and Politics in a New York Metropolitan Community*. Baltimore, MD: Johns Hopkins University Press, 2001.

McFarlane, Larry. "British Investment and the Land: Nebraska, 1877–1946." *Business History Review* 57, no. 2 (Summer 1983): 258–272.

——. "British Investment in Midwestern Farm Mortgages and Land, 1875–1900: A Comparison of Iowa and Kansas." *Agricultural History* 48, no. 1 (January 1974): 179–198.

McGirr, Lisa. *Suburban Warriors: The Origins of the New American Right*. Princeton, NJ: Princeton University Press, 2001.

McKee, Elmore. *The People Act: Stories of How Americans Are Coming Together to Deal with Their Community Problems*. New York: Harper and Brothers, 1955.

McKenna, Rebecca Tinio. *American Imperial Pastoral: The Architecture of US Colonialism in the Philippines*. Chicago: University of Chicago Press, 2017.

Meisner Rosen, Christine. "'Knowing' Industrial Pollution: Nuisance Law and the Power of Tradition in a Time of Rapid Economic Change, 1840–1864." *Environmental History* 8, no. 4 (October 2003): 565–597.

Melamed, Jodi. "Racial Capitalism." *Critical Ethnic Studies* 1, no. 1 (Spring 2015): 76–85.

Meyer, Stephen G. *As Long as They Don't Move in Next Door: Segregation and Racial Conflict in American Neighborhoods*. Boston: Rowman and Littlefield, 2000.

Michney, Todd. *Surrogate Suburbs: Black Upward Mobility and Neighborhood Change in Cleveland, 1900–1980*. Chapel Hill: University of North Carolina Press, 2017.

Michney, Todd, and LaDale Winling. "New Perspectives on New Deal Housing Policy: Explicating and Mapping HOLC Loans to African Americans." *Journal of Urban History*. Advanced online publication January 9, 2019. https://doi.org/10.1177/0096144 218819429.

Mills, Quincy T. *Cutting Along the Color Line: Black Barbers and Barber Shops in America*. Philadelphia: University of Pennsylvania Press, 2013.

Ming, William R., Jr. "Racial Restrictions and the Fourteenth Amendment: The Restrictive Covenant Cases." *University of Chicago Law Review* 16, no. 2 (1949): 203–238.

Moehring, Eugene. *Urbanism and Empire in the Far West, 1840–1890*. Reno: University of Nevada Press, 2003.

Molina, Natalia. *Fit to Be Citizens? Public Health and Race in Los Angeles, 1879–1939*. Berkeley: University of California Press, 2006.

Mollett, Sharlene. "The Power to Plunder: Rethinking Land Grabbing in Latin America." *Antipode* 48, no. 2 (2016): 412–432.

Monchow, Helen. *The Use of Deed Restrictions in Subdivision Development*. Chicago: Institute for Research in Land Economics and Public Utilities, 1928.

Moreton, Bethany. *To Serve God and Wal-Mart: The Making of Christian Free Enterprise.* Cambridge, MA: Harvard University Press, 2009.

Moudry, Roberta. "Gardens, Houses, and People: The Planning of Roland Park." MA thesis, Cornell University, 1990.

Muhammed, Khalil Gibran. *The Condemnation of Blackness: Race, Crime, and the Making of Modern Urban America.* Cambridge, MA: Harvard University Press, 2010.

Murphy, Sharon Ann. "Securing Human Property: Slavery, Life Insurance, and Industrialization in the Upper South." *Journal of the Early Republic* 25, no. 4 (Winter 2005): 615–652.

Neagle, Michael E. *America's Forgotten Colony: Cuba's Isle of Pines.* Cambridge: Cambridge University Press, 2016.

Ngai, Mae. "Chinese Gold Miners and the 'Chinese Question' in Nineteeth-Century California and Victoria." *Journal of American History* 101, no. 4 (2015): 1082–1105.

——. *Impossible Subjects: Illegal Aliens and the Making of Modern America.* Princeton, NJ: Princeton University Press, 2004.

Nicolaides, Becky. *My Blue Heaven: Life and Politics in the Working-Class Suburbs of Los Angeles, 1920–1965.* Chicago: University of Chicago Press, 2002.

Nightingale, Carl. *Segregation: A Global History.* Chicago: University of Chicago Press, 2012.

——. "The Transnational Contexts of Early Twentieth-Century American Urban Segregation." *Journal of Social History* 39, no. 3 (Spring 2006): 667–702.

O'Connor, Alice. *Poverty Knowledge: Social Science, Social Policy, and the Poor in Twentieth-Century U.S. History.* Princeton, NJ: Princeton University Press, 2001.

Olson, Joshua. *Better Places, Better Lives: A Biography of James Rouse.* Washington, DC: Urban Land Institute, 2003.

Olson, Sherry. *Baltimore: The Building of an American City.* Baltimore, MD: Johns Hopkins University Press, 1980.

O'Mara, Margaret. *Cities of Knowledge: Cold War Science and the Search for the Next Silicon Valley.* Princeton, NJ: Princeton University Press, 2004.

——. *The Code: Silicon Valley and the Remaking of America.* New York: Penguin Press, 2019.

Orenstein, Dara, and Aaron Carico. "Editors' Introduction: The Fictions of Finance." *Radical History Review* 14, no. 118 (2014): 3–13.

Orleck, Annelise. *Storming Caesar's Palace: How Black Mothers Fought Their War on Poverty.* Boston: Beacon Press, 2006.

Orser, Edward. *Blockbusting in Baltimore: The Edmondson Village Story.* Lexington: University Press of Kentucky, 1994.

Ott, Julia. *When Wall Street Met Main Street: The Quest for an Investors' Democracy.* Cambridge, MA: Harvard University Press, 2011.

Papenfuse, Eric Robert. *The Evils of Necessity: Robert Goodloe Harper and the Moral Dilemma of Slavery.* Philadelphia: American Philosophical Society, 1997.

Perkiss, Abigail. *Making Good Neighbors: Civil Rights, Liberalism, and Integration in Postwar Philadelphia.* Ithaca, NY: Cornell University Press, 2014.

Peterson, Jon. "The Birth of Organized City Planning in the United States, 1909–1910." *Journal of the American Planning Association* 75, no. 2 (Spring 2009): 123–133.

Pietila, Antero. *Not in My Neighborhood: How Bigotry Shaped a Great American City.* Chicago: Ivan R. Dee, 2010.

Power, Garrett. "The Advent of Zoning." *Planning Perspectives* 4, no. 1 (1989): 1–13.

——. "Apartheid, Baltimore Style: The Residential Segregation Ordinances of 1910–1913." *Maryland Law Review* 42, no. 2 (1983): 289–328.

——. "The Unwisdom of Allowing City Growth to Work Out on Its Own." *Maryland Law Review* 47, no. 3 (1988): 626–674.

Pritchett, Wendell E. "The Public Menace of Blight." *Yale Law and Policy Review* 21, no. 1 (2003): 1–52.

Radford, Gail. *Modern Housing for America: Policy Struggles in the New Deal Era.* Chicago: University of Chicago Press, 1996.

Reps, John W. *The Making of Urban America: A History of City Planning in the United States.* Princeton, NJ: Princeton University Press, 1965.

Robb, George. "Ladies of the Ticker: Women, Investment, and Fraud in England and America, 1850–1930." In *Victorian Investments: New Perspectives on Finance and Culture,* ed. Nancy Henry and Cannon Schmitt, 120–140. Bloomington: Indiana University Press, 2009.

Roberts, Samuel, Jr. *Infectious Fear: Politics, Disease, and the Health Effects of Segregation.* Chapel Hill: University of North Carolina Press, 2009.

Robinson, Cedric. *Black Marxism: The Making of the Black Radical Tradition.* Chapel Hill: University of North Carolina Press, 2000.

Rockman, Seth. *Scraping By: Wage Labor, Slavery, and Survival in Early Baltimore.* Baltimore, MD: Johns Hopkins University Press, 2009.

——. "What Makes the History of Capitalism Newsworthy?" *Journal of the Early Republic* 34, no. 3 (Fall 2014): 439–466.

Rosenzweig, Roy, and Elizabeth Blackmar. *The Park and the People: A History of Central Park.* Ithaca, NY: Cornell University Press, 1992.

Ryan, Mary P. *Taking the Land to Make the City: A Bicoastal History of North America.* Austin: University of Texas Press, 2019.

Rydell, Robert. *All the World's a Fair: Visions of Empire and American International Exhibitions, 1876–1916.* Chicago: University of Chicago Press, 1984.

Samuels, Warren J. "Markets and Their Social Construction." *Social Research* 71, no. 2 (2004): 357–370.

Sandoval-Strausz, A. K., and Nancy Kwak, eds. *Making Cities Global: The Transnational Turn in Urban History.* Philadelphia: University of Pennsylvania Press, 2018.

Satter, Beryl. *Family Properties: How the Struggle Over Race and Real Estate Transformed Chicago and Urban America.* New York: Metropolitan Books, 2009.

Schlack, Harry G. "Planning Roland Park, 1891–1910." *Maryland Historical Magazine* 6, no. 4 (Winter 1972): 419–428.

Schwarz, Kirsten, Michail Fragkias, Christopher G. Boone, et al. "Trees Grow on Money: Urban Tree Canopy Cover and Environmental Justice." *PLOS One* 10, no. 4 (2015): 1–17. https://doi.org/10.1371/journal.pone.0122051.

Self, Robert. *American Babylon: Race and the Struggle for Postwar Oakland.* Princeton, NJ: Princeton University Press, 2005.

Shah, Nayan. *Contagious Divides: Epidemics and Race in San Francisco's Chinatown.* Berkeley: University of California Press, 2001.

Shermer, Elizabeth Tandy. *Sunbelt Capitalism: Phoenix and the Transformation of American Politics.* Philadelphia: University of Pennsylvania Press, 2013.

Sies, Mary. "North American Suburbs, 1880–1950." *Journal of Urban History* 27, no. 3 (March 2001): 313–346.

Silver, Christopher. "The Racial Origins of Zoning in American Cities." In *Urban Planning and the African American Community: In the Shadows,* ed. June Manning Thomas and Marsha Ritzdorf, 23–42. Thousand Oaks, CA: Sage, 1997.

Smith, Jason Scott. *Building New Deal Liberalism: The Political Economy of Public Works, 1933–1956.* Cambridge: Cambridge University Press, 2006.

Smith, Keithlyn B., and Fernando C. Smith. *To Shoot Hard Labour: The Life and Times of Samuel Smith, an Antiguan Workingman, 1877–1982.* Scarborough, ON: Edan's Publishers, 1986.

Smith, Preston H., II. *Racial Democracy and the Black Metropolis: Housing Policy in Postwar Chicago.* Minneapolis: University of Minnesota Press, 2012.

Snowden, Kenneth. "Covered Farm Mortgage Bonds in the United States During the Late Nineteenth Century." *Journal of Economic History* 70, no. 4 (December 2010): 783–812.

Stach, Patricia Burgess. "Real Estate Development and Urban Form: Roadblocks in the Path to Residential Exclusivity." *Business History Review* 62, no. 2 (Summer 1989): 356–383.

Stern, Walter. *Race and Education in New Orleans: Creating the Segregated City, 1764–1960.* Baton Rouge: Louisiana State University Press, 2018.

Strom, Sharon H. *Beyond the Typewriter: Gender, Class, and the Origins of Modern American Office Work.* Urbana: University of Illinois Press, 1992.

Sugrue, Thomas. "Jim Crow's Last Stand: The Struggle to Integrate Levittown." In *Second Suburb: Levittown, Pennsylvania,* ed. Dianne Harris, 175–199. Pittsburgh: University of Pittsburgh Press, 2010.

——. *The Origins of the Urban Crisis: Race and Inequality in Postwar Detroit.* Princeton, NJ: Princeton University Press, 1996.

Surillo Luna, Gricel M. "Moving Forward: Railways in Puerto Rico." PhD diss., City University of New York, 2017.

Taylor, Dorceta E. *The Rise of the American Conservation Movement: Power, Privilege, and Environmental Protection.* Durham, NC: Duke University Press, 2016.

Taylor, Keeanga-Yamatta. *Race for Profit: How Banks and the Real Estate Industry Undermined Black Homeownership.* Chapel Hill: University of North Carolina Press, 2019.

Teaford, Jon. *Municipal Revolution in America: Origins of Modern Urban Government, 1650–1825*. Chicago: University of Chicago Press, 1975.

——. "Urban Renewal and Its Aftermath." *Housing Policy Debate* 11, no. 2 (2010): 443–465.

Thomas, George. *The of Institutions Under Irrigation*. New York: Macmillan, 1920.

Thurston, Chloe N. *At the Boundaries of Homeownership: Credit, Discrimination, and the American State*. Cambridge: Cambridge University Press, 2018.

Traflet, Janice. "Gendered Dollars: Pin Money, Mad Money, and Changing Notions of a Woman's Proper Place." *Essays in Economic and Business History* 26 (2008): 189–202.

——. "'Never Bought, Always Sold': Salesmanship, the Small Investor, and the Early Postwar Surge in Mutual Fund Participation." *Essays in Economic and Business History* 27 (2009): 5–14.

Trotter, Joe. "The Great Migration, African Americans, and Immigrants in the Industrial City." In *Not Just Black and White: Historical and Contemporary Perspectives on Immigration, Race, and Ethnicity in the United States*, ed. Nancy Foner and George Frederickson, 82–99. New York: Russell Sage Foundation, 2005.

Trouillot, Michel-Rolph. *Silencing the Past: Power and Production of History*. Boston: Beacon Press, 1995.

Vill, Martha J. "Building Enterprise in Late Nineteenth-Century Baltimore." *Journal of Historical Geography* 12, no. 2 (1986): 162–181.

Von Hoffman, Alexander. "Enter the Housing Industry Stage Right: A Working Paper on the History of Housing Policy." Joint Center for Housing Studies, Harvard University, 2008.

——. "A Study in Contradictions: The Origins and Legacy of the Housing Act of 1949." *Housing Policy Debate* 11, no. 2 (2000): 299–326.

Vose, Clement. *Caucasians Only: The Supreme Court, the NAACP, and the Restrictive Covenant Cases*. Berkeley: University of California Press, 1967.

Waesche, James. *Crowning the Gravelly Hill: A History of the Roland Park–Guilford–Homeland District*. Baltimore, MD: Maclay and Associates, 1987.

Warner, Sam Bass. *Streetcar Suburbs: The Process of Growth in Boston, 1870–1900*. Cambridge, MA: Harvard University Press, 1962.

Weiss, Marc. "Real Estate History: An Overview and Research Agenda." *Business History Review* 63, no. 2 (Summer 1989): 241–282.

——. "Richard T. Ely and the Contribution of Economic Research to National Housing Policy, 1920–1940." *Urban Studies* 26 (1989): 115–126.

——. *The Rise of the Community Builders: The American Real Estate Industry and Urban Land Planning*. New York: Columbia University Press, 1987.

Weiss, Marc, and John T. Metzger. "The American Real Estate Industry and the Origins of Neighborhood Conservation." In *Proceedings of the Fifth Annual Conference on American Planning History*, ed. Society for American City and Regional Planning History, 753–784. Hilliard, OH: Society for American City and Regional Planning History, 1993.

Wexler, Alice. *The Woman Who Walked Into the Sea: Huntington's and the Making of a Genetic Disease*. New Haven, CT: Yale University Press, 2008.

Wiebe, Robert. *The Search for Order, 1877–1920*. New York: Hill and Wang, 1967.

Wiese, Andrew. *Places of Their Own: African American Suburbanization in the Twentieth Century*. Chicago: University of Chicago Press, 2004.

Wilkins, Mira. *The History of Foreign Investment in the United States to 1914*. Cambridge, MA: Harvard University Press, 1989.

Williams, Rhonda. *The Politics of Public Housing: Black Women's Struggles Against Urban Inequality*. New York: Oxford University Press, 2005.

Woods, Louis Lee, II. "The Federal Home Loan Bank Board, Redlining, and the National Proliferation of Racial Lending Discrimination, 1921–1950." *Journal of Urban History* 38, no. 6 (November 2012): 1036–1059.

Worley, William S. *J. C. Nichols and the Shaping of Kansas City*. Columbia: University of Missouri Press, 1990.

Wright, George C. "The NAACP and Residential Segregation in Louisville, Kentucky, 1914–1917." *Register of the Kentucky Historical Society* 78, no. 1 (Winter 1980): 39–54.

INDEX

Printed in the USA
CPSIA information can be obtained
at www.ICGtesting.com
JSHW021432131223
53760JS00004B/212